OCEAN DEVIL

JAMES MacMANUS

Ocean Devil

THE LIFE AND LEGEND OF GEORGE HOGG

HARPER PERENNIAL
London, New York, Toronto, Sydney and New Delhi

Harper Perennial
An imprint of HarperCollins*Publishers*
77–85 Fulham Palace Road, Hammersmith, London W6 8JB

www.harperperennial.co.uk
Visit our authors' blog at www.fifthestate.co.uk

First published in Great Britain by Harper Perennial 2008

1

Copyright © James MacManus 2008

James MacManus asserts the moral right
to be identified as the author of this work

A catalogue record for this book is available from the British Library

ISBN 978-0-00-727075-0

Set in Linotype Minion by
Rowland Phototypesetting Ltd, Bury St Edmunds, Suffolk

Printed and bound in Great Britain by Clays Ltd, St Ives plc

Mixed Sources
Product group from well-managed
forests and other controlled sources
www.fsc.org   Cert no. SW-COC-1806
© 1996 Forest Stewardship Council

FSC

FSC is a non-profit international organisation established to promote the
responsible management of the world's forests. Products carrying the FSC
label are independently certified to assure consumers that they come
from forests that are managed to meet the social, economic and
ecological needs of present and future generations.

Find out more about HarperCollins and the environment at
www.harpercollins.co.uk/green

For Emily, Elizabeth and Nicholas

CONTENTS

LIST OF ILLUSTRATIONS 9

LIST OF MAPS 11

PROLOGUE 15

1 *The Road to China* 21

2 *Shanghai* 44

3 *Hankow* 54

4 *The Fall of Hankow* 80

5 *Gung Ho!* 111

6 *Ocean Secretary* 138

7 *On the Road* 150

8 *The Headmaster* 192

9 *Journey Over the Mountains* 220

10 *Shandan* 243

EPILOGUE 263

ACKNOWLEDGEMENTS 275

A NOTE ON THE TEXT 278

SOURCES 279

INDEX 283

ILLUSTRATIONS

The young George Hogg in the garden at Red Gables in Harpenden.

George takes tea with his father Robert and brother Stephen.

George's mother Kathleen with his brothers Daniel and Stephen.

Rosemary, Daniel, Stephen, Barbara and George in 1922.

George aged seventeen, as captain of the St George's school first rugby XV.

George in 1934, during his first term at Wadham College, Oxford.

The Wadham rugby XV, 1936–37.

George's aunt Muriel Lester, the 'Mother of World Peace'.

Agnes Smedley. *(Martin Harris, Time-Life Pictures/Gettyimages)*

Rewi Alley. *(Alexander Turnbull Library, Wellington, New Zealand)*

Kathleen Hall, the New Zealand missionary nurse who restored Hogg to health after he contracted typhus in 1939.

George Hogg with commander Nieh Rong Zhen of Mao Tse-tung's Eighth Route Army.

Hogg addresses troops of the Eighth Route Army.

George in Xian in 1940.

Hogg in Baoji in 1941. *(Carl Mydans, Time-Life Pictures/ Gettyimages)*

George in 1942, cradling the youngest of his four adopted sons.

The convoy carrying the school struggles across the Wu Ling Pass, on the last stage of the arduous seven-hundred-mile journey from Shuangshipu to Shandan in the winter of 1944–45.

Xiao Ren and three of George Hogg's adopted sons standing by Hogg's grave in Shandan.

The watercolour of George Hogg that hangs in the small museum near his grave in Shandan.

Six of Hogg's 'old boys' photographed in spring 2007 in the city of Xian Yang, near Xian.

The bust erected in Shandan to commemorate Hogg's memory.

Jonathan Rhys Meyers as George Hogg in a scene from the 2008 film *The Children of Huang Shi*, based on Hogg's life. *(zero fiction film GmbH)*

MAPS

China in the 1940s   12–13

Japanese-occupied areas of China, 1937–45   52

George Hogg's journey from Shuangshipu to Shandan,
    January–March 1945   239

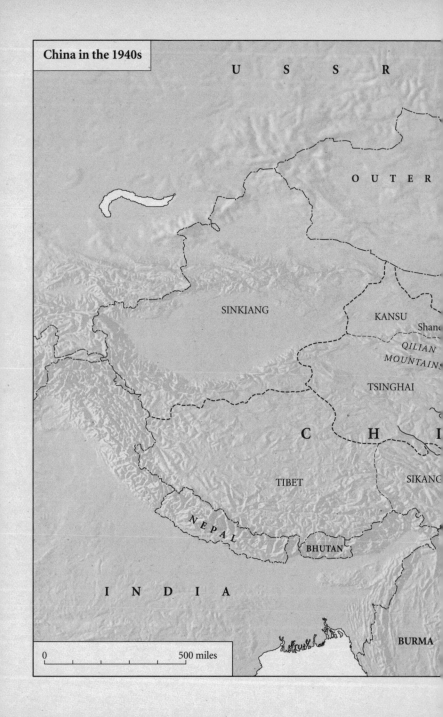

China in the 1940s

U S S R

OUTER

SINKIANG

KANSU

Shane

QILIAN
MOUNTAINS

TSINGHAI

C   H   I

TIBET

SIKANG

NEPAL

BHUTAN

I   N   D   I   A

BURMA

0   500 miles

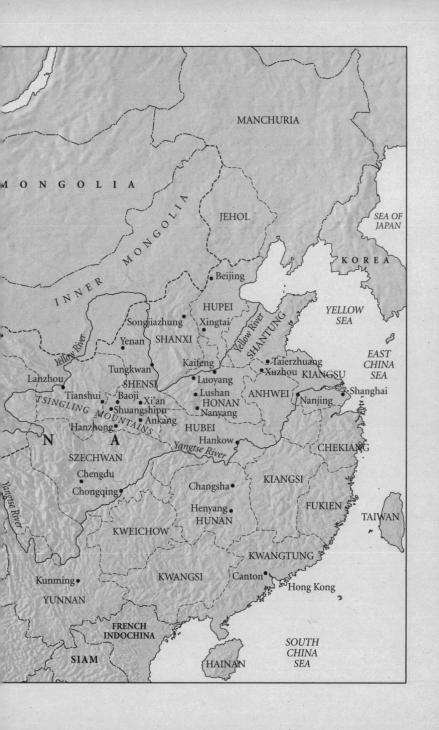

PROLOGUE

In the spring of 2007 in a crowded Beijing restaurant an elderly Chinese man rose to his feet and silenced his fellow diners with a song he had learnt as a child:

> *Three blind mice, three blind mice,*
> *See how they run, see how they run*
> *They all ran after the farmer's wife*
> *She cut off their tails with a carving knife*
> *Three blind mice, three blind mice.*

Although seventy-five years old, Nieh Guanghan had a strong tenor voice, and to the bafflement of the restaurant he reeled off a number of other English nursery rhymes, finishing with a rousing rendition of:

> *London's Burning,*
> *London's Burning,*
> *Fire! Fire!*

The elderly Chinese guests had all learnt those and other songs by heart as children. They had gathered to share their memories of the man who had taught them to sing English nursery rhymes, and to whom they owed their lives, a young Englishman who became both their headmaster and their adoptive father at the height of the Sino–Japanese war in the 1940s.

His name was George Aylwin Hogg, and in a few brief years during the three-sided war in China he achieved legendary status in the north-west of the country. Although unknown in his own homeland he remains well loved and remembered by those he met and cared for in the brief years he worked in China before his death in July 1945.

It was in China in 1984 that I had first come across the story of Hogg, when I was working for the London *Daily Telegraph* as holiday relief in the Beijing bureau. After several barren days searching for a decent story I went to the British Embassy Club for a quiet beer. There I overheard a British diplomat complain that he had to fly to the town of Shandan in the remote north-west of the country, because the Chinese authorities had erected the bust of an Englishman in the town.

Strange things were happening in Beijing at the time. Mao Tse-tung had died in 1976, allowing Deng Xiaoping to return from disgrace and begin the economic liberalisation that was to set China on the path to today's burgeoning market economy. The first McDonald's had opened in Beijing. Cars were just beginning to challenge the many millions of bicycles on the streets of the capital. Western businessmen were arriving with every flight at the international airport. Nevertheless, the idea that China would honour an unknown Englishman with a bust seemed preposterous.

But it turned out to be true. In August that year some eighty elderly gentlemen gathered in Shandan to join local officials and a number of VIPs from Beijing to mark the reopening of a school and library. There were eloquent speeches to mark the reconstruction of a tomb and gravestone desecrated by Red Guards during the Great Proletarian Cultural Revolution of the 1960s.

Flowers and wreaths were laid on the grave. A statue was unveiled. Old men shed tears.

The man whose memory was being was honoured had ended an epic journey – and his life – in this remote region of China in 1945. George Hogg's work in the Chinese co-operative movement in the 1940s, and later as headmaster of a school for war orphans, would always have earned him the tribute of later generations. But what made him a hero to the Chinese was the ten-week journey he made in 1945, against all odds, over the highest mountains in western China with a school of young boys in the worst winter for twenty years, seeking and finding sanctuary from the Japanese on the edge of the Gobi desert. The elderly men who had travelled to Shandan in the summer of 1984 were all Hogg's old boys who survived that terrible journey nearly forty years earlier.

Sadly, I did not have time to take the two internal flights and make the then sixteen-hour car journey to join them at the graveside ceremony. The *Telegraph* had cut short my stint in China with a characteristically curt instruction to go to Hong Kong. I only had time to file a news story about the honour paid to an unknown Englishman before heading for Beijing airport.

Back in London, I took a closer look at George Hogg, and discovered that he had been a great deal more than the heroic headmaster of a school in wartime China. In a book, in his letters and through his journalism he had left behind a record of China at war with itself as well as with Japan in the years 1938–45. He reported the conflict through the eyes of the people who bore the brunt of its savagery: the peasant farmers, the school teachers, the women and children everywhere in the countryside.

No one sent George Hogg to China. It was pure luck that brought him to Shanghai at such an extraordinary time. He rode his luck for eight years, surviving a medical dictionary of serious diseases, countless brushes with death and terrifying journeys over the mountains of western China on every conceivable type of transport. Young, confident and courageous, he ignored the risks he was running. But he did once confide that sliding and skidding over icy mountain roads in ancient trucks was a good deal more frightening than slipping through the Japanese lines at night.

His journalism and regular letters home are a record of a young man struggling to come to terms with the brutality of a war in which some fifteen million people lost their lives between 1937 and 1945. He witnessed repeated atrocities inflicted upon defenceless civilians. The massacres in Nanjing in 1937–38, when as many as 260,000 people died at the hands of the Japanese, were not isolated war crimes. They were an extreme example of routine tactical terror to break popular resistance to the Japanese plan to turn China into a servile client state.

Occasionally – usually when spattered with mud and blood in some bombed-out village – Hogg yearned for the dreamy world of Oxford and the comforts of the middle-class life in the home counties that he had left behind. But he never lost his enthusiasm for his work in China. In his heart he knew he would never return home.

While working as a news agency stringer Hogg found time to write a book, *I See a New China*. It was favourably reviewed on both sides of the Atlantic, although one reviewer criticised the author's 'adolescent tone' in writing about the twists and turns and endless atrocities of the Sino–Japanese war.

But that was the whole point of George Hogg. He bounded out of Oxford with all the enthusiasm and naïveté that three years in a great university confers upon a self-confident young man of twenty-two. He had been brought up from childhood to think the best of people, and to do his best for them. Throughout the eight years he spent in China his letters are coloured by cheerful exuberance, a belief in the essential benevolence of humanity and a refusal to be downcast by evidence to the contrary.

He travelled light as he crisscrossed north-west China, moving from one war zone to another; but whether on foot, on horseback or on top of an ancient truck, he always found room for his typewriter. Hogg never stopped writing: letters, short stories, news stories and features. His reporting of the developing industrial co-operative movement in China, which had been initiated in 1938 to replace the country's shattered manufacturing base, led to a job offer that was to change his life. He joined the movement as a publicity director, with the title 'Ocean Secretary', in 1941. The title reflected the general use of the term 'ocean' in Mandarin to denote anything foreign – foreigners throughout Chinese history have been known as 'ocean devils'. This led him in 1942 to become headmaster of a co-operative training school in the remote mountain town of Shuangshipu. It was here, at the crossroads of the Tsingling mountains in north central Shanxi province, that George Hogg found his destiny.

When I travelled to China in 2007 to talk to his old boys, and to the woman he had loved and had hoped to marry, it was clear just how much the man and the moment had come together in Hogg's headmastership. In Beijing and Xian four of his old boys spoke of the love they still felt for the man who became their adoptive father and headmaster. Looking back, they found it extraordinary that an unknown Englishman should have emerged as their saviour at a critical moment in their young lives.

Because 'Hogg' is not a name that is easy to pronounce in Chinese, the boys called him by a Mandarin approximation, 'Ho Ke' (pronounced Ho-cur). Nieh Guangchun, the eldest of Hogg's boys, who was seventy-nine when we met, said: 'Ho Ke was gentle, he was kind. We had had other headmasters, all Chinese, who punished us. Ho Ke didn't do that. He was firm but he became a friend. He did everything with us. He taught us English songs, Chinese liberation songs, traditional songs; he loved singing. When we went over the mountains with him we didn't really know why. We were too young. But we just followed him. We had never met anyone like him. We never will.'

Hogg's work and memory were vilified during the years of the Cultural Revolution. His grave was desecrated by Red Guards, and his former students were tracked down and forced to denounce their old headmaster. But during the 'Beijing spring' of the late 1970s Deng Xiaoping repudiated the Cultural Revolution and personally signalled the rehabilitation of George Hogg, saying in a speech that he deserved 'immortality as a great international fighter'. The restoration of his burial place in Shandan was accompanied by a long eulogy in the country's leading newspaper, the *People's Daily*, which echoed the tributes paid by former colleagues and pupils to his achievements. As the *People's Daily* pointed out, the real memorial to George Hogg lies not in a graveyard in a remote Chinese town, but in the lives of the children he saved and in the lives of their children.

Nieh Guanghan, the fine tenor at our reunion lunch, said: 'George saved many of our lives. I think many of us would have died one way or another if he had not taken us over the mountains. Our children, their children and future generations will be able to look back on a young Englishman and say without him we would not be here.'

So who was this Englishman who aroused so much love and admiration among boys grown to men whom he had taught in a remote town in China in the 1940s? And what had he done to be singled out by name by the man who led China out of the chaos and cruelty of the Mao era?

ONE

The Road to China

'He seemed to have some inner vision of his own.'

George Hogg was born on 26 February 1915 in a large rented house in Harpenden, Hertfordshire, the youngest child of a prosperous middle-class family. His father Robert ran a well-known tailoring business, Hogg & Sons, in Hanover Square in the heart of London's West End. George was given the middle name of Aylwin, an old family name, by which he was always known at home.

There were six children: the eldest, Gary, Barbara and Daniel, were separated by a gap of several years from Stephen, Rosemary and George – affectionately known as 'Stake', 'Roke' and 'Hake'. They all had the advantages bestowed by class and wealth: a nanny and private education first at St George's School in Harpenden and then, for the boys, Wadham College, Oxford. There were summer holidays in Salcombe, Devon, and winter sports breaks in Switzerland.

The Hoggs lived the life of a conventional middle-class family in the late Edwardian era. In one respect, however, they were very different. The Victorian age had bequeathed English society three overarching institutions: the monarchy, the Anglican Church, and the Empire. In this respect the Hoggs were non-conformists. The family's political views were shaped by the Quaker pacifist philosophy which George's mother Kathleen and his unmarried aunt, Muriel Lester, had embraced from an early age. Muriel campaigned on pacifist and anti-empire platforms all her life. She was briefly jailed in Holloway prison in London, and in Trinidad, on charges of sedition. She became a friend of Gandhi, and founded the Kingsley Hall mission which still continues its work as a community centre in East London.

Muriel Lester was very close to her sister Kathleen, and she was to have an early and powerful influence on her youngest nephew. Indeed, George's first memory was of being taken to a beach by his mother and Aunt Muriel in the summer of 1918, when he was three, and given a sign to hold up which read 'No More War', while the ladies tried to impress their pacifist message upon the crowd of holidaymakers. George grew up in a family in which pacifism and international peace, very much the language of the left in the twenties, were advocated by the parents and absorbed by the children. Mealtimes in the Hogg household were serious affairs. There was always time for light-hearted family banter, but Kathleen made sure that the great issues of the day were discussed and debated. This was especially true when Aunt Muriel made one of her regular visits.

Muriel and Kathleen's politics had been shaped by the poverty they saw in the East End of London in the last decade of Queen Victoria's rule. They and their sister Doris were born in the 1880s in Loughton, in the Epping Forest area of Essex. Their upbringing was affluent, both their father and their grandfather having prospered from shipbuilding. The family were leading Baptists, and had moved to Loughton because it was a stronghold of Protestant non-conformism, with a Baptist church erected in 1813. The three sisters were baptised into the Church in 1898.

The arrival of the railway saw Loughton become a popular destination for East Enders. It soon became known as 'Lousy Loughton', a reference to the lice and fleas the impoverished visitors supposedly brought with them.

In her early teens, Muriel occasionally travelled through the slums by train when returning home from London. From the window of her first-class carriage the sight of shoeless children in ragged clothes playing in front of homes that were little more than hovels (and the unsympathetic comments of her fellow travellers) profoundly influenced her. She decided to become a social worker in the East End. Around this time she read the works of Tolstoy, notably his non-fiction masterpiece *The Kingdom of God is Within You* (1894), which was to become a vital text for Christian pacifists, second only to the Bible. Muriel later wrote, 'It changed the very quality of life for me. Once your eyes have been opened to pacifism, you can't shut them again.'

The Fellowship of Reconciliation, established in December 1914, gave Muriel Lester an international platform for her pacifist ideals. The organisation had been formed following a chance meeting at Cologne station in July that year between an English Quaker, Henry Hodgkin, and a German Lutheran, Friedrich Siegmund-Schultze. The two men talked while waiting for a delayed train, and found common cause in their detestation of the coming war. They parted with the words, 'We are one in Christ and can never be at war.' By the end of the war the Fellowship of Reconciliation had become an international body, with the three Lester sisters enthusiastic supporters. The ideals of the Fellowship and the moral imperative of pacifism were drummed into the young George Hogg from an early age.

The Hogg family moved to Harpenden before the First World War, and lived first in the rented house, 'Red Gables', where

George would be born. Later they would build their own house in the town, 'Wayfarings'. Harpenden changed little as the Hogg children grew up through the war years and the 1920s. It was a tight-knit commuter community, just thirty-five minutes by rail from central London. George's father, like many of his friends, took the early train to London every day, leaving Kathleen and the nanny in charge of the children. With a population of only ten thousand, Harpenden still called itself a village at the time when George was growing up. The main street and surrounding residential areas quickly gave way to the green fields of Hertfordshire. Harpenden was well known for its school, St George's, but was otherwise an unremarkable county town.

A group of families who shared the Hoggs' Christian outlook formed the social world in which the children grew up. The Hunters, Nelsons and Proctors lived close to the Hogg home, and their children were in and out of each other's houses at weekends. From an early age George formed close friendships with a group of boys with whom he went through school. David 'Dippy' Proctor, Robert 'Bosh' Nelson and Roger Hunter were sporty, naughty boys, typical of their generation. The honorary girl of the group, Bosh's sister Winifred, known as 'Muff', was to become George's first serious girlfriend.

The political views of George's parents were something of a joke among his friends, and probably an embarrassment to him, since he recalled having to hide the family's regular newspaper, the left-wing *Daily Herald*, when they came round.

Kathleen Hogg brought up her family in a strict, almost puritanical regime that would be regarded as repressive today. She is remembered by her nephews and nieces as a difficult, somewhat eccentric woman, who insisted on the observance of strict rules of behaviour, especially on Sundays and religious holidays. The Hogg family attended three services at Harpenden's Methodist chapel on Sundays, and for the rest of the day were required to read improving books – the Bible, the prayer book or works by well-known missionaries. Any other book they chose to read had to be covered in brown paper and read well out of their mother's view. As well as religious attendance, Sundays meant homework and piano practice. Kathleen was well remembered by her children and grandchildren seated at the top of the stairs brushing her hair and offering a stream of critical comments while listening to one of the children playing the piano.

This was an obviously loving family, but by all accounts Kathleen showed little emotion towards her children 'There was no kissing and no hugging of the children,' George's great-niece Hilary Jarvis says. 'It was very much a family of its time; showing emotion was not the done thing at all; manners were important, it was on the surface very stiff.'

George was very much his mother's boy. He grew up as the adored youngest child, and can be seen in the family album dressed in velvet suits with a shining aureole of golden curls standing in a well-kept garden with various much older brothers and sisters. He soon learnt how to get round his mother's stricter rules. He had a natural sense of fun, which bubbled through the gloomy Sundays with their required reading and long silences. George and his sister Rosemary, who was three years older, and to whom he would always be closer than to any of his other siblings, would frequently skip the longer Sunday-morning service at the Methodist chapel and go to play with neighbours' children. Aware of this mischief, Kathleen, who stayed at home to prepare the lunch, would begin the meal by quizzing the children on the nature of the lengthy sermon. Fire-and-brimstone sermons were very much to Kathleen's taste and she was determined that her children should benefit from them. George and Rosemary persuaded their elder brother Stephen, who had to attend chapel because he was in the choir, to report on the highlights, which were then dutifully repeated at lunch.

For all the strictness of the regime at home, George Hogg had a very happy childhood. He was once overheard saying to Rosemary, 'If heaven isn't much nicer than earth I shall ask God to let me come back.' He was remembered by his nephews and nieces as the 'the golden boy' who was marked out by his parents at an early age for success. Given his later achievements this might be attributed to hindsight, but from the observations of his teachers at the time, and later those of the Warden at Wadham College, the great Maurice Bowra, it seems clear that there was something special about the youngest Hogg.

From the age of six George was taught at home by a governess. At ten he was sent to a school at Gland, on the shores of Lake Geneva in Switzerland, which had been set up on pacifist principles. Rosemary was returning for her second year, and had begged to be allowed to take her brother with her. The school's aim was to break down all barriers of age, sex, class and nationality. All the staff shared the housework with the children.

The main effect on George of his Swiss education seems to have been liberation from the strict regime at home. At weekends he would go off hiking, bicycling or skiing with other boys, while Rosemary remained behind to wash and mend his clothes. Once a week there was a school meeting at which the pupils were free to criticise their masters and mistresses, and even the head, and to express their views on anything they thought unfair or wrong. To the young George Hogg this was revolutionary, and he was to introduce exactly the same practice when he became headmaster of his own school in China.

The year of emancipation ended with George's return to England, where he joined his siblings at the co-educational St George's school in Harpenden. The headmaster, Cecil Grant, was one of the great educationalists of his time, and his school provided imaginative teaching, designed to bring out and develop talent.

George showed promise as a writer for the school magazine. His parents were already convinced he had a gift for words. When he was ten his father had read him aloud Tennyson's 'The Eagle' and asked him to describe an eagle. After a moment's thought George replied: 'A whirring mass of fierce glory.'

All the Hogg children had done well at St George's, but the youngest child proved the ablest pupil. He was nicknamed 'Pig' at school – not because of his surname, but because of a characteristic sinal snort. The other name given him by his rugby-playing friends was self-explanatory: 'Tuff'. Both on and off the playing field George proved a natural leader. His sixth-form master wrote of him many years later:

> *I sensed in him great reserves and a high sense of purpose. He was modest to a degree and showed true humility. Quiet and unassuming he nevertheless was a dominant influence in the form. It was a joy to observe in the years after he left a new generation of prefects, showing traits of character which they had unconsciously copied from him, so that his influence lived on. It was equally a feature of his [rugby] football that in the hardest game he always had something in reserve to call on in an emergency.*

The golden boy had his mischievous side. One night he and his friends Roger Hunter and David Proctor stole a car belonging to Miss Terry, the French teacher. George, who had learnt to drive his father's car at the age of sixteen, drove them to a scout troop camp, where they let the tents down and fled. George was demoted as a prefect for a fortnight, and caned by the head-master.

At St George's the youngest Hogg grew into a tall, good-looking young man who delighted in singing and showing off his skills at the monthly Saturday-night dances. He was head boy at the age of seventeen, and almost naturally began a relationship with the head girl, Winifred 'Muff' Nelson.

The Nelsons provided a second home for the Hogg children in Harpenden. Although practising Christians, they were more relaxed in their observance of the faith, and their cheerful and fun-loving family life – a considerable contrast to the strict regime of his own home – made a big impression on George. So did another family in Harpenden, the Hunters, who also provided a home from home.

Muff Nelson, who had gained her nickname through her childhood affection for the nursery rhyme 'Little Miss Muffet', was a good-looking redhead with a great sense of fun. A year older than George, she had been drawn to him from the time they had played together as young children. She shared his passion for sport, and his love of dancing and singing. As an old woman looking back over her life Muff wrote to a friend: 'I adored the boy and always hoped we would grow up together and get married.' After his death she wrote rather more formally in the school magazine: 'There were nothing but words of admiration and affection for George both while he was at the school and after he left it. We all associate George with the headmaster's well remembered cough followed by the quiet words, "Well done, boy." '

Although he and Muff were very much regarded as a couple at school, that did not prevent George from casting his eye over some of his friends' girlfriends. St George's golden boy, head of school, captain of the rugby XV, a dazzler on the dance floor and with a fine singing voice, knew he was attractive to women.

On his last night in England before leaving for China, George,

Muff and other friends held a farewell at the Silver Cup pub in Harpenden. He promised her he would return within a year. She was devastated when he did not come back, and more so when it became clear that he had found a new and exciting life in China, and had no intention of returning to resume their relationship. Nothing survives of their correspondence while he was in China, but George's letters home reveal that two years after he left he became aware that Muff had developed a relationship with his good friend Roger Hunter.

Muff's sadness at the long separation from George had been compounded by the death of her elder brother Robert, a marine commando who was killed at Deal in Kent in 1940 as a result of one of the very few Italian air raids of the war. In the summer of that year the invasion scare was at its height, and the Battle of Britain had yet to be won. In these circumstances it is perhaps not surprising that Muff reached for the security of marriage, even if it was to the best friend of the man she really loved. Almost from the beginning the marriage was a disaster, and Muff soon moved back from married quarters at a coastal command base to her parents' home in Harpenden.

Understandably, it was the more thoughtful side of George's character that his contemporaries remembered when they paid tribute to him in the school magazine after his death. His close friend David Proctor said: 'My impression of him was of a thinker. He strove for perfection. He was a man of few words but those words always made sense.' Maurice Bowra wrote to Kathleen: 'He had great reserves of character and seemed to have some inner vision of his own which showed him where to go and what to do.' This was a remarkable tribute, given that Bowra had many letters of condolence to write to parents of his former students who died in the war.

*   *   *

In September 1934, at the age of nineteen, George Hogg arrived at Wadham College to read 'modern greats', as it was then called (it evolved into what is now known as PPE – politics, philosophy and economics). He was by now an assured young man, over six feet tall. He had fair hair which had never quite shaken off its childish waves. It was no surprise that he walked into the college rugby first XV, and went on to captain the team in his last year. Had he been more heavily built he would certainly have got his 'blue'. As it was he played regularly for the university's second team, 'The Greyhounds'.

Wadham, one of the smallest of the Oxford colleges, was an eccentric place in the 1930s, with an admissions policy that depended on the whim of the examiner rather than academic ability. Michael Mann, a contemporary of Hogg's, recalls going up to Wadham on the recommendation of an old waiter in the King's Arms pub, where most Wadhamites did their drinking. Mann had taken a room at the pub while trying various colleges for a scholarship in Spanish. The waiter told him Wadham had the best course, and Mann found himself sitting the exam with two other candidates, without any sign of an invigilator. One candidate seized the entire supply of writing paper and refused to surrender so much as a page. Mann tracked down the senior tutor and complained. He was sent to a stationer's in town with half a crown to buy paper, and given an extra fifteen minutes to complete the exam. He got the scholarship, which was not surprising: of the other two candidates, one thought he was sitting for a Hebrew scholarship, and the other left the exam early.

Hogg's time at Wadham was dominated by one of the great Oxford figures of the twentieth century, Maurice Bowra. Bowra did not become Warden of the college until 1938, a year after Hogg had left Oxford, but in a sense he had already fulfilled the role for years. Even as a Fellow he cast a long and lively shadow over college activities, influencing most aspects of undergraduate life. His riotous parties for students and distinguished guests were famous for his practical jokes. Among other things Bowra would make up fictitious careers and achievements for his guests, and then introduce them to each other, enjoying the subsequent confusion.

In the 1930s Bowra personified Wadham College. He was a celebrity don who set out to shock. With a characteristic touch of high-table humour he declared himself anti-prig, anti-elitist, anti-solemn and very anti-Balliol. The purpose of a university, Bowra believed, was to break down barriers of class, convention and national sentiment, and to 'revel in the uninhibited exercise of the mind'. His attractive view of life appealed to many of his students, and George Hogg was certainly among them. Bowra could have been talking of Hogg when he described the aim of university life as being 'to take young men who arrived in Oxford suppressed and unselfexpressed and recast them into individuals with something to say'. Bowra had been born in China, where his father worked as a customs officer, and this gave him a special interest in Hogg's later work and wanderings.

George's sister Rosemary, known to the family as 'Roke' or 'Posie', was three years older than him, but they had spent their childhoods together and had formed the closest relationship in the family circle. They adored each other, and during his Oxford years when Hogg wrote home to catch up with family news it was always Rosemary who was on his mind. She remembered him talking with huge enthusiasm about college life, and about Bowra's role as both a tutor and party host. She said: 'You could not say that Oxford made him, because there were so many other early influences, but he loved his time there, he loved everything about the place, especially the freedom.' Oxford gave him the chance to get away from the enclosed world of home and

Harpenden. He had never openly rebelled against the inhibitions of life at Wayfarings, but like most young men of eighteen he wanted freedom. No more grim and gloomy Sundays being forced to read one of his mother's 'Sunday books'.

George Hogg was not by nature a political animal, although the mix of liberal and left-wing views he grew up with at home would have been reinforced at Oxford. His student generation was highly political, and vociferous about the big issues of the day: the infamous Oxford Union debate 'That this house will in no circumstances fight for its King and Country' had taken place in February 1933, the year before Hogg went up. The majority of 275 for the motion, with 153 against, was a gift for the news editors of Fleet Street, created a national furore, and was roundly condemned by the political establishment. Winston Churchill, then a backbencher in his wilderness years, termed it 'abject, squalid and shameless'.

The big issues of the day dominated the student union debates and inspired long and self-regarding editorials in the student newspapers: the powerlessness of the League of Nations as Japan, Italy and Germany trampled on the international agreements that they had signed in the decade following the First World War, the Spanish Civil War, and the question of rearmament in the face of the rise of Nazi Germany.

The views of the majority of students were predictable. They backed the republican side in the Spanish Civil War and roundly condemned the Italian invasion of Abyssinia. The League of Nations was damned as ineffectual. Some of those who had supported the King and Country resolution would later claim in *The Times* that they had really been voting for collective security and a stronger League of Nations. It was a thin argument which convinced no one. The two Oxford student magazines, *Isis* and *Cherwell*, published lengthy leaders questioning whether students were truly serious about such matters or were merely posturing.

As far as Wadham was concerned, much of the student debate took place in the King's Arms or the college dining hall. There were no noisy demonstrations outside the Spanish or Italian embassies in London, nor angry letters to the national papers. George Hogg's Oxford may have been a noisy, political place, but his own memories of his time there dwell on student pranks such as burning lavatory seats, the pleasures of toasting muffins in front of the fire, and the hard work of trying to get a rugby blue. His name appears in the college gazette, and occasionally in the student newspapers, but only to report his prowess on the rugby pitch. It is hard to avoid the conclusion that he was more concerned with having a good time than with worrying about Abyssinia or the struggle against fascism in Spain.

With the help of Maurice Bowra, Hogg took the best that Oxford had to give. It was an enchanted world, and one he recalled with great affection throughout his brief life. The experience did not, and indeed could not, have prepared him or any of the university's graduates for the realities of a world in which fascism was building a powerful popular appeal in a Europe racked by depression; in which the militarism in Japanese culture was about to embroil China and the whole Pacific region in a tide of warfare; in which centuries of feudalism in the most populous nation on earth, China, were being bloodily replaced by a modern totalitarian political concept.

The political ideas that Hogg took to Oxford, pacifism and the Christian socialism of the Fellowship of Reconciliation, remained intact if dormant during his student years. As a tutor Maurice Bowra equipped him to test the ideals drummed into him by his mother. Oxford's real gift to Hogg was to give him the freedom to live and enjoy himself beyond the confines of a repressive home life.

Rugby was probably as important as anything else for him at Oxford. Gerald Parker played in the college team with him, and in 2007, at the age of ninety, he recalled his captain well: 'The Wadham team did very well against the other colleges in the two years I played with the team. Hogg was a very good captain and led by example on the field. There were no long pep talks before the game, it was pretty much "Follow me and do what I do on the field." As a team we always had some beers together afterwards. We were not a political bunch really – rugby was the thing.'

Hogg spent his long vacations travelling. In 1936 he set out on a hitch-hiking tour of central and south-eastern Europe with £4 in his pocket and a Rhodes Scholar as a companion. The violent and sectarian politics of the Balkans, the hotbed of nationalist rivalries elsewhere in eastern Europe and the racism and militarism of Nazi Germany opened his eyes to the real world beyond the dreaming spires of Oxford.

In the early summer of 1937 Hogg left Oxford with a second-class degree (two of his brothers, Stephen and Daniel, had obtained third-class degrees, while the eldest brother, Gary, got a second) and returned home to plan his future. He did not really know what to do. His friends were planning to disappear into the civil service or the City. The world around him offered little inspiration. In May the coronation had taken place of King George VI and Queen Elizabeth at Westminster Abbey. A month later the former King Edward VIII, now the Duke of Windsor, married the woman for whom he had abdicated, Wallis Simpson. While these royal events attracted widespread public attention and comment, they probably did not elicit much interest in the Hogg household, where Aunt Muriel's views on the British Empire were firmly in place.

The Hoggs' daily newspaper, the *Herald*, presented a bleak view of the world that summer. Hitler and Mussolini stated publicly that they would intervene in Spain after General Franco had suffered a setback at the battle of Guadalajara. In Russia, Stalin's purge of the army led to a wave of executions of senior officers. A brief news agency item from Berlin stated that Heinrich Himmler, chief of the German police, had announced the establishment of a new concentration camp at Buchenwald to house those considered enemies of the state. Camps at Dachau and Sachsenhausen had already been set up. At the end of August most British newspapers carried a dramatic picture of a badly burnt Chinese baby crying in the wreckage of Shanghai's bombed-out south railway station. The battle for the city had begun, and Japanese planes were being used to clear a path for their advancing army. Two thousand British women and children were evacuated from the city aboard the P&O liner *Rajputana*. A British battalion arrived to reinforce the garrison and protect the remaining expatriate population.

Aunt Muriel came to stay at Wayfarings in August. By now she was known to the press as 'Mother of World Peace', and regularly travelled the world on lecture tours. Untroubled by the outbreak of hostilities in the Far East, indeed probably because of them, she announced her intention to travel across America to Japan, China and India to promote her pacifist message. Japan was the rising imperial power, and Muriel wished to make contact with the Christian co-operative movement there. She believed that while the government might pursue the politics of imperial aggrandisement, the Japanese people wanted peace.

Kathleen was a passionate gardener, and took her sister into the garden to discuss the plan over some serious weeding. Muriel had taken George's elder brother Daniel to India to meet Gandhi a few years previously. Why not take George with her on this latest journey?

George jumped at the idea. The problem was money. The

Hoggs had few savings left after educating six children privately, and taking expensive annual winter holidays in Switzerland. Then there was the question of George's career. The idea of taking time off after university to travel was a novel one. Most of George's university friends were going straight into the professions. The Depression was far from over, unemployment was still high, and the international outlook was threatening. This did not seem the time to be travelling the world seeking adventure.

George solved the money problem by cashing in a small legacy. This would cover the £18.10s. third-class single fare to New York, and the passage from San Francisco to Japan. What little was left over would cover his expenses while he hitch-hiked across America to rejoin his aunt for the voyage across the Pacific. As for the return journey, he would find a way of earning his passage back from India.

It was settled that aunt and nephew would sail on the *Queen Mary* for New York in September 1937. The night before he left, George said his farewells to Muff Nelson and other friends in the Silver Cup (which is still one of the better pubs in Harpenden). The following day he was so engrossed in the new American best-seller that had just been published in Britain, Margaret Mitchell's *Gone with the Wind*, that he had to be dragged from his armchair for the drive to Southampton.

There is, or was, in the Hogg family album a faded Box Brownie photograph of members of the family standing on the dockside at Southampton that September day, with the *Queen Mary* in the background. The group are facing a westering sun, with George in the middle, wearing a snappy trilby and suit, and his parents and Rosemary and Stephen around him.

Third-class cabins on the *Queen Mary* were at the front of the ship, and thus experienced the worst of the pitching and rolling in rough weather. And the weather was bad throughout the six-day voyage. Many of the 580 third-class passengers were European migrants to North America, and for their convenience the menus in the ship's restaurant were printed in both English and French. No one read them. The restaurant was largely deserted, as the passengers remained confined in their cabins. The little deck space available to third class was closed. While Aunt Muriel took to her cabin, George talked his way into the second class and the chance of some fresh air.

In New York George went straight to a Fellowship of Reconciliation conference before he took to the road. To everyone's surprise a delegate from China made a speech damning the Japanese attack on Shanghai and defending China's right to meet force with force. He then resigned from the Fellowship. This triumph of nationalism over pacifism stunned the meeting.

George wrote to his mother, 'I don't think there are many real pacifists in the world . . . Aren't you glad when you hear China has pulled off something good in the war?' It is not recorded how this letter went down at Harpenden, nor whether George told Muriel that he had begun to question the politics with which he had grown up. But he consistently distanced himself from the family's pacifist beliefs throughout his time in China, although return letters from his mother never challenge his apostasy.

Hogg spent several months in the autumn of 1937 hitch-hiking across and up and down the USA. By his estimate he covered 5,500 miles by car and lorry, sleeping where he could. On several occasions when he could not find anywhere to stay he was given a cell for the night by the local police. The experience was not always pleasant. He described one of his jailors, a police sergeant, as 'a most sinister man. A steel tube took the place of a severed right hand and he was driving nails into the wall with it; no hammer was necessary. The bare room [of the police station] contained a few people standing around the stove; they spat expertly

37

and frequently. "If you are in more of a hurry than I am," said the sergeant, "there is always the sidewalk outside." Only pride forbade an immediate retreat. His face was as hard as his steel tube hand; eyes blue, when you saw them, hollow cheeks and an Irish jaw. He showed me a musty pile of blankets in a filthy cell. "Up at four and we don't feed anyone, get that straight," he said.'

In the Deep South an introduction from Muriel took him to the Delta co-operative farm in Rochdale, Mississippi, where black and white sharecroppers were working together to pay off their debts and buy their land. The co-operative had been founded the previous year to take in workers who had been sacked from cotton farms after trying to start a union, and it made a big impression on the English visitor: here was theory in practice, an ideal that had actually been translated into working reality.

Still immersed in *Gone with the Wind*, Hogg travelled through the states and cities in which Margaret Mitchell had set her novel. He went to Richmond, Charleston and Savannah. The widespread evasion of the Prohibition laws, still supposedly in full force, made Hogg laugh: 'Tennessee is dry!' he wrote. 'They voted dry because everyone makes a good profit out of illegal drink. The state police make good tips, the people get cheap liquor and the bootleggers make big profits. But the drink is still very cheap because the state can't tax it!'

The final leg of his journey across the United States brought a stroke of extraordinary luck, the same good fortune that would carry him through his perilous years in China. Some days before he was due to meet Aunt Muriel in San Francisco, Hogg found himself well over a thousand miles to the east, in the plains of Texas. Forced to stand outside city limits because hitching was against the law in the city, he spent day after day watching cars accelerate past him. Finally one car stopped. The driver said nothing, but drove west for a half an hour before asking his passenger where he was going.

'To Japan and China with my aunt,' replied Hogg. After considering this statement the driver said, 'I'm on my way to China too. I'm travelling with an Englishwoman named Muriel Lester.' It turned out that the driver was a Dr Lacey from the American Bible Society, and that he was taking a shipment of Bibles to Japan. George went with him for the remaining 1,600 miles, and met his aunt on the quayside.

A fortnight later, in mid-November 1937, aunt and nephew arrived in Yokohama, and went to the port city of Kobe to stay with their host in Japan, Dr Toyohiko Kagawa. This remarkable man was a Christian leader in a nation where the Emperor was considered divine, and Shinto, the worship of ancestral and other gods, was the state religion. He preached pacifism in a society that been indoctrinated in the militaristic ethic, and had twice been imprisoned for trade-union activism. Kagawa had been born in 1888, orphaned at an early age, and brought up by American missionaries. Disowned by the rest of his family after his conversion to Christianity, he went to theological colleges in the United States and Japan, but rejected the endless doctrinal arguments and decided instead to work among the poor in the slums. He played a major role in the successful campaign for universal adult suffrage in 1925, and would go on to publicly apologise in 1940 for the Japanese invasion of China. This inevitably led to further arrest and imprisonment.

Among his other activities, Dr Kagawa had spent twenty years developing a co-operative system among farmers and small businessmen around Kobe. While Aunt Muriel sought meetings with government officials to give them the benefit of her views on militarism, George was shown co-op banks, farms, restaurants and market gardens. He also learnt from Dr Kagawa how a government dominated by the military had drawn on a deep-rooted cultural and religious belief in Japanese racial superiority to sanctify, and thus legitimise, the Chinese campaign in the eyes of the people. Japan projected its role in China as a civilising mission, designed to bring peace and prosperity to a country racked by warlordism and corruption. The message resonated deep within the Japanese national psyche.

Hogg found himself in a nation gripped by chauvinist hysteria. The slow-moving invasion of China had begun in the 1890s, with an encroachment into the north-eastern region of Manchuria. But from 1931 the pace of conquest quickened. By the time George and Aunt Muriel arrived, Japan had occupied large areas of China, established a puppet state, Manchukuo, in the north-east, and taken control of the old imperial capital Beijing, then called Peking.

In Japan, criticism of the government was forbidden. Anyone who dared to publicly question official policy was dismissed from his or her job, and even risked assassination. Newspapers and radio were heavily censored. Foreigners could be accused of spying on the slightest pretext. Schools and universities used textbooks with strong nationalistic overtones, and many foreign academic works were banned. Even children's hour on the official radio station almost always contained a story about the civilising mission of the brave Japanese soldiers in their struggle with the treacherous Chinese.

It would have been impossible for a visitor to be untouched by the mood of isolationism and paranoia. Hogg picked up a smattering of spoken Japanese, and his hosts translated press reports for him on a regular basis. He would thus have been aware of the portrayal of China, on radio and in the newspapers, as a nation torn apart by civil strife and liable to follow Russia into a Bolshevik revolution. It was effective propaganda, because it was partially true. The other side of this coin was the message that Japan's mission in China was a civilising one. The purpose of the military intervention had been to stop a bloody civil war, and to prevent China from going communist. Japan certainly wanted to stop the spread of communism in China, but the propaganda masked Tokyo's true aim, which was the establishment of regional hegemony, with China in the role of a vassal state.

Since the early 1930s Japan had been falling under the control of a fanatical wing of the army, bent on imperial expansion. The economic pressures of the Depression had revived age-old dreams of national glory. The war minister General Minami and his senior officers did much to create, and take advantage of, the climate of political extremism. The modest advances towards a parliamentary democracy and the development of pluralist politics in the 1920s were overwhelmed by the wave of nationalism that broke over Japanese politics in the last years of that decade. The civilian politicians in the cabinet provided little opposition as relatively junior officers, none too discreetly backed by their commanders, revived ambitions for Japan to assume its rightful place as ruler of the Asian mainland.

The apostles of empire were easily able to manipulate a long list of grievances to justify their pursuit of territorial ambition. School history lessons hammered home the message that Japan's legitimate imperial ambitions in the nineteenth century had been thwarted by the greed of Britain and the other European powers. The list of grievances was long. Australia and America had introduced quotas on Japanese immigration after the First World War. These injected a new racial element into relations, since in their dealings with the Western powers the Japanese had previously sought, and often received, the status of Europeans in Asia due to their perceived social and economic superiority. New trade tariffs designed to protect the US economy from Japanese competition in the twenties only fuelled Tokyo's resentment towards the West.

China was easy prey for the militant political class and war-minded army officers in Japan at the start of the 1930s. The Chinese offered only impotent protests as Japanese troops advanced into Manchuria and Tokyo made plain its plans for further territorial conquests. Boycotts of Japanese goods and repeated anti-Japanese demonstrations had had little effect. The social and political chaos in China in the 1920s, as the nationalist government of Chiang Kai-shek struggled to assert itself over regional warlords and the fast-growing Communist Party, merely accelerated Japan's ambitions.

On 18 September 1931, using the flimsy pretext of 'Chinese provocation' near the Manchurian town of Mukden, the Japanese began military operations to complete the conquest of Manchuria. The invasion was ordered by the army command, not the cabinet. The government was only consulted when it came to the question of reinforcements. From that moment until the Japanese defeat at the end of the Second World War the military were effectively in charge of the Japanese government.

The Christian co-op movement in Japan was one of very few voices raised against the government. But it was a weak and muted voice. Christianity had only been made legal in Japan in 1878. Shinto, the state religion, was a traditional set of beliefs rooted in the worship of spirits and of the Emperor, whose divinity was unchallenged. For centuries Shinto had co-existed with Buddhism, and had to some extent incorporated Buddhist beliefs. From the late nineteenth century it was used as a means of rallying the nation against Western imperialism. It focused on emperor-worship, and thus became a more overtly political religion. The core Shinto philosophy held that the Japanese emperor was descended directly from the Sun Goddess; that he was therefore of divine descent; that the Japanese islands and people were also of divine descent; and that Japan was therefore superior to other nations.

With his strong Baptist upbringing, George Hogg took a keen interest in the travails of the Christian Church in a country dominated by an alien and aggressive religion. There were only 300,000 Christians in a nation of seventy-three million. Persecution in the seventeenth century had wiped out most Christians, and the small community that had emerged after the legalisation of the faith was scattered, frightened and demoralised.

Fearful that history might repeat itself, Dr Kagawa and other Christian leaders worked hard to find an honourable compromise with the government's aggressive nationalism. They carefully avoided condemnation of Japan's military operations in China, causing Hogg to note wryly that at least the Church had not gone so far as to pray for a Japanese victory.

TWO

Shanghai

'No poppa, no momma, no whisky soda.'

George Hogg left Japan on the French ship *Président Doumer*, and arrived in Shanghai in February 1938. He only intended to stay for two weeks before rejoining Aunt Muriel in Japan, from where they planned to travel together to India, and then return to England. Since the First World War Shanghai, styling itself 'the Paris of the East', or 'the Pearl of the Orient', had become a favourite destination for well-heeled international travellers. There were three million Chinese and seventy thousand foreigners in the city, with miles of slums concealed behind a façade of tall and elegant buildings on the north bank of the Huangpu River, a tributary of the Yangtse. Now the tourists, along with the cruise liners that used to tie up at the Bund, had gone, but Shanghai still clung to remnants of its old lifestyle.

On the eve of the Japanese take-over Shanghai was essentially three cities: the international settlement, under the joint control of the British and the Americans, covered an area of eight square miles on the bank of the Huangpu. The commercial, industrial and shipping businesses were all centred here, as were most of the foreign residents, who lived a life totally divorced from the

Chinese population around them. Policing and taxation were controlled by the international powers, and the Chinese contribution to the lifestyle of the expatriates lay largely in the provision of cheap labour and domestic servants. The French concession was smaller, but similarly organised. Beyond that lay the teeming Chinese quarter.

George Hogg stayed with missionary contacts of Aunt Muriel. Frank and Aimee Millican were American Methodists who had been in China since 1907. The Reverend Millican organised the church and distributed Christian literature in the city, while his wife ran a Christian broadcasting station.

In Shanghai Hogg received a brutal introduction to what Japan's civilising mission meant on the ground. Japanese forces had taken all but the international settlements of the city in fighting that summer, while Hogg was mulling over his future in Hertfordshire. He was studying the co-operative movement with his Christian hosts in Japan when Tokyo's troops stormed the Chinese capital Nanjing in mid-December 1937. The massacres that followed lasted seven weeks, and were still continuing while Hogg began to grapple with what had happened in Shanghai.

He found a city crowded with refugees and devastated by war. Scores of desolate, ruined villages lay just beyond the city limits. Within the French concession and the international settlement there were sandbags at the entrances of all the main buildings, pillboxes on street corners and sentries with fixed bayonets everywhere. He wrote home remarking on the swarms of urchin children who attached themselves to any foreigner, crying, 'No poppa, no momma, no whisky soda.'

Hogg liked Shanghai. He found the city strangely exhilarating. This was no leisurely hitch-hike across the United States, no guided tour of the co-ops in Japan. He had been pitched in among a population which was fighting to survive. The streets of the international settlement had become home for tens of thousands of refugees driven from their villages in the countryside. For the first time in his life Hogg saw human degradation at first hand. The refugees ate, slept, made love, gave birth and died on the pavements of the city. Old newspapers were fought over by the street people because the scant warmth they provided could mean the difference between life and death during the bitter nights.

Everything in Shanghai was for sale. Hogg described street sellers touting fried eels in one hand and fountain pens in the other. In between there was nothing that was not on offer. There was no luxury that could not be bought, no whim that could not be satisfied. This was an aspect to life in the city that even a naïve young Englishman could not have missed, although he took good care not to mention it in his letters home.

Hogg arrived in the city only weeks before W.H. Auden and Christopher Isherwood, who had been commissioned to write a travel book about China. The book would be called *Journey to a War*, and in researching it the two writers joined the growing foreign press corps in China, of which George Hogg was about to become a very junior member.

Auden and Isherwood had known each other since they were both at St Edmund's school, at Hindhead in Surrey. They had achieved literary fame – and had become lovers – during the thirties, that 'low, dishonest decade', as Auden was to describe it a year later. Isherwood had already published his best-known works, *Mr Norris Changes Trains* (1935) and *Sally Bowles* (1937; later included in *Goodbye to Berlin*). The two men collaborated on three plays, and enjoyed a sporadic sexual relationship throughout their long friendship.

Isherwood immediately saw through the 'impressive façade of a great city'. Shanghai was nothing more, he thought, than a collection of semi-skyscrapers dumped on an 'unhealthy mud bank'. Behind the façade lay a sordid and shabby mob of smaller buildings: 'Nowhere a fine avenue, spacious park, an imposing central square. Nowhere anything civic at all.'

Despite this indictment of China's greatest city, the literary couple found plenty to distract them: 'The tired or lustful businessman will find everything here to gratify his desires,' wrote Isherwood. 'You can attend race-meetings, baseball games, football matches. You can see the latest American films. If you want girls, or boys, you can have them, at all prices, in the bathhouses and brothels. If you want opium you can smoke it in the best company, served on a tray, like afternoon tea. Good wine is difficult to obtain but there is enough gin and whisky to float a fleet of battleships. Finally if you ever repent there are churches and chapels of all denominations.'

Hogg was concerned less with the decadence of the city than with the desperation of its citizens. Through Aunt Muriel, one of the great networkers of her time, he established contact with the *Manchester Guardian*. The paper had given generous coverage to Miss Lester's campaigns for the Fellowship of Reconciliation and to her friendship with Gandhi. At the time it had no regular correspondent in China. The editor, William Crozier, agreed to take the unknown and inexperienced Hogg on trial as a non-staff correspondent.

This was an extraordinary coup. The *Manchester Guardian* had achieved national and international recognition under the editorship of C.P. Scott, who held the post for fifty-seven years from 1872. In those days every correspondent, however junior and remote from the Manchester office, was made aware of Scott's famous dictum which appeared in an article he wrote to celebrate the centenary of the paper in 1921: 'Comment is free, but facts are sacred . . . The voice of opponents no less than that of friends has a right to be heard.'

As Hogg was to discover, the then editor took this principle very seriously. The *Manchester Guardian* was a high-minded paper whose leaders inclined towards moral posturing. The paper had long refused to provide coverage of horse-racing, on the grounds that it encouraged gambling. But it insisted on giving a fair hearing even to its political enemies, and Mr Crozier made that point in a letter to his new China correspondent early on in Hogg's career with the paper.

After writing a first piece in February 1938 for his new employers about the frenzied daily struggle for existence in Shanghai – which the paper did not print – Hogg found little to do. The city was packed not only with refugees but also with missionaries who, he observed, 'were only too willing to do anything that had to be done'. There was starvation in the Chinese quarter and death on the streets of the international settlement, but the restaurants and cabarets remained open. There was plenty of good food and entertainment for those with money. Hogg had just received a cheque from home for the large sum of £10, and was well able to afford good restaurants. 'Chinese meals are absolutely enormous!' he wrote home, unconscious of any irony. 'Dish after dish comes in and the idea is to take a little of each. This has great effect in preventing indigestion but is rather unsatisfactory otherwise – I prefer a good tuck in on a few things.'

Thanks to the Millicans and a visit to the imposing British embassy, where he was received by the lowliest of third secretaries, Hogg began to understand the complex sequence of events that had led to the destruction of much of Shanghai. He, like his missionary hosts and other members of the foreign press corps, was also hearing reports that tens of thousands of civilians were being slaughtered on the streets of Nanjing – reports that the expatriate population in Shanghai simply did not believe at first.

The Sino–Japanese war, which was to cost an estimated fifteen million Chinese lives and to last eight years, began on 7 July 1937. Under the terms of a treaty imposed on China in 1901, the Boxer Protocol, Japan had stationed troops in north China between the port of Tientsin and Beijing. That night Japanese forces claimed to have been fired on by Chinese troops, and stormed a local garrison in search of a missing soldier. The history of Japanese aggression towards China leaves little doubt that this was deliberate provocation. Within days the two nations were at war, formalising a conflict that had been intensifying since Japan occupied Manchuria in 1931.

On 7 August the leader of China's nationalist government, Chiang Kai-shek, and his top advisers announced a national war of resistance. Chiang then took a military gamble that has been debated ever since. He decided to shift the major battleground of the war from north China to Shanghai.

The thinking was that while Japanese mechanised forces, backed by air power, would be undefeatable on the plains of north China, the restricted area of China's major sea port would nullify their superiority in armour. Equally, Chiang reckoned that an attack on the Japanese settlement in Shanghai – one of several autonomous zones granted to foreign powers – would force Japan to switch forces from the north, relieving pressure on the Chinese army there.

Making a stand in Shanghai had the added advantage of rallying public opinion behind a government embroiled in a civil war with communist guerrillas. Above all, Chiang Kai-shek thought that any battle for Shanghai, under the eyes of the large foreign community, would draw the attention, sympathy and possibly the intervention of the Western powers. What Chiang and his commanders had overlooked was the sheer ferocity of the Japanese response. This was to lead to huge civilian and military casualties, culminating in the massacre of hundreds of thousands of civilians in the capital Nanjing.

On 11 August Chiang moved three of his best German-trained and -armed divisions inside the limits of Greater Shanghai, although outside the areas of foreign concession. The Japanese were caught by surprise, and rushed reinforcements into their sector. The fighting between the two sides began on 13 August.

The use of heavy weaponry and air power took a terrible toll on both armies, and on the civilian population of Shanghai. In three months of fighting the majority of the nationalist army troops, the nucleus of Chiang's modern army, were killed or wounded. Japanese casualties were over forty thousand. Thousands of civilians were killed. Large portions of the city outside the Western concessions were destroyed. Beaten and disorganised, the Chinese forces fell back towards Nanjing, the nationalist capital.

The Tokyo government offered to settle what it called 'the China incident' by negotiation, setting out a series of demands which in effect amounted to Chinese recognition of Japanese control over large areas of northern China. When Chiang Kai-shek did not deign to respond, the government in Tokyo announced that it would 'annihilate' the Chinese government. The true meaning of that announcement became clear within days at Nanjing, the Chinese capital, which the government had hastily evacuated as the Japanese advanced. The city fell on 12–13 December 1937, and what followed was one of the most shameful chapters in the history of twentieth-century warfare.

The 'Rape of Nanjing', as it became known, to this day clouds relations between Beijing and Tokyo. Despite the diplomatic blandishments and the economic and strategic imperatives that bind the two nations in a close regional relationship there is no mistaking the deep and enduring Chinese anger at Japan's refusal to explain or apologise for what happened in Nanjing. In seven weeks of savagery Japanese troops, under the clear control of their commanders, indulged in an orgy of rape and killing. The slaughter was carried out with unimaginable brutality. Thousands were buried or burnt alive. An international tribunal later estimated that more than 260,000 non-combatants had been killed – more than four times the number of British civilians killed during the entire Second World War.

A number of foreigners in the city, including two American correspondents, Tillman Durdin of the *New York Times* and Art Steele of the *Chicago Daily News*, witnessed the senseless slaughter. And it was senseless. There was no military reason for exacting revenge on Nanjing. Indeed, some of the inhabitants had actually welcomed the Japanese as a means of ending weeks of fighting. Nor was the wave of terror and slaughter inflicted upon a civilian population the arbitrary behaviour of drunken troops. Day after day, week after week, for almost two months, Japanese soldiers committed mass murder and mass rape with methods, and on a scale, that defy description and logic.

The Chinese decision to defend the city was also incomprehensible. Nationalist commanders first torched all the villages and suburbs around Nanjing, then ordered their troops, with no means of resupply or escape, to make a stand in the walled city. Thus fifty thousand Chinese troops were surrounded and trapped by an enemy that could bombard them at will from the air, from the river and from ground batteries. According to Tillman Durdin, about two-thirds of the defenders were executed by the Japanese after the city had fallen. Young men were hunted down, stripped of their shirts, and those found with the tell-tale strap marks indicating military webbing were shot out of hand.

Durdin, who escaped Nanjing on an American ship moored on the Yangtse on 22 December 1937, filed a graphic series of reports. In summing up what he had seen, he set the tone for much of the

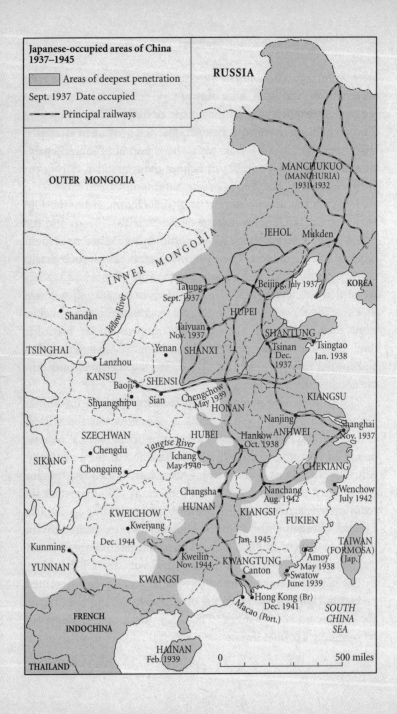

Japanese-occupied areas of China
1937–1945

Areas of deepest penetration

Sept. 1937 Date occupied

Principal railways

RUSSIA

OUTER MONGOLIA

MANCHUKUO
(MANCHURIA)
1931–1932

INNER MONGOLIA

JEHOL   Mukden

Shandan

Datung
Sept. 1937

Beijing, July 1937

KOREA

HUPEI

TSINGHAI

Yenan   SHANXI

Taiyuan
Nov. 1937

SHANTUNG

Tsinan
Dec.
1937

Tsingtao
Jan. 1938

Lanzhou

KANSU   SHENSI

Baoji

Sian

Chengchow
May 1939

HONAN

KIANGSU

Shuangshipu

Shanghai
Nov. 1937

SZECHWAN

HUBEI

Hankow
Oct. 1938

ANHWEI

Nanjing

Chengdu

Yangtse River

SIKANG

Ichang
May 1940

CHEKIANG

Chongqing

Changsha

Nanchang
Aug. 1942

Wenchow
July 1942

HUNAN

KIANGSI

KWEICHOW

FUKIEN

Kweiyang

Dec. 1944

Jan. 1945

TAIWAN
(FORMOSA)
(Jap.)

Kunming

Kweilin
Nov. 1944

KWANGTUNG

Amoy
May 1938

YUNNAN

KWANGSI

Canton

Swatow
June 1939

Hong Kong (Br)
Dec. 1941

Macao
(Port.)

SOUTH
CHINA
SEA

FRENCH
INDOCHINA

THAILAND

HAINAN
Feb. 1939

0   500 miles

international reaction to the Japanese atrocities: 'The wholesale execution of prisoners, the slaughter, rape and looting by the Japanese after their occupation of the city all seem to belong to a more barbaric, vanished period.' The Sino–Japanese war had begun with an atrocity that was to be repeated time and again, although on a smaller scale, throughout the conflict.

The Japanese did not take the international settlements in Shanghai until after Pearl Harbor in December 1941. Old Shanghai had gone, but until hostilities between Tokyo and the Allied powers were formalised, life in the international settlement staggered on. The bar of the Cathay Hotel, the hub of all gossip and intrigue, nightly entertained the usual cast of spies, philanderers and fraudsters, sometimes all three in one. This is where Richard Sorge, one of Stalin's most successful double agents, who certainly recruited agents within the press corps, spent his time. For four years, from 1937 to 1941, when he was arrested, he kept the Kremlin informed of Japanese and German moves in the Far East. He was hanged in Tokyo in 1944.

With the Chinese retreat from Shanghai and the massacre at Nanjing, the war entered a new phase. George Hogg had realised, as had Auden, Isherwood and every other journalist in the city, that there was no point staying in Shanghai. A new and supposedly final battlefront had formed. Chiang Kai-shek had moved his government to a new capital, and the Japanese were once again rolling their armoured and infantry columns westwards. The Chinese government prepared to defend the next major city in the line of attack, and pledged not to give it up as lightly as they had Nanjing.

The new Chinese capital, and the place every journalist wanted to be, was Hankow.

THREE

Hankow

'Hankow is the most interesting place on earth.'

Hankow was one of three cities at the confluence of the Yangtse and the Han, 450 miles from the coast. It was here, halfway down the Yangtse on its journey from the Himalayas to the sea, that Chiang Kai-shek's nationalist government retreated after the loss of Shanghai and Nanjing. The new seat of government, together with Wuchang and Hanyang, was part of a three-city complex known today as Wuhan, the capital of Hubei province.

The only way to get to Hankow from Shanghai in 1938 was by steamer to the British colony of Hong Kong, and then by plane or train. George Hogg left Shanghai aboard the Japanese steamer *Suwe Maru* on 9 March. On arrival in Hong Kong he immediately took the train to Hankow. On the two-day, five-hundred-mile journey he talked his way from his highly uncomfortable third-class berth into the first-class compartments. There he met a smartly dressed Chinese businessman who sold newsprint for a Dutch firm with a branch in Shanghai. Learning that his new English acquaintance was looking for a job, the man made him an immediate offer. It would greatly impress his clients, he explained, if he took an English secretary to meetings. Thus George Hogg's first letter home from Hankow was written on the grand stationery of Van Reekum Bros Ltd, and enabled him to describe himself as a businessman.

With equal good luck, Aunt Muriel had again used her contacts to find a rented room for him in a city where the hotels were turning away even celebrity guests. The room was in the Lutheran mission, which was run by an American bishop and Oxford graduate, Logan Roots: 'your utter charmer, a very good fellow', Hogg called him. The mission owed nothing to the Christian ethic of frugality, and a great deal to the large funds the Church had raised in the US. Standing on several acres on the edge of the city, it was surrounded by a moat-like canal and large red-brick walls. Within the enclosure lay flower and vegetable gardens, tree-lined walks and tennis courts. Several buildings contained classrooms and dormitories for students. The mission ran an elementary school in English and a seminary for the graduates of Chinese high schools.

The Bishop, who was within a few weeks of retirement after a lifetime in China, had good political contacts with Chiang Kai-shek's circle. In the spirit of Christian liberalism, and perhaps political opportunism, he also entertained senior communists and rented rooms to known communist sympathisers. Chou En-lai, then leading the communist delegation in Hankow, would drop in for tea, as would the government's Premier, H.H. Kung. Chou spoke good English, and made a point of seeking out journalists staying at the mission.

Hogg had certainly landed on his feet. Within days of arriving he wrote home to say that the city was 'the most interesting place on earth'. And he was right. Hankow's history as a concession port, its neoclassical European architecture and its teeming Chinese slums had plenty to interest an enquiring journalist.

The provisional capital was one of the Yangtse River cities

opened up to foreign trade by the 1858 Treaty of Tientsin. The treaty had been imposed upon the Emperor in Beijing after the British inflated a minor incident into a major diplomatic confrontation. Not to be left out, the French seized on the murder of a missionary in a part of China not yet opened to the West, and joined the negotiations. Germany and the United States followed suit. Ten new ports were opened to the Western powers along the Yangtse River. In each a number of concessions were granted, allowing the British, French, Germans and Russians to create foreign enclaves with wholly independent powers of policing and taxation. The enforced granting of extra-territorial concessions was humiliation enough for the Emperor. The affront was sharpened with a clause in the treaty which opened all of China to foreign missionaries, Catholic and Protestant alike.

The Bund, or river embankment, at Hankow was a metaphor for the imperial *diktat* that Europe had imposed upon China. The elegant buildings that lined the river not only reflected Western tastes in architecture, but as far as possible were made off-limits to Chinese. The banks, offices, government buildings and the great homes of the wealthy merchants were all lovingly created to mirror the taste and style of home. The heart of the city, with its high-rise buildings, theatres, cinemas, cafés, broad boulevards and bustling riverfront was wholly European in style and layout, even though surrounded by China. Horse-racing at an elegant track on the city outskirts was a focal point of the social scene, and the club buildings, the stands and the surrounding parkland had been designed to lead the spectator to believe that he was in the heart of Surrey.

George Hogg's lifestyle at the Lutheran mission compound may not have been up to the expatriate standards of comfort, but there were servants to look after him, good food at the Bishop's table and a laundry service. In his first letter home he described other foreigners who had also taken advantage of the Bishop's hospitality. Among them were Peg Snow, wife of the American correspondent and author Edgar Snow, famous for his book *Red Star Over China* (1936), and, as Hogg put it, 'an American woman authoress who at one time rode all over the place with Mao's Eighth Route Army'.* The woman was Agnes Smedley, and she was to play a crucial role in the next few months of Hogg's life. A self-proclaimed communist supporter, and author of the best-selling autobiographical novel *Daughter of Earth* (1929), Smedley had become a leading member of the fast-growing Hankow press corps.

Hankow was the wartime capital of China for the first ten months of 1938. It was a Mecca for foreign correspondents, diplomats, hangers-on and spies, and therefore a natural destination for any young journalist looking to make his name and earn some money. Franco's victory in Spain that year had left famous correspondents, small-time stringers and a host of photographers all looking for the next war. While Hankow remained in Chinese hands it became another Madrid, another beleaguered capital making a final and, as it turned out, doomed stand against the forces of fascism. Many of the journalists who arrived were battle-hardened veterans of the Spanish Civil War. They needed a new war, preferably one that offered their readers moral certainties.

When George Hogg arrived the front line was still several hundred miles distant. The fighting would remain far from the

* The communists' army which made the Long March in 1934–35 comprised some sixty thousand troops by the time Mao Tse-tung established his new base in the north at Yenan. In 1937 they were renamed the Eighth Route Army and placed under the control of Mao's most senior commander, Zhu De. The ten thousand guerrillas who had been left behind in the eastern Yangtse valley were renamed the New Fourth Army.

new capital for months thanks to an important, and rare, Chinese victory over the Japanese army at a small town called T'aierh-chuang, which meant the nationalist government was able to delay the final assault on the city until the autumn.

After their conquest of Nanjing, the Japanese had pushed north in an effort to take the important railway centre of Xuzhou in Jiangsu province, which would give them control of the north–south rail links through the heart of China. The ancient brick-walled settlement of T'aierhchuang, on the banks of the Grand Canal, stood in their way. After two weeks of street fighting, which destroyed much of the town, the Chinese appeared to retreat. Two days later, on the evening of 6 April, thirteen divisions of Chinese troops counter-attacked, led by the 31st Division, so famed for night assaults that they were called 'the sleep robbers'. In an overnight battle the Japanese were routed, losing ten thousand killed or captured out of a force of thirty thousand men.

Robert Capa, a twenty-four-year-old photographer already famous for his work in the Spanish Civil War, had gone into action with the Chinese troops, carrying only his camera. *Life* magazine, whose editor and proprietor Henry Luce was taking a close interest in the conflict, spread the photos over two pages, beginning the accompanying story with a battle-cry of an opening paragraph: 'To the names of small towns famous as turning points in history, Waterloo, Gettysburg, Verdun add still another. It is T'aierhchuang.' History was not to be as kind to the Chinese army as it was to the victors of those earlier battles.

The front and the fighting may have been far away, but Hankow had plenty to offer a young man trying to break into journalism. The city provided the influx of famous correspondents with a perfect vantage-point for the next stage of the struggle by a united Chinese front against the forces of fascism. The communist–nationalist front was probably more genuine at this period than at any other time in the years 1938–45. Chou En-lai and a large communist delegation had moved into Hankow to take up their roles in the front government. There was also a big German military delegation in the city, led by a German World War I hero and former Nazi, Captain Walter Stennes, who was advising Chiang Kai-shek.

Above all there was a great cast of foreign correspondents, mainly American, who had assembled in the city: Haldore Hanson of the Associated Press, Edgar Snow of the *Saturday Evening Post* and the *Daily Herald* in London and his wife Peg, otherwise know by her *nom de plume* Nym Wales, Jack Belden of United Press International and later *Time* magazine, Tillman Durdin of the *New York Times*, Art Steele of the *Chicago Daily News*, Agnes Smedley for a range of American radical magazines, and Freda Utley of the *News Chronicle* in London.

The arrival of Peter Fleming of the London *Times* with his actress wife Celia Johnson was a publicity coup for the Chinese government. Fleming was a well-known figure on London's literary and social scene and had received acclaim for his first book, *News from Tartary*, describing a journey from Peking to Kashmir, published in 1936. Although later overshadowed by his elder brother Ian, the creator of James Bond, it was Peter who first became famous. His marriage in 1935 to Celia Johnson, who would star in *Brief Encounter* with Trevor Howard in 1945, was a high-society wedding that had greatly excited the gossip columns of the day. Celia Johnson was a star in her own right who had performed leading roles in a series of West End stage hits; her film career did not begin until 1941.

Christopher Isherwood and W.H. Auden arrived in the city on 8 March 1938 and were quick to meet up with the Flemings. The *Times* correspondent had clearly overdressed for the occasion: 'In his khaki shirt and shorts, complete with golf stockings, strong suede shoes, waterproof wristwatch and Leica camera, he might have stepped straight from a London tailor's window, advertising Gents' tropical exploration kit,' wrote Isherwood in the diary that would form part of *Journey to a War*. Isherwood also decided that, despite their earlier reservations about the perils of wartime China, they were in the right place: 'Today Auden and I agreed that we would rather be in Hankow at this moment than anywhere else on earth.'

Like many other new journalists in Hankow, Auden and Isherwood contacted Agnes Smedley soon after arriving. They found her in her room at the Lutheran mission, where she immediately began to cross-examine them on their political views. Smedley did not have a lot of patience with those who did not agree with her radical opinions. She had already met George Hogg at the mission, and saw in him a naïve, unformed, innocent abroad who was prepared to approach the war in China with an open mind. She also saw a tall, good-looking young Englishman. They became friends as well as colleagues, but although Smedley was famously liberal with her sexual favours, it is unlikely that they became lovers.

Hogg described her as 'tall, rather grim and Eton cropped, about forty, an ardent communist of the Chinese not the Russian variety'. He was certainly awestruck by the strength of her views and the way she furiously argued her case with other members of the US press corps. Smedley believed that the government of Chiang Kai-shek was a crypto-fascist organisation, and that the communists held out the only hope for China. This was not a popular view at the time, but Smedley made it her life's work to offend those in power, those she worked with, and most of her friends.

It was remarkable that a flamboyant feminist and radical activist who became a publicly outspoken supporter of the communist cause in general, and Mao's brand of Chinese communism in particular, should have formed a friendship with a rather naïve young Oxford graduate. But Smedley was an unusual woman, with an extraordinary past. Her latest biographer, Ruth Price, presents a well-documented case that Smedley was in fact an agent of the Comintern, the organisation set up in Moscow in 1919 to foment communist revolution around the world.

She had been born in rural poverty in Missouri in 1892, and when she was ten her family had moved to the coal country of Colorado. Her father was a labourer by profession and a drunk by inclination. Her mother died from malnourishment when Agnes was sixteen. Her father rifled the few savings she had hidden away – $45 – and went to get drunk with the boys. Agnes was left at home with a younger sister and two brothers. She also had charge of a baby born to an elder sister who had died in childbirth. She took a decision then that she was to live by all her life. She would not play by society's rules. She would not live as other women did, and certainly not as a drudge looking after four children and a drunk of a father.

Making rudimentary arrangements for the children, Agnes left home to begin a life of semi-vagabondage that was to last for years. She arrived in New York in her early twenties, worked as a waitress during the day and by night studied at New York University. Here, during the years of the First World War, she became politically active among Indian exile nationalists seeking to overthrow the British Raj. Typically, Smedley was not content with political posturing. In 1918 she was convicted and jailed for gun-running and violating America's Neutrality Act. Thus began her life as a radical, which was only to end with her death in 1950, while she was under investigation for espionage.

Her biographer Ruth Price described Smedley as 'a virago who challenged the world . . . Smedley sparked intense, divergent responses in a tremendous range of people in her lifetime.' Political conservatives saw her as either a dizzy camp-follower of the Chinese communists or a dangerous revolutionary to be suppressed at all costs. Fellow journalists dismissed her fervent reportage as wholly slanted; others were offended by her morals: she publicly boasted of sleeping with 'all colours and shapes'. Those who actually knew her saw either a troubled and unstable eccentric or an impossibly soft-hearted dreamer. 'I may not be innocent, but I am right,' was one of her sayings, but it might well have been, 'I went too far – and then further.'

By the time Smedley arrived in China in 1929 she had already been branded a dangerous radical by conservatives. The *Frankfurter Zeitung* refused to publish her first reports of Japanese atrocities after the invasion of Manchuria. But she was proved right, and became a leading correspondent for the paper until the Nazis took power in 1933. Her London publisher, Victor Gollancz, drew her to the attention of the *Manchester Guardian*, which also appointed her a correspondent in China.

As in every other city that has hosted journalists in a time of crisis – Saigon and Salisbury, Rhodesia, in the 1970s, Jerusalem at almost any time and Beirut in the eighties – the foreign correspondents gathered at one particular watering hole to gossip, drink, fall in love and betray each other. In Saigon it was the bar of the Continental Palace, in Salisbury the Quill Club, and in Beirut the Commodore Hotel. In Hankow it was both the US naval canteen and the nearby Terminus Hotel. The modern history of Hankow is closely connected with that of the Yangtse Patrol, a US naval detachment which was there to protect the American presence and personnel in the city, and whose fleet of gunboats operated from the riverfront. As far as the press was concerned the real contribution of the patrol was its canteen, which like the US Navy was supposed to be dry. Since the Hankow press corps spent so much time there, one assumes they managed to circumvent the rules.

Smedley was a key figure among the correspondents who gathered in the naval canteen or the Terminus Hotel, where strong drinks were obligatory. She introduced George Hogg to the other members of the press corps, and he quickly found himself a novice member of their fraternity.

Years later Rewi Alley, a New Zealander and communist sympathiser who was also in Hankow at the time, and who was to play a crucial role in Hogg's life in China, commented on Hogg's relationship with Smedley.

> *George was amazed at the liberated nature of Smedley's social life and the openness of her communist views. She liked him because he wasn't like others in the press corps. He had brought no views of his own to China apart from the pacifist ideals of his family. And Smedley thought those were faintly ridiculous because the Chinese were fighting for their survival. She believed that you had to fight for everything that you got in life. And he agreed with her. They were friends but I think that was all.*

Smedley liked Hogg, and wished to convert him to her own view of communism. She also let him use her bank account in Hankow to cash cheques, and became a source of good advice on where to go to find the story. George had known and loved strong, unconventional and 'difficult' women all his life. His mother and aunt were strong-minded people with unconventional views for the era in which they lived. Smedley was like a more dangerous version of Aunt Muriel, without, however, the strict middle-class manners and morals with which the Hogg family were brought up.

There was another larger-than-life figure who enlivened and

illuminated the Hankow scene. Sir Archibald Clark-Kerr had been appointed British Ambassador to China in early 1938, just after the embassy moved from Nanjing to Hankow. Clark-Kerr was an unconventional and colourful character. He and his blonde Chilean wife Tita made a point, both in Hankow and later in Chongqing, of holding parties that mixed nationalists, communists, journalists and businessmen. With golden curls, tiny, perfect features and the trace of a Spanish accent, Lady Clark-Kerr looked like an exotic doll. Behind the baby-doll image lay an intelligent and well-informed woman. The Ambassador and his wife were prominent members of Hankow's social life, and made a point of forging good relations with the press corps.

Agnes Smedley was almost as surprised as the other guests when she was invited to dine at the Ambassador's imposing residence one night. She turned up in a borrowed dress, expecting to be vilified for her views on the British Empire. She had after all been jailed twenty years earlier in New York for gun-running for the nascent Indian nationalist movement. But Sir Archibald surprised her. She found him to be 'a lean brown Scotchman with a keen tough mind and a scintillating sense of humour' who clearly, if discreetly, shared her views on the nationalist government. Unable to reconcile his charm and sympathetic political views with his role as British Ambassador, Smedley concluded that he was a 'good Scotchman fallen among diplomats'. More importantly for George Hogg, that night Clark-Kerr revealed two important facts that Smedley would pass on to him. They would change his life.

The Ambassador told his guests that he was an enthusiast for a plan to set up industrial co-operatives in rural areas to replace China's shattered industrial infrastructure and to help arm and equip the forces fighting the Japanese. Silence fell over the table as he explained that he had been much impressed by the New

Zealander Rewi Alley, who was trying to persuade the government to back the idea. According to Smedley, one of the guests spluttered that Alley was an illusionist chasing a will o'the wisp. In that case, said the Ambassador, it might not be a bad idea if more people pursued that will o'the wisp.

Clark-Kerr made it clear to his guests that he was going to help Alley, and would promote the idea of industrial co-ops to Chiang Kai-shek and his wife Soong Meiling. He was true to his word. The wife of the Chinese leader became an enthusiastic supporter and organiser of the plan to create small-scale factory workshops in rural areas. She was crucial to the early successes of the movement.

Alley at that time was working as a municipal employee, inspecting factories in Shanghai. But he moved to Hankow for several weeks in 1938 to work on the co-operative project, and there he briefly met George Hogg. Smedley, who was also an enthusiast for co-ops, introduced the two men in the hope that Hogg would write an article about the project. He made a note to investigate the supposed rural renaissance of China's industry, and left it at that.

Having found lodgings at the Lutheran mission, Hogg had next to find the money to pay the rent. Bishop Roots may have been a good Christian, but he wasn't in the business of giving free accommodation to itinerant journalists. And money remained a problem.

Hogg's job with Van Reekum Bros required him to spend from 9 a.m. to noon at a smart Hankow hotel where the Chinese businessman saw his customers. His wages just covered his rent, leaving no money to buy an essential piece of equipment for any freewheeling journalist in the city, a bicycle. He was so short of money that instead of the promised fortnightly letters home, he told his parents that they would get a longer monthly letter to save on postage. He also urged them to use lightweight paper and envelopes, as he had discovered to his dismay that he was charged for items over a certain weight. It is one of the more extraordinary features of the war years in China that the postal service insisted on such bureaucratic niceties, and indeed managed to function at all. But function it did, and although some of Hogg's parents' letters to Hankow failed to get through, many of them did reach their destination. Letters from the UK to China went by sea via Hong Kong, and thence by train. After the fall of Hong Kong to the Japanese in 1941 the main postal route to China from England was via a long and unreliable overland journey through Russia.

Hogg tried to raise money by teaching English at the Russian diplomatic mission, and then at Hankow's university. He signed up to teach courses in English and economics in the new academic year which was to begin in September – but by then the Japanese were at the gates of the city, and the university closed.

However, his problems were partly solved, and his life changed, when he was offered a job as a stringer, or part-time correspondent, for United Press International. It came with a monthly retainer of US$80, a reasonable sum given that the local currency was in the grip of rampant inflation. Hogg immediately gave up his job with the Chinese businessman and bought a bicycle.

UPI, whose motto was 'Around the world around the clock', already had, in Jack Belden, a famous full-time correspondent in Hankow, and from time to time the agency sent out other star correspondents, such as Betty Graham, to cover the conflict. Belden was part of Agnes Smedley's 'Hankow gang' and it is probable that it was she who introduced the young Englishman to the veteran American reporter. Belden would have been only too happy to have a young trainee to do the legwork around town for him.

The UPI job was a huge stroke of luck for Hogg. It gave him

press accreditation, which provided access to people and events that were shaping the course of the war. It gave him all-important status in the press corps. Above all it gave him an education in the bedrock of journalism, news reporting. UPI had been founded in 1907 as a rival to Reuters and the Associated Press, and challenged their supremacy with livelier, more colourful stories. Roy W. Howard, the UPI chief in Washington, believed that rival agencies were far too sombre and boring in their reporting, and encouraged his correspondents to inject colour and human interest into their despatches.

George Hogg's UPI reports have long since been lost, but his writing for the *Manchester Guardian* and in his letters home show how quickly he absorbed the demands of his editors in Washington. The new job ended plans for a teaching career. For the next eighteen months he would learn the art and craft of being a foreign correspondent. It was hard work, which brought scant praise from his editors. But he learnt how to shape a short news item, and how the right quote or telling detail can illuminate and enliven the most mundane story.

Hogg was lucky. There was nothing mundane about the story he had to cover. From the moment he set foot in China the undeclared war between Japan and China had gathered pace, providing gruesome copy for the newsmen as the casualties and the atrocities mounted.

In May 1938 the Japanese finally took the railway town of Xuzhou. After the brilliant rearguard action at T'aierhchuang, the Chinese commanders had failed to follow up their advantage. The nationalist armies were soon continuing their retreat across central China, taking up new positions in the great ring of mountain ranges that surround Hankow and its two sister cities.

The Japanese were now in full pursuit. Unabashed by appalled Chinese reaction to the Nanjing atrocities, and encouraged by the comparative lack of any international condemnation, the Japanese forces used the same terror tactics of mass executions of wounded and captured troops, and the mass murder of the civilian population in towns and villages, as they swept inland. Everywhere they went the army of Emperor Hirohito created brothels and filled them with Chinese women for the troops.

In retaliation, and to slow the advance, in early June 1938 the Chinese dynamited the great Yellow River dykes, causing the river to burst its banks and sweep across the path of the advancing armies. The surging river carved a new course to the sea across the plains of Honan, drowning thousands of Japanese soldiers, miring armoured vehicles in mud and cutting rail and road communications. The loss of civilian life was massive as the floodwater swept away eleven large towns and four thousand villages. Two million people were left homeless and destitute. The number actually drowned remains a matter of controversy, but figures as high as 325,000 have been given. In military terms the tactic was a success, and the final assault on Hankow was delayed by at least three months. But, embarrassed by the civilian casualties, the nationalist government denied for years that it had deliberately breached the dykes.

As the Japanese pressed forward Generalissimo Chiang Kai-shek ordered all industrial machinery in the Hankow region to be dismantled and transported further inland. This was part of a broader strategy to remove population, government, schools and factories from the vulnerable coastal areas to the interior. It was a dramatic move. China's economic and political life sprang from her great cities on the coast and in the river valleys in the centre and south of the country. The vast provinces of the interior, Szechuan, Yunnan, Kwangsi, Hunan, Shanxi and Gansu, were now to become the base for the fight against the Japanese. Faced with Japan's better-equipped and -trained armies, Chiang

Kai-shek had chosen to use China's vast territory and limitless supply of manpower to engage the invader in a war of attrition.

In the spring of 1938 Chiang was fifty years old, a professional soldier who had gained international recognition as the leader of the world's most populous nation. But his control over party and country had never been complete, and was continually challenged. He had entered the army at the age of nineteen, and emerged from the anarchic years that followed the collapse of the Manchu dynasty* in 1912 as a protégé of the nationalist leader Sun Yat-sen, generally acknowledged as the father of modern China. Sun Yat-sen was a Methodist Christian who had received much of his education outside China, in Hawaii. In 1912 he forged a number of revolutionary republican splinter groups into the Nationalist Party (Kuomintang, or KMT), with the aim of overthrowing the old imperial order and creating a modern republic on the European model. Elected as provisional president of the republic of China a year later, Sun Yat-sen found himself powerless in the face of regional warlords, and was forced to resign within months of taking office.

The decade that followed was one of humiliation and anarchy. Lacking any kind of central government, China fell under the control of regional warlords and foreign powers. The two men whose destinies were entwined in what would prove a long and murderous struggle for supreme power emerged from the years of darkness on separate paths to leadership.

* The Manchu dynasty (also known as the Qing dynasty) provided the Chinese Empire with its rulers from 1644 to 1911. The Manchus were not ethnic Chinese, unlike the majority Han population, but came from the remote border area of north-east China. The collapse of the dynasty ended two thousand years of imperial rule and ushered in a period of anarchy, invasion and civil war culminating in the communist victory in 1949.

In 1921 a stocky young man who had worked as a teacher, a librarian, a bookseller and a journalist joined the new Chinese Communist Party in Shanghai. His name was Mao Tse-tung, and at the age of twenty-seven he would abandon his previous careers and become a professional revolutionary.

The following year Chiang Kai-shek was sent to Moscow to seek support and funds for the KMT. He returned to report that communism was simply tsarism under a different name. Russia's real interest, he argued, lay in sovietising China. In 1924 Chiang became director of the Whampoa Military Academy, a training school for the new class of officer in a national army. It was no surprise that when he assumed control of the KMT after Sun's death in 1925 he consolidated power in a divided party by breaking with the communists. To enhance his political legitimacy in the eyes of his party he then married Sun's sister-in-law Soong Meiling in the same year. Meiling's family were Christian, and Chiang was converted and baptised in 1929. But it was not until March 1938, at an extraordinary congress of the KMT in Hankow, that Chiang was finally accorded the title of Director General. This was the office through which Sun Yat-sen had wielded dictatorial powers. Chiang's dominance of the party, but not of the country, was complete.

The politics of the nationalist government did not, however, concern George Hogg. He and the Hankow press corps were interested in only one story – the war. The fighting was coming closer as spring turned to summer in 1938, but the conflict was still difficult to cover with any accuracy. The real front line throughout the war was anywhere Japan chose to deploy its airpower. Although thwarted in their advance on the city, the Japanese were able to bomb Hankow at will. Hogg had witnessed the after-effects of artillery and mortar fire in Shanghai. Now for the first time he found himself in the line of fire.

In May, June and July 1938 squadron after squadron of Japanese bombers flew over the three cities in the Hankow complex at heights of between ten and fifteen thousand feet, above the range of Chinese anti-aircraft batteries. The planes flew with perfect precision in parallel lines, and first targeted Hankow's airfield and then largely, but not exclusively, the poorer Chinese areas of the three cities.

Writing from Shanghai, Hogg had been careful not to alarm his parents with stories about the violent world in which he found himself. From Hankow he began to expose them to the reality of what was happening around him. The adolescent tone of his letters began to change as he adapted to life under almost daily air attack. The golden boy who went to Oxford and the naïve young graduate who left to travel the world had been transformed into a hard-working reporter covering the grisly aftermath of air raids on a rusty bike. On one occasion he followed up a brief agency report that no damage had been done when a Japanese plane released its bombs over open countryside. In fact a small village had been hit. He sent the story, called 'No Damage', to the *Manchester Guardian*.

The little Chinese house of wattle and straw stood alone on a dry patch of ground among the rice paddies. Through years it had seen nothing but the daily lives of its farmer folk and their domestic capital. Men and women scarcely distinguishable, a succession of children, a few pigs, ducks and water buffalo, had been indiscriminately sheltered – from the oldest toothless one down to the latest baby, litter or calf. But on this sunny morning something was wrong with the old house.

Jagged cracks ran slantwise down its walls, and it was perched askew on its raised hillock like an old and disreputable hat. Evidently it had achieved sudden fame, for a crowd of excited people was milling round it, and more could be seen coming from all directions along the paths between the rice paddies.

Nicely arbored between the two projecting wings of the house and almost entirely filling the courtyard, lay the huge carcass of a water buffalo; this seemed to be the centre of interest, but some way off a small group had discovered a pair of hairy hind legs, emerging from a bundle of red crushed meat. Attention was suddenly diverted from these as a woman raised the side of an overturned wheelbarrow to reveal a mangled human body. She held the barrow up for the crowd with one hand, using the other to help her in a mumbled incantation. The crowd peered curiously at the remains and went off in little groups to swap emotions at a safe distance; some of them threw the woman a few pennies before leaving. Meanwhile the mourners' dirge and the smoke from burning paper money came from a half-open door into the house itself where the body of a woman, perfectly unhurt save that it had no head, was lying fully clothed on the floor. The sight of her unshrouded body, headless and thick with child, excited only a sort of pitying wonder. It was at once too near the ordinary, and too far beyond the limits of ordinary experience, to bring horror.

Hogg was now working hard to win the acceptance of both his fellow journalists in Hankow and his editors in Washington. He was just twenty-three years old, and very inexperienced to have found himself a member of such a prestigious press corps. Like most young men in that position, he probably did not realise the extent of his good fortune. But he certainly made the most of it.

Many of the press corps were veterans of the Spanish Civil War, and they recognised that the Japanese tactics of 'total war' were based on those of General Franco in Spain. Japan's air campaign was influenced by German advisers who used methods that had already been tested in Spain. One of these was that Japanese planes always bombed munitions stores and factories before attacking military or civilian targets in a given area. The aim was to cripple efforts at reconstruction after the raids.

As in the Spanish Civil War, the press corps did not aspire to neutrality. Thus, when on 29 April 1938, the Emperor Hirohito's birthday, the Chinese hit back against the Japanese there was general rejoicing among the journalists in Hankow. On that day a spectacular dogfight took place over the city, involving fifty Japanese bombers supported by fighters against eighty planes of the Chinese air force, piloted by Russians. The Chinese claimed that in the thirty-minute duel twenty-one Japanese planes were shot down, for the loss of seven of their own. Russian pilots in the Chinese air force were joined by US pilots in what the press called 'the flying foreign legion', a motley group that included volunteers from France, England and New Zealand. They flew and fought for China for the first five months of 1938, before being disbanded due to indiscipline.

At a time when the Chinese government badly needed propaganda victories to bolster its authority, it scored a triumph in May 1938, when its planes attacked mainland Japan. Hogg was in Hankow at the time, and he, like every other correspondent, missed the biggest story in the air war between Japan and China.

Flying from their base at Hankow, Chinese air force crews in two giant US-made Martin bombers flew a three-thousand-mile round trip to a number of Japanese cities including Kyushu, Nagasaki and Fukuoka. The bombers, which refuelled twice on their way to the Chinese coast, only dropped propaganda leaflets printed in Japanese and describing atrocities committed against the Chinese civilian population. The need for extra fuel tanks for such a long mission prevented them from carrying out the original plan, which was to bomb Japanese bases. Details of the mission were kept secret for several days, and were only released for publicity to offset the news of the Japanese victory at Xuzhou.

Throughout the spring Hogg worked closely with Jack Belden, who would go on to become a famous correspondent for *Time* magazine. Belden, born in Brooklyn and educated in New Jersey, spent his college vacations travelling the world as a seaman, and fell in love with the Far East while in Hong Kong. After graduation he shipped out as crew on a cargo boat to the British colony, and stayed on in China. He learnt the language fluently, became an English teacher and wandered into work for UPI.

Belden possessed two big advantages over the rest of the Hankow press corps. He could speak Mandarin fluently, and he was a close confidant and friend of the US military attaché Colonel Joseph Stilwell. The two men gained access to front-line areas denied the rest of the press corps, although Stilwell insisted that the information he gave Belden was shared with them.

Hogg concentrated on reporting the harrowing situation in Hankow while Belden, five years his senior, filed from the battle-front. It was a winning combination for UPI. For Hogg it was a compressed education, and not just in war reporting. Belden had assumed the role of his mentor. Hogg, who only a year earlier had donned mortarboard and gown to receive his degree from Oxford, was now sitting at the feet of a moody, alcoholic boss who wrote from the battlefield with poetic insight.

The eight months that Hogg spent in Hankow proved a transforming experience. His initial orders from the UPI desk in Washington were to report on the disease and epidemics that were rife among the population. He arrived as spring transformed the city at the end of a long and bitter winter. The trees were in leaf, the gardens were in bloom and the temperatures climbed to those of England in July, although the heat was close and clammy. Rickshaw coolies stripped to the waist and ran sweating through the streets. Chinese troops switched to light tropical uniforms and the foreign community, at least the men, suddenly appeared in white shorts and jackets.

From the journalists' point of view the change in weather was a boon. It increased the tempo of news, bringing epidemics of dysentery and cholera to the shanty towns and, under clearer skies, heavier Japanese air attacks. It was a toss-up as to which posed the greater threat. 'The chances of catching malaria, cholera, and typhus are as great as those of being hit by a piece of shrapnel or of being caught in the wreckage of ancient wooden buildings,' Hogg wrote in a letter home.

He spent his days investigating death by disease in the cities of Wuchang and Hanyang across the river, while at night he was out reporting on the victims of the latest bombing raids. He travelled on his bicycle and on the military trucks that ferried the wounded to hospitals. With Bishop Roots' daughter Frances and a couple of musicians he met at the Lutheran mission he formed a jazz quartet. In both Chinese and English, the group would perform impromptu concerts at schools and hospitals. Hogg had a good voice for jazz. 'Show that man a piano and he will give you a song,' a colleague said.

Throughout the spring and early summer Hankow turned itself into a city under siege. Fortifications and machine-gun positions appeared at key points across the city. Large reinforced wooden gates set in concrete beds were placed at the ends of the main streets, which were lined with double rows of barbed wire to prevent the rapid movement of enemy troops through the city. The foreign-controlled concessions began planning 'safety zones' which, it was hoped, would guarantee the security of those inside if the Japanese stormed the city.

This was a year before the outbreak of the war in Europe, and two and a half years before the Pearl Harbor attack in December 1941. The two major foreign concessions in Shanghai were still in

Western hands, and like Hong Kong would remain inviolate until they were attacked and taken hours after Pearl Harbor.

The Chinese business community believed that the number of foreigners and foreign-owned businesses in Hankow would save it from the fate of Nanjing. Every conceivable excuse was found either to paint foreign flags on, or fly them from, the bigger buildings. Large inscriptions in Mandarin and English were painted on foreign-owned offices and banks stating that the property was mortgaged to, or owned by, a foreign company.

In public at least the communists and their senior partners and implacable enemies in the united front, Chiang Kai-shek's nationalists, insisted that the army would fight for the capital. The Generalissimo, as Chiang Kai-shek was known, was rarely seen in Hankow, preferring to remain in his headquarters across the river on the south bank. He had good reason to avoid open movement through his capital. The Japanese had numerous agents in the city, and had placed a large price on his head. Tokyo's spies were not discreet about their activities. Hogg and his colleagues would watch during night air raids as rockets were fired into the sky to guide the bombers to strategic targets such as the power station by the river.

In contrast to her husband, Chiang's wife Meiling was to be seen everywhere, travelling on foot, by rickshaw or in her official car. Dressed impeccably, she visited schools, hospitals and factories and bombed-out slum areas. She became the public and compassionate face of a government that showed little concern for the suffering of its civilian population.

Meanwhile, on his daily journeys across the two rivers Hogg found that Hankow's twin cities were dying under the weight of air attacks and disease. He wrote home: 'You can walk for hours between ruined houses in the musty smell of rotten woodwork and rubbled plaster. Here and there you will find a family camping in what was once its own home or an old woman mumbling to herself as she pokes among the ruins of her past.'

Most of the population of the two cities had sought refuge in the countryside or had crossed the river to seek shelter on the streets of the foreign concessions. Government officials, foreign missionaries, rickshaw men, beggars and refugees moved into whatever quarters they could find in Hankow. In the summer heat the streets became a battleground between pedestrians and every kind of transport. In the midst of this frenzied city life, 330 British sailors busied themselves building barbed wire fences around the British consulate. Their gunboats were moored along the Bund and, like the Chinese troops in and around Hankow, they spent the steamy summer awaiting events.

Most days the press would meet at lunchtime in the US naval canteen, where alcohol was strictly on a bring-your-own-bottle basis, and by night at the Terminus Hotel, where the reverse applied. The journalists took grim satisfaction in reminding themselves what had happened in Nanjing and agreeing that the Chinese efforts to hold Hankow were doomed. With the mixture of cynicism and pessimism that is a hallmark of their tribe, they speculated endlessly about what the Japanese would do once they had taken the city. Everyone else was playing the same guessing game. The brutal Japanese behaviour in the field since Nanjing had been fully reported in the local papers, heightening fears among the Chinese of what would happen if the Japanese penetrated the defences of the city, whose population had swollen to 750,000.

In this doom-laden atmosphere Hogg and other journalists formed a 'Last Ditchers Club' which met regularly at 'Rosie's Dine, Dance and Romance Restaurant'. In every city at war the press always finds or creates a 'Rosie's Restaurant'. There would be farewell dinners for the 'deserters' who were leaving town, and bets were placed on who would hold out the longest. As it happened, UPI's young English correspondent would be among the small group who did hold out the longest.

While in Hankow, Mao's chief representative, Chou En-lai, took great care to cultivate the Western press. He met journalists regularly at the Communist Party's headquarters, and encouraged his aides to be as helpful as possible with briefings. Chou was always careful not to criticise the nationalist government, and to stick to the united front policy positions. Throughout his life the one principle from which he never wavered was the party line, and his slavish obedience made him the ideal apparatchik in Mao's eyes. To the Western press he was a charming and skilful spokesman for the communist cause. To Mao he was an invaluable organiser and enforcer.

Chiang Kai-shek, on the other hand, tended to regard most of the Western press corps as dangerous subversives. And in his terms he was not wrong. The collective sentiment in the foreign press corps when the war started was anti-Japanese; as the conflict continued and the united front began to crumble, so the bulk of the foreign press became more openly hostile to the nationalist government, and more sympathetic to the communists and their guerrilla armies.

While Chou En-lai received the more important correspondents, especially the Americans, Chiang Kai-shek saw only favoured visitors such as the proprietor of *Time* and *Life* magazines, Henry Luce. The government's trump card as far as the media was concerned was the Generalissimo's wife, Meiling. She spoke perfect English, and became skilled at presenting the government's case to the American public; in turn she became the subject of admiring interviews.

In June, before the Japanese closed in on Hankow, Hogg managed to make a train journey north to Xian, and thence by truck to the new communist headquarters at Yenan. It was here that Mao Tse-tung had retreated with his forces after the Long March in 1934–35. Agnes Smedley set the journey up for him, but Hogg delayed his departure for days, torn between his desire to see the communist base and his reluctance to leave his friends and colleagues in the beleaguered city.

Expressing these concerns in a letter home on 3 June, he also gave his parents their first view of his new friend Smedley. With schoolboy enthusiasm he wrote:

> *This Smedley is a real revolutionary. She has given every penny more or less to those projects I told you of (refugee organisations), has collected thousands of dollars for them but made no provision for herself. She is known as a communist by the foreigners so they won't have much to do with her. She cannot have Red army status because they don't have any foreigners except doctors. Because she is known to be connected to them she cannot even get a job with the Russian embassy who are scared of getting into bad odour with other consular and ambassadorial staffs. Her new American passport which she got after great trouble from the American officials was stolen on delivery by Chinese fascist detectives ... if the Japanese come they will undoubtedly kill her.*

And the Japanese were coming; the large Japanese press corps, comprising some five hundred newsmen, photographers and broadcasters, were poised behind the lines, ready to be flown in to report the latest Japanese victory. They had to wait. The mighty Yangtse, and the effect of the Yellow River floods to the north, as much as the Chinese armies, had slowed the advance.

FOUR

The Fall of Hankow

'Time to sell what you had, take up baby and bedroll,
time to go.'

In June 1938 Hogg quietly left Hankow, taking the train north. The nationalist government had banned all Western correspondents from visiting the communist base at Yenan, and threatened to withdraw the accreditation from those who did so. Journalists working for the major US newspapers could afford to ignore the ban – although most abided by it. As a mere stringer, Hogg had to be more careful.

The train took two days to reach the ancient imperial capital of Xian, whose huge walls had risen and fallen with the city's fortunes over two thousand turbulent years. Xian boasted that its walls had been built to the width of three oxcarts and the height of ten men. As Japan intensified its air attacks on major cities under Chinese nationalist control, the walls once more became the city's first and final line of defence. Far below the castellated ramparts lay dark, damp, rat-infested catacombs which provided the only haven from the aerial bombardment. Tens of thousands of people crowded into these underground shelters every night. Two years later the citizens of another ancient and once-walled city on the other side of the world were to seek shelter underground in very similar circumstances.

From Xian a Red Cross lorry took Hogg 250 of the three hundred miles north to his destination. The passengers who lay sprawled over the baggage inside the vehicle included a honeymooning couple, the bridegroom's sister, two young women refugees and a group of Red Cross nurses. For the first time Hogg experienced the pull that the communist headquarters was exerting on young Chinese. The passengers' eyes shone with idealism; they were fired with a passionate desire to help their country. Hogg only spoke limited Chinese at this stage, but he knew enough to realise that this mixed group of young people were being drawn north to Yenan by the dream of national salvation, not by communist ideology. The journey provided material for an article which the *Manchester Guardian* published later that month. Hogg was developing an eye for background colour, as in this description of the countryside:

> We passed over a plain studded with the giant mounds of ancient mausoleums, over rivers red with the rains. Later as we reached the mountain country, each climb was a gamble as the lorry slowed from a roar to a grind and from a grind to an angry growl with the block bearer crouching anxiously behind the rear wheel. Deep-cut valleys and crenellated skylines, geometrical fields in light greens and rusty reds, terraces rising in regular proportion to the plateaux in relief gave the whole sense and air of detached symmetry which is common to all loess country.*

* Loess is fine silt blown from eroding rock formations over millennia. North China is rich in this light soil, which the winds shape into a constantly changing landscape.

By the afternoon of the third day the tyres had been shredded and the driver had given up. The group gathered their possessions and began the fifty-mile walk along a crowded road. Fleets of military trucks crawled their way in both directions through clouds of dust. Convoys of mule carts carrying prized local goods such as matches headed south to Xian. Hundreds of wheelbarrows, their axles shrieking under the loads of flour and vegetables, headed north, bound for Yenan.

And everywhere on the dusty road, Eighth Route Army volunteers joined thousands of students heading for the communist base. The young army of migrants was penniless, and many of them carried no more than a toothbrush, a tin mug and a towel. They were all heading for the one place in China that seemed to offer a beacon of hope for the disillusioned young.

Yenan was Mao's master stroke. The nine years in which the communist leadership used the city as their base were the making of the man who was to lead China from 1949 to his death in 1976.

Mao had been born to a prosperous peasant family who were able to give him an education denied most children of his background. At the age of seventeen, in the spring of 1911, he arrived in the provincial capital of Changsha just as a wave of republicanism was breaking over the old Manchu dynasty. Years later the political path which began in the medieval streets of the city would take him to a meeting with Professor Chen Tu-hsiu, a leading radical intellectual. The professor gave his young admirer a job selling Marxist books and literature back in Changsha. Mao welcomed the job. He loved books, and had spent six months working as a librarian in Beijing some years previously.

The Bolshevik revolution in 1917 made the revolutionary philosophy of Marxism increasingly attractive to intellectuals and much of the educated professional class in China in the early 1920s. Widespread public anger at the terms of the Versailles

Peace Treaty had triggered unprecedented student demonstrations in Beijing on 4 May 1919. The catalyst for the public protest was the Allies' refusal to support China's demands that Japan be forced to cede Shandung province in the north-east, which it had seized during the war.

The 4 May protests signalled an intellectual uprising among the urban, educated classes across China. Nationalism, the ideology that had alternately inspired and convulsed Europe in the nineteenth century, found popular appeal in China in the first decades of the twentieth. From 1919 intellectual Chinese of varying persuasions saw it as their mission to redeem their country from the twin evils of imperialism and warlordism. To the outside world, and especially to the new Bolshevik regime in Moscow, conditions in China looked ripe for Marxist revolution.

The country was mired in an anarchic conflict between warlords. Much of this power struggle involved political shadow-boxing rather than open hostilities, but the fact remained that the last vestiges of central power had collapsed with the Manchu dynasty in 1912. The republic that succeeded it proved to be a makeshift transitional arrangement that was unable to exert its authority. At the same time the representatives of the Western powers and Japan clung to their privileged status in their concessions while the peasantry remained locked in a feudal lifestyle that had prevailed for centuries.

Spurred by the influx of foreign ideas and ideologies, two opposing views on national regeneration emerged: a pragmatic evolutionary model that was at least partially accepted by the Nationalist Party of Sun Yat-sen, and the Marxist revolutionary model of the Chinese Communist Party which was to find its leader in Mao Tse-tung.

The Chinese Communist Party (CCP) was formed in August 1920 in Shanghai by a group of eight Marxists led by Mao's mentor Professor Chen Tu-hsiu. His avowed aim was to replicate the success of the Bolshevik revolution in Russia. The new Soviet government in Moscow was heavily involved in the establishment of the party, and remained its moving force and source of funding for many years. Mao Tse-tung was one of the thirteen people who attended its first full congress in 1921. The Russian emissaries who organised the congress insisted that the CCP be regarded as a branch of the Comintern, a notion angrily rejected by Chinese delegates. Thus began a fraught relationship which would finally end in the Sino–Soviet split of the late 1950s.

In 1924 a loose three-way alliance emerged which laid claim to be the government of China. Moscow helped broker a united front between Sun Yat-sen's Kuomintang government and members of the then tiny Communist Party. Soviet Russia had provided the third leg of the very shaky stool on which the national governance of China rested. Sun Yat-sen died in 1925, aged fifty-eight, before he could take on the warlords and begin the task of uniting the country. The military mission and the mantle of nationalist leadership fell upon Chiang Kai-shek, then director of the Whampoa Military Academy, on an island near Canton.

The inevitable split between nationalists and communists followed Chiang's successful blitzkrieg from 1926 to 1928, which saw the KMT gain control of the southern half of China. The success of the follow-up 'northern expedition' meant that by 1929 the greater part of China lay under the control of Chiang and his nationalist forces. Nanjing was the country's new capital, and the old imperial capital, Peking, was renamed Peiping.

The international recognition accorded Chiang as China's leader set the stage for the next round in the confrontation between nationalist and communist forces. After successive offensives from 1930 to 1934, nationalist forces had penned the communists into a base area around the town of Ruijin, the capital of their 'Red State' in Jiangxi province. From here the Communist Party controlled an area of thirty thousand square miles with a population of around four million. A final offensive in 1933–34 brought the Red State, its party and army to the verge of defeat. In October 1934 eighty thousand communist soldiers and followers set out on what would be a six-thousand-mile journey from south-east to north-west China. The original aim was to find safety on the Russian border.

Mao was not among the leaders of the party at the outset of the 'Long March', and had spent weeks under effective house arrest by the pro-Soviet wing of the party. But it was on the march that he emerged as the party's leader, and from it he created a political mythology – that of the great survivor, the great helmsman – that he brilliantly manipulated ever after.

Disease, starvation and attacks by nationalist forces and local warlords took a heavy toll of the communist columns as they struggled north. When they arrived in the north-west province of Shanxi, only eight thousand survivors remained. This was the nucleus from which Mao and his army commander Zhu De rebuilt the communist movement. Veterans of the Long March would dominate the Chinese Communist Party until the purges of the Cultural Revolution thirty years later.

The Long March was one of two events crucial to Mao's ultimate victory in the civil war: the other was the undeclared war between China and Japan which began on 8 July 1937. The outbreak of hostilities thwarted Chiang Kai-shek's ambition to bring the greatly weakened communist forces to a final and conclusive battle. He had to settle instead for another united front with his foes.

As part of the deal the nationalist government recognised communist control of fifty thousand square miles of territory in the northern Shanxi province. Yenan, a small town of eight thousand people before the arrival of Mao in December 1937, was to be the red army's capital, and would remain the nerve centre of the CCP until 1947. The ancient city enclosed by massive castellated walls looked to one American correspondent like 'an ogre's castle'. A large nine-storey pagoda dominated the skyline, and in the centre stood a Spanish Franciscan cathedral, completed in 1935 and taken over by a local communist leader the next year. Oil had been discovered in the area, but the oilmen, like the wealthy residents, had moved out as the communists moved in.

The city provided a secure base for the CCP, well out of the way of the main fighting, but still subject to heavy bombing. Such was the damage that the rapidly expanding population had taken to the caves carved out of the soft loess cliffs in the surrounding mountains where the local people had lived for centuries. Surrounded by a chain of hills and straddling a small river, the city was an attractive setting for the next stage in Mao Tse-tung's path to power.

By the time Mao and the eight thousand survivors of the March reached Yenan, his quest for supreme power over the Communist Party was almost complete. During the year-long march he had defeated his political rivals and assumed control of a three-man military group with his close ally Chou En-lai. The military group was the effective source of power in the CCP, and in Yenan Mao was able to restructure the party organisations and create new social and political institutions very much as he wished.

Intellectually, Yenan provided Mao with the time to adapt the urban-orientated Soviet model of Marxist Leninism to the Chinese revolutionary experience and to the particular circumstances of the war against the Japanese. In practice this meant that the party placed 'peasant radicalism' at the forefront of its thinking; theories of land reform, including rent-reduction policies, were now turned into practical programmes.

Mao was one of the first political leaders to understand the political importance of the media. Favoured correspondents and guests were invited to the new headquarters and granted long interviews, if not with Mao himself, with senior party figures. Image was important, and in keeping with the communist ethos personal luxuries were forbidden. Even the top leaders lived Spartan lives, with little to distinguish their dress or lifestyle from those of the soldier or the peasant.

The Yenan years also gave Mao time to build up his armed forces. The Eighth Route Army was scattered over the north-west, with many guerrilla units operating further east behind Japanese lines. Keeping in radio contact with Yenan at all times, commanders such as Zhu De and Nieh Rong Zhen repeatedly crossed Japanese lines while developing their successful insurgency.

For a generation of Chinese students and intellectuals who had grown up in the chaos of the twenties, the politics of change being shaped at Yenan proved highly attractive. This was hardly surprising. The contrast between Nationalist and Communist Parties, between the secretive Chiang and the apparently open Mao, between Hankow with its poverty and disease and the new, efficiently run Yenan, was striking.

The Kuomintang was viewed as the party of the landlord, the warlord and the businessman. Most foreign correspondents had discovered that Chiang Kai-shek's administration was deeply corrupt. Fraud and incompetence pervaded the nationalist government from senior to local government level. Chiang's military commanders largely treated their troops with callous contempt. This was especially true of the new conscripts, who were often regarded as little more than military slave labour.

Little wonder that by the time George Hogg arrived in Hankow in March 1938 the foreign press had reached broad conclusions about the two parties within the united front. The nationalist government and its capital represented old feudal China, corrupt, backward and inward-looking. By contrast, at Yenan the communists, in the words of Peg Snow, were 'reaching out for a bridge to the Western world through their Marxian concept and were trying to become men of their own century'. In her book *Inside Red China* (1939) she went further, saying that in Yenan the Chinese Communist Party was developing 'a new mind and a new people, creating a new world in the heart of the oldest and most changeless civilisation on earth'.

One did not have to be a communist in China in the 1930s, nor indeed to share the utopian idealism of Edgar Snow and his wife Peg, to see the appeal of the political model being developed by Mao and his party. His international image and his attraction to the foreign press had been hugely helped by the publication in 1936 of Snow's *Red Star Over China* – a book that had been pressed upon George Hogg by Agnes Smedley at their first meeting, and which was seminal in shaping American opinion about Mao and his communist guerrillas, at least among the liberal intelligentsia.

The communist leadership went to great lengths to secure the result they wanted – a book which promoted the CCP as a dynamic indigenous force, a Communist Party with austere principles and a dedication to the well-being of the broad mass of the people and to the fight against the Japanese. The series of interviews that Mao gave the Snows at Yenan was rigorously orchestrated. Questions were submitted in advance, and answers carefully prepared. Mao and his advisers demanded and were given sight of the draft text of the book, and asked for changes to which Snow readily agreed. There is no question that the communists manipulated Snow. But he submitted to the restrictions imposed upon him in order to gain unprecedented access to a man who was a mystery to the outside world. *Red Star Over China* was a propaganda triumph for Mao, but it was also the first book to illuminate the background, the personal history and the thinking of the man who would emerge as China's first modern leader.

At a violent period in China's history, when repression and political killing were commonplace, it is perhaps not surprising that the communists acted no differently from any other political organisation as they struggled to survive nationalist repression in the twenties and thirties. Yet Edgar Snow, like every other journalist who visited Yenan, failed even to allude to Mao's brutal treatment of his political adversaries. The evidence was readily available for those who chose to look. Mao and other communist leaders had treated the local population in the 'Red State' they created and controlled in large parts of the provinces of Jiangxi and Fujian from 1930 to 1934 as little more than slave labour. In their recent acclaimed biography of Mao, Jung Chang and Jon Halliday describe the communist-controlled areas at this time as 'run by terror and guarded like a prison'.

Snow was the first to break the government embargo on contact between the communists and the foreign press, and he paved the way for a series of interviews that Mao and his commanders gave to Western journalists from 1937 onwards. None was on the scale of the Mao–Snow discussions, but all, like him, burnished the image of the communists as a force for revolutionary change in the context of a nationalist struggle against the invading Japanese and a wider struggle against the feudal past, and as the true inheritors of the Sun Yat-sen revolution – and not as a Marxist Leninist party in thrall to Moscow. Ironically, Mao himself, with one eye on his all-important relationship with his Russian allies, publicly rejected the notion that there was any difference between Moscow's brand of Marxist Leninism and his own.

George Hogg was lucky to be among the early journalists to visit Yenan, but he arrived with Marx far from his mind. His group straggled into the town on foot on a Saturday evening. His first impression was that the centre of Yenan looked like a London park: basketball and football matches were being played on a wide parade ground. A large crowd looked on while referees' whistles cheeped officiously. Riders were trotting their mounts up and down beside the road. Booths selling green tea and noodles added to the holiday atmosphere.

Hogg spent three weeks in the communist capital in the early summer of 1938. If Hankow had been his crash course in journalism, Yenan provided a steep political learning curve. The guides attached to foreign journalists spent hours explaining the party's policies and system of government. The message was simple: while the 'special area' under communist control was very much joined with the nationalist government in the anti-Japanese crusade, it was different. Its laws were the same, but better enforced. Its system of government was similar, 'although a little more democratic'. Its economy used the national currency, but it was self-sufficient. The clear meaning of these polite homilies was that the communists were offering the change that China needed to break with its feudal past.

In the subterranean cool of one of the hundreds of caves dug out of the hillside, Hogg listened to such lectures as he sipped his green tea and made notes for his letters home and articles for the *Manchester Guardian*. He realised he was being fed party propaganda, but his eyes and ears told him that much of it was grounded in reality. Like more experienced journalists and observers who visited Yenan, he was impressed by the order, the simplicity of life and the strength of the political message that was being delivered.

Hogg's family would have considered themselves political.

His mother's strong Quaker views were grounded in socialism. But Hogg himself noted with a certain irony that his family's left-wing politics were conditional. They were not allowed to interfere with the Hoggs' middle-class values, or their sense of their station in society.

Hogg's travels across the United States, his experience of co-operatives built by sharecroppers in the Deep South and close contact with the formidable Aunt Muriel had certainly shaped his political thinking. By the time he reached Hankow he was receptive to the whole spectrum of views that he found in the press corps, from Agnes Smedley's open communism to the liberal-left views of most of the American correspondents. He was young and, as Smedley noted, politically unformed.

Therefore the time he spent in Yenan made a powerful impression; but as this letter home on 3 July 1938 reveals, he remained his own man. Having seen a modern Chinese opera with a powerful anti-Japanese theme, he wrote:

> ... *it is propaganda* ... *but everything here is propaganda. There are about 8000 students feeding on nothing else but millet and propaganda (they are allowed about a halfpenny a day for vegetables, fuel etc). It is a fairly good type of propaganda, not based on hate. The whole machine is directed versus Japanese imperialism and the Japanese people are represented as potential friends and allies.*

The large numbers of students drawn to Yenan from all parts of China and from Chinese communities in the Philippines, New Zealand and Hawaii were not on the whole communist, Hogg noted. They had come because the Eighth Route Army had shown itself to be master of the only tactics that might defeat the Japanese – surprise attacks on rural bases and supply lines,

followed by swift retreat into the countryside. They were, however, also drawn by the idealism of the communist philosophy
and the simple life it offered its adherents. Hogg was sympathetic,
although he was aware that both positions – support for the war
and the communist way of thinking – would be anathema in
Harpenden, Hertfordshire.

As all the visitors to Yenan noted, and as their guides were
anxious to stress, there was no Soviet influence in the development of the Chinese communist ideal. 'The orthodox communist
wouldn't find very much to please him here,' Hogg wrote home.
'No communist industry nor agriculture, nor even a communist
form of soviet government.'

In his letters home he tried to describe what was happening at
Yenan, and took another tilt at his parents' pacifism:

*It is amazing, the number of students and young people of all
classes – from all parts of the country as well as from Singapore,
Manilla, New Zealand, and Hawai, etc., [who] are attracted here.
There are two ex-film stars (women) for instance! Only about 10%
of the students or less are communist. They come largely because of
the enormous reputation which the Reds gained when fighting the
Kuomintang (Chang Kai-Shek) before the Xian Coup; because the
Red Army was at that time the originator of the guerrilla tactics
which are now recognised as the only way in which to fight Japan . . .*

*If you're not a pacifist you could hardly wish to find a better place.
If you are it is difficult to know what to say. Most of your arguments,
as well as those of . . . A [Aldous] Huxley about war leading to
fascism, etc, don't work here. This war will, if it is carried out as these
people want it to be, lead increasingly to democracy. Their ideal
is a new kind of totalitarianism – not that of the highly organised
super-capitalist country working like a machine in centralisation but
that of small groups of decentralised units, part time soldiers, part*

time peasants . . . politically conscious of the need for democracy and
for breaking the Japanese lines by surprise attacks. Well I don't think
you are interested in any kind of war are you?

One big surprise about Yenan was that many of the population had been ordered to learn Japanese: special schools had been built, and everyone from government officials to lowly students was required to study the language of the invader. The idea was to counter Japanese propaganda that depicted the Chinese troops as animals who would inflict terrible torture on their prisoners before killing them. Japanese troops were indoctrinated with this view to prevent them from allowing themselves to be taken prisoner. Most preferred a bullet from their own gun to capture.

For propaganda reasons, and to reinforce the internal message that the war was against the Japanese military machine, not its people, the communist guerrillas were ordered to take prisoners where possible. Using loud-hailers, or merely shouting when the lines were close, Chinese troops encouraged Japanese soldiers to surrender, telling them that they would not be harmed. In a report for the *Manchester Guardian*, Hogg said that Mao Tse-tung had described this policy to him and stressed the importance of taking prisoners. Since he mentioned meeting Mao nowhere else, it is more likely that he attended a speech the communist leader gave on the subject.

Hogg interviewed six Japanese prisoners at length, and wrote a short story about their fate. The group had performed a play in front of party leaders at a theatre evening in Yenan. The audience included Chairman Mao, as he was now styled, who stamped his feet, cheered and laughed uproariously with the rest of the crowd. Hogg described how after months of re-education the six prisoners were released by the Chinese. They were sent back to their own lines, greeted with joy by their old comrades – and promptly executed.

Everyone at Yenan, senior party figures, officials and students, lived in the caves surrounding the city. Wedged in a narrow river valley between two ranges of hills, and fearful of bombing, the people of Yenan had not dared to expand their city beyond its fortified walls. Instead they had burrowed deep into the soft earth of the hillsides. By the time George Hogg arrived the communists had expanded the network of caves to include schools, hospitals and at least some of the offices and lecture halls of the five colleges in the city. The caves were cool in the searing heat of the summer and not too cold in winter. Hogg wrote in a letter:

Looking out from one of the caves you see right over the city roofs to hills across the valley, whose outer surface is also honeycombed with rows of caves at various levels. There are many beautiful old temples on the hills round about. One most startling thing is the Printing Press – it turns out a couple of newspapers a week and many books and pamphlets. It is situated in some massive caves called Buddha caves. Very gloomy as you go in. When your eyes get used to it, you see first a huge Buddha high up at the back gazing meditatively in front of him. Then far underneath, scurrying printers devils, bales of paper and huge presses in clanking motion.

Yenan was to become the point of contact between President Roosevelt's administration in Washington and the Chinese communists. The US Marine Corps Captain Evans Carlson had been the first American official to be allowed by the Chinese government to visit the communist area, in 1937. His highly sympathetic reports stressed the excellent relations between the guerrillas and the peasantry, and the moral conduct and political consciousness of the communist troops. His findings were to be echoed by later American visitors, but it was not until 1944 that Roosevelt secured the consent of Chiang Kai-shek to open a US military mission in the city.

For Mao, the 'Yenan experience' during the nine years he lived in the city was one of high achievement. He used the time to lay the foundation for the new and what at least appeared to be highly pragmatic system of Chinese communism. He received a flow of important visitors, both journalists and diplomats. Mao had never left China, and was only ever to do so twice, visiting Moscow in December 1949 and again in 1957. He used the interviews to question journalists closely on events and politics in their own countries. The main point of these sessions was to reinforce the message that the Communist Party and guerrillas formed the most disciplined and aggressive anti-Japanese force in north China. The strength of this message was that it was partially true, and that it was delivered by Mao in person.

Journalists such as Hogg's friend James Bertram were received in Mao's own quarters, a roomy cave-dwelling burrowed out of Yenan's towering cliffs. Bertram was a New Zealander who won a Rhodes scholarship to Oxford and joined *The Times* in London as a sub-editor, and was writing from China as a freelance. As he reported in his book *Unconquered: Journal of a Year's Adventure Among the Fighting Peasants of North China* (1939), the interviews were carefully staged to create a dramatic effect: 'We would begin talking in the early evening and often carry on far into the night, with the candles guttering on the table between us, throwing grotesque shadows across the curving roof. The room was piled high with despatch boxes, and radio messages arrived constantly, which Mao read in the intervals between answering questions.'

George Hogg's enthusiasm for what he saw in Yenan was echoed by his more senior colleagues, and also by visiting diplomats. With hindsight it is easy to see that they were naïve in their uncritical evaluation of Mao and his 'Chinese communism'. Correspondents such as James Bertram, Edgar Snow and Jack Belden were to be accused of being little more than propagandists for the communist cause when the great debate over 'Who lost China?' erupted in the US after the communist victory in 1949. They certainly did not hide their distaste for Chiang Kai-shek's government, or their sympathy for the guerrilla cause. The reason for the collective failure of the press corps was their assumption of knowledge they did not have. Journalists work hard to convince their readers, listeners or viewers that they know what is happening: 'I don't know what is really going on here' is not a line of copy that has ever been filed or broadcast.

Emily Hahn, for many years a distinguished *New Yorker* columnist, author and journalist, observed the foreign press corps at close quarters while in China in 1940. In her bestseller *China to Me* (1944) she described the American correspondents as

> *inclined to be leftist out of a frustrated sense of guilt, a superior view-point of things as they are and a tendency to follow the crowd – of newspapermen. Most newspapermen don't know anything more about the Communists in China than you do. They hear rumours. They try and get permission to see these people and once in a while somebody does. But the chances of seeing what really goes on among the Chinese communists are even less than of seeing the inside of Russia. If you live in Chongqing you can always interview Chou En-lai. That is what he is there for. But if you think China is going to give you all the answers you are as innocent as – as an American newspaperman.*

But the fact is that Mao offered, both in policy and in practical programmes, a real break with China's feudal past. In the context of the war with Japan and the hopeless corruption of Chiang

Kai-shek's government, Mao's communism seemed to be the peasant agrarian socialism that many took it for.

The success of the CCP's rural programmes meant that despite the loose nationalist blockade, Mao was able to extend his territory during the Yenan years so that by 1945 he controlled nearly 400,000 square miles, containing over a hundred million people. He had in fact created a state within a state, and one that had won quasi recognition from Washington.

Late in July 1938 Hogg made the return journey to Hankow, to find a city convulsed by rumour and convinced that a final Japanese assault was imminent. The evacuation of refugees south to Changsha and west to Chongqing was in full swing. Three boats left upriver daily, refugee trains rolled out of the city every evening, and a walking party of several thousand marched out every night to avoid Japanese strafing on the road by day. Hogg spent a day walking with the refugees, and reported that they were well looked after, with tea halts every four miles and food stations every ten.

Not all the refugees were being sent aimlessly into the interior. Some at least were going to appointed destinations to start small mobile industrial co-ops. This was further evidence of official support and funding for a movement that was to spread through much of central and north-western China.

Meanwhile, daily Japanese air raids devastated Hankow's twin cities across the river. The raids on 10 and 11 August were the heaviest, killing 1,500 people. Armed with his camera, Hogg visited the scenes of the bombing the moment the planes had left: 'a gruelling and gruesome business', he called it. He was filing almost daily for UPI. The agency looked to its star writer Jack Belden for the big stories, but the editors in Washington liked their new stringer's copy. His work was to earn him a bonus of an extra month's retainer after the fall of the city.

By late summer almost all foreign wives and children and the families of senior Chinese officials had been evacuated. Chou En-lai had left with his delegation in June. In the summer heat the remaining foreign community of several thousand men consoled themselves with the belief that their presence would enable Hankow to avoid the fate of Nanjing. Much faith was placed in a demilitarised 'safety zone' which, it was hoped, would remain free from bombing and attack in the final assault on the city. Chinese were kept out of the zone, leading to pitiful scenes during bombing raids when Chinese women thrust their children over the barred entry gates only to have them roughly bundled back. The Japanese air force mostly respected the foreign safety zones, but the bombers knew exactly where the Chinese quarter lay, and attacked it mercilessly. Their aim was to drive the Chinese population of Hankow's two sister cities across the Yan and Yangtse Rivers into the countryside, and to take over a depopulated Hankow as a going concern. But while Wuchang and Hanyang were being systematically destroyed from the air, most of their populations actually fled into Hankow itself, swelling the population as the Japanese advanced up the Yangtse valley.

At the end of August Chiang and his commanders made the secret decision not to fight for their capital. While continuing to fortify the city and refusing to discuss terms with the Japanese, the Chinese command planned to evacuate their forces rather than risk a further costly defeat. The lessons of Shanghai and Nanjing had been learnt.

As part of a scorched-earth policy – called 'Leave Nothing to the Japanese' – the Chinese did, however, decide to dynamite buildings and installations not directly owned by foreigners. In the event the controversial policy was largely thwarted by British sailors who removed the demolition charges after the Chinese troops had left. Elsewhere the scorched-earth policy was to be bungled, with devastating results.

Shortly after the fall of Hankow, which would take place on 25 October, government forces torched Changsha, the capital of Hunan province, which was supposedly the next major population centre in the line of the Japanese advance. Lying 430 miles south-west of Hankow, Changsha was an important trading centre on the Xiang River, with a population of three to four million. Among the many thousands of refugees scattered by this senseless act was a young woman named Xiao Ren, one of six children. Their father worked in a flour mill as a manager, while their mother did her best to make ends meet at home. Xiao Ren was twenty-one when her home city was almost totally destroyed by government arson. The population fled to the countryside, where, with limited support from the government which had made them homeless, they attempted to scratch a living as peasant farmers.

Xiao Ren had been active in anti-Japanese campaigns in Changsha, so her family decided that she should be taken for her safety to Baoji, a small but important road and rail junction several hundred miles to the north, near the city of Xian, at the start of the silk route to Europe. Here her aunt placed her in an organisation for women refugees that was to become part of the co-operative movement. And it was here that, late in 1939, she would meet and fall in love with a young Englishman who had also made his way north after the Japanese victories in central China.

In her book *Battle Hymn to China* (1944; reissued in 1984 as *China Correspondent*), Agnes Smedley described the camaraderie among the foreign journalists in Hankow as they worked out strategies for survival when the Japanese arrived: 'We were like passengers on a ship foundering in a stormy sea who had at last found their humanity and clung to each other ... in the tense atmosphere of war even poetry, song and wit blossomed among us and a magical glow shone over our friendship.'

The plight of the refugees had led Smedley to take a Red Cross job which meant long hours working in harrowing conditions in the city's crowded and filthy hospitals. The chaos and the mounting refugee problem on the streets contrasted sharply with the lifestyle of those who had enough money to enjoy themselves in the restaurants and nightclubs. Hogg made the point in a report for the *Manchester Guardian* at the end of August:

> *After dark, activity becomes more marked than ever. The pavements are crowded with beggars and their children. The nightclubs and cinemas are packed every night both with Chinese and foreigners. Recently a 'Thrift Campaign' was launched in the press and many a rich Chinese was startled to see in the local paper the amount of money he had spent in entertaining and the amount of mileage he had covered in his official car on official petrol. Accompanying the description was the threat to disclose identities next time.*

As August turned to September and the Japanese closed in, there were an estimated 750,000 people left in the city. Foreigners formed committees to organise emergency supplies of food and fuel. Those Chinese who had not joined the exodus waited stoically, counting on the presence of large numbers of Westerners to prevent civilian massacres.

By this stage Agnes Smedley had been forced to leave her lodgings in the Lutheran mission. Bishop Roots had deemed her behaviour to be immoral, due to the number of overnight visitors to her room. This might explain the fact that while she thought some of the younger missionaries 'progressive and divinely discontented', her view of their older, more established colleagues, including Bishop Roots, no doubt, was less charitable: 'I have never, anywhere or in any profession met more viciously re-actionary or bigoted men than among some of the more elderly foreign missionaries.'

To bring home to his readers the reality of the evacuation, Hogg followed his first rule of journalism: to live the life of the people he was writing about. He took a refugee train out of the city, using the experience to produce a graphic feature for the *Manchester Guardian* called 'Last Train'.

Local gossip had it that the Chinese government was beginning to evacuate Hankow; that the Japanese would approach the city from all sides; that indiscriminate bombing would soon begin; that poison gas would be used on the city; that the dykes would be cut for defence purposes regardless of low lying Chinese dwellings . . . and a hundred other things. Anyhow for those who wished to make the north west their new home it was time to get moving. Time for bundle and basket, string and strap; time to sell what you had, take up baby and bedroll, time to go.

Tired refugee eyes looked out from the train as it rolled slowly over the flat plains. 'Not much to stop the Japanese here,' they seemed to be thinking. More people pile in at every station until there seems to be not an inch of space left uncovered. The floor is already quite taken up with people sitting on their luggage. Late at night a smiling face appears at our window, then a man's whole body, then case after case, roll after bale after box, each new imposition on us being made with a nervous laugh and 'Bu yao chin, bu yao chin.' 'It doesn't matter, not at all.' As though he were the one to decide what mattered and what did not! For a time I refused to co-operate having been bred to the belief that you should stick to your rights for a seat if you have paid for a ticket. But after a time I thought that maybe this doesn't apply to China in war-time, and by the time he had begun to bring his whole family connection through the window, from toothless mother-in-law to squawking baby I was helping to stow away his belongings with a certain zest . . .

A second night passed in fitful sleep. There was driving rain, and the crush was increased by those people from the top of the train who forced their way inside. A bowl of water at a country station and the crisp dawn air soon removed dust from within and without.

At Luoyang, reached by mid-morning, halfpenny bowls of rice and egg soup cooked individually on a brazier while you wait, ripe peaches at twelve a penny, hard-boiled eggs, tea and bread of dubious cleanliness could all be purchased from picturesque characters along the platform. Here there was an air-raid warning. As we leapt from the windows three planes were already circling over the city and anti-aircraft shells bursting around them. Rough trenches were prepared beside the line, into which those who could get off the train in time (the campers on top were mostly left at the mercy of machine-gunners from the air) flung themselves. I was glad enough to be at the bottom of the pile of others. Bombs exploded on the station as we lay face downwards breathing deeply the scent of the damp earth. Then we could hear the drone approaching us until it was low overhead. Would they attempt to bomb the train and the line? Would the quantity of soldiers on the train tempt them to sweep it with machine-gun fire? Timeless seconds of apprehension passed before we were cautiously turning our heads to watch them fly away. Back at the station we found the line quite unharmed. But some distance away a column of smoke meant homelessness, death, and a numb hate for these inaccessible and all-powerful visitants from the sky.

The train now travelled swiftly westward out of the Japanese sphere of influence. The countryside took on the aspect of the Pyrenean foothills in Catalonia. Hills and houses were of a dusty brown; arid terraced fields yielded sparse crops of wheat, potatoes and turnips. Donkeys and mules appeared in place of water buffalo and oxen, light green and brown for the luscious rich green of the rice in the riverbeds, geometrical shapes of mountains in purple, green and brown for the uniformity of the plains.

The four days' journey culminated in the sight of the massive gates of Xian, towering over the city walls and the surrounding country. 'Tao liao!' 'We've arrived!'

Hogg does not record how he was able to get back into Hankow, but he was lucky to do so. His next and last letter from the city records how the provisional capital was completely cut off. Writing on 13 October, just twelve days before the Japanese entered the city, he seems shocked by the realisation that while all his energies have been focused on the war in China, events in Europe were threatening to become just as dangerous.

Dear Mother and daddy,

Thanks for your letter of October 5th about the crisis in Europe. It must be awful, I didn't realise that they had given out gasmasks and everything. It's difficult to feel what it is really like but your letter really brought it home ... There is a war on here too. It is coming closer. Everyone is dashing off with bundles and bales slung over their shoulders often with no money, families getting all split up etc because some are required to stay here, some (children, skilled workers factory girls of capable age) have special organisations to look after them. Now we are pretty well cut off.

The Japanese had cut the railway link to Canton, which was to fall shortly after Hankow. The railway line north had also been cut. The Chinese had put a boom across the Yangtse upstream of the city to deny access to Japanese gunboats, but all it did was to limit the flow of river traffic carrying refugees, and further increase the sense of isolation in the city.

The night before Hankow fell to the Japanese, Hogg sent the *Manchester Guardian* a graphic last look at the city:

Night of October 24th. The mayor reports that a population of about half a million remains in Wuhan. That means that over a million have evacuated. A week ago movement was desultory. Children still played familiarly among the trenches and sandbags; dance-halls were filled with hay-makers and the last sun-flowery girls whose limbs peeped provokingly from their side-split skirts, and business men profiting by the times. But for the last three days the roads have borne a steady stream of traffic.

At night the automobiles of the fortunate bump uncomfortably into the country; they travel in the dark to avoid Japanese planes flying low over the road to strafe anything that doesn't take cover quickly enough. In daytime the poorer citizens set out. Carrying spring beds, tables and chairs, cooking utensils, invalids on litters, babies in baskets, all slung on stout poles across their shoulders, their rhythmic 'Ho-hee ho-ho' will echo with every step for hundreds of miles along the refugee trails . . . Today the last boat left up river; disconsolate families who were unable to push their way aboard in the seething mass of people and baggage, sat on the fore-shore watching their hopes of safety sail away. Meanwhile those who are staying behind – including over 1,000 foreigners – were frantically busy, or keeping themselves artificially busy to avoid thinking of the guns that could sometimes be heard down the river.

The night is deep and dark. We are in the heart of a great city, the capital of a people which loves noise, but it is as quiet as midnight on the plains of Arizona. Wounded soldiers are lying along the bund hoping to be evacuated in junks. Groups of farmer folk hurry through the city driving their cattle in front of them. Small pathetic lines of refugees pass quickly in no set direction, like sheep. Soon they will lie down fatalistically to wait in the street . . . Sleep is uneasy in Hankow

tonight. It may be interrupted by the explosions of the 'scorched earth'
policy. In the small hours guns from the river will become audible.
And tomorrow? The generalissimo is gone! Long live Emperor Meiji!**

Generalissimo Chiang Kai-shek had indeed gone. His decision
not to fight for Hankow spared the population the horrors of
Nanjing, and brought a relatively peaceful take-over of the city.
The diplomats and most of the journalists had left by boat upriver
to Chongqing, the new provisional capital. Agnes Smedley, as ever
pursuing her own path, travelled north to the communist areas.
A group of eighteen 'Last Ditchers' remained, including Hogg.
Although the Japanese had no intention of repeating the atrocities
of Nanjing, they had no wish to subject their actions to the
scrutiny of the foreign press. The remaining journalists were
quickly rounded up and put on a military plane for Shanghai.

Seven months earlier, it had taken Hogg two weeks to work
his way from Shanghai to Hankow, via Hong Kong. The journey
back took just two hours and fifty-seven minutes. The flight took
the journalists over a countryside scarred with trenches, bomb
craters and burnt-out villages, the battlefield they had been
reporting on for months.

Back in Shanghai, Hogg filed an angry story for the *Manchester
Guardian* which the paper turned into a lead letter. Titled 'A View
of Empires in Action', it was an account of the cynical action
of the foreign powers in protecting their own interests rather
than the Chinese population when the Japanese entered Hankow.
He described how the Italian Consul, in full dress uniform, had

---

* Hogg was being ironic. Emperor Meiji had been the great modernising
Emperor of Japan from 1868 to 1912, and had committed the country to act
in accordance with international law. Hirohito was the Japanese Emperor
during the war with China.

welcomed the Japanese commanders personally, while British naval officers and men prevented Chinese troops from carrying out the planned destruction of strategic buildings in the city. Instead of acting to protect the civilian population, American gunboats stationed themselves by the Standard Oil installation and National City bank on the Bund.

There were still half a million civilians in Hankow, many of whom had congregated in the 'safety zone'. Although foreign businesses had encouraged them to stay and to believe that they would be protected, the Japanese kicked them out immediately. They were, Hogg reported, no more than an unsanitary nuisance to foreigner and Japanese alike. The refugees were sent to a new zone in deserted slums:

Long trails of them – all the oldest and most feeble who were unable to evacuate – could be seen struggling along the road to their new quarters: pregnant mother led blind grandmother, grandfather bent almost double under the weight of the family belongings, small daughter carried the baby. Their misery was extreme and they bore it with typical Chinese stoicism. As they walked through thin rain I saw one Japanese soldier trying to take a family's bedding, another begin to take away a refugee woman and girl lying desperately ill on the pavement.

As well as his bonus, the quality of Hogg's reporting from Hankow earned him an undertaking from UPI that they would be glad to take further contributions from wherever he chose to base himself in China. He rented a room at the Shanghai YMCA – which surprisingly came with a gym and squash courts attached – and planned his next move.

The brief visit to Yenan had fired his interest in north-west China, and he decided that that was to be his destination. He planned to spend Christmas in Japan, then travel to Beijing and cross the Japanese lines to link up with the 'government within a government' in communist-controlled areas. He also wanted to find Rewi Alley. He had briefly met the New Zealander in Hankow, and had heard he was working with the industrial co-operatives somewhere in north-west China. But no one knew where.

A case of paratyphoid, usually contracted through drinking contaminated water, changed his plans. Hogg ended up in hospital, where he spent nineteen days in a state of delirium. He was lucky to survive, given the depleted medical supplies in Shanghai at the time. His old Methodist missionary friends, Frank and Aimee Millican, took him in. They knew how to nurse typhoid patients, and probably saved his life.

Hogg's life was twice saved by Protestant missionaries during his years in China, and he always recognised the debt he owed them. Only later would he come to realise the deep-rooted popular resentment aroused by the work of the Western Churches in China. Catholic missionaries had been active in the country, although on a small scale, since the sixteenth century. At every stage of the long series of humiliations that Western powers heaped on China, the missionaries strengthened their position. Thus when China lost the First Opium War (1839–41) the imperial court in Beijing was forced to cede five ports plus Hong Kong to the Western powers, and agree to allow the extension of missionary activity to major cities such as Canton, Amoy and Shanghai. The Second Opium War (1856–60) ended with China's enforced acceptance of further freedom of action by the missionaries and the guaranteed right of Chinese citizens to convert to Christianity.

Missionary activity continued to expand after the Taiping Revolution of 1850–65 and the Boxer Rebellion of 1899–1901.

Hostility to the missionaries, and resentment at the challenge to traditional faiths, played a major part in these uprisings: some thirty thousand Chinese Christians died in the Boxer revolt. Renewed activity by conservative evangelical and social gospel movements followed in the first decades of the twentieth century, and by 1930 there were over eight thousand Protestant missionaries in the country, and an estimated Chinese Protestant community of half a million. The larger Catholic community was estimated at two million in 1949.

After assuming power in that year, the communists began to restrict religious freedoms and to expel foreign missionaries. In 1951 diplomatic relations with the Vatican were severed. This was scarcely surprising, since the Catholic leadership had largely supported the Chiang Kai-shek regime, and to some extent continued to do so. The long repression of the Christian Church in China had begun.

The Millicans ran a Christian radio station, and kept their visitors in touch with events in China and the outside world. They also served as a *poste restante*. When he had recovered, Hogg was handed a number of letters which brought him up to date with news from home. It was his sister Rosemary rather than his mother who told him that his old girlfriend Muff Nelson was in a relationship with his good friend Roger Hunter. He also learnt that his brother Stephen had married in August that year, and that his eldest brother Gary had separated from his wife. It cannot be said that these family events greatly moved him. 'Too bad about Gary and Dorothy,' was his comment. Gary was fourteen years older than George, and had formed little part of either his childhood or his later development. As for Stephen, George remarked upon his mother's joke about the small-sized morning suit he had worn to his wedding. Barbara, George's eldest sister, had married Donald Thomas, another St George's boy from

Harpenden who had suffered from polio as a child and who worked as a military censor at the *Manchester Guardian* for much of the war. His brother-in-law's reports from China would have crossed his desk.

Rosemary, the much-loved 'Roke' of George's childhood, had begun a romance with a bank manager from Bristol. Kathleen, ever the fierce matriarch of the family, proved uncharacteristically understanding of the fact that Rosemary's suitor, Cyril Baker, was still legally married, even though he had separated from his wife. Kathleen clearly had high hopes for this relationship, since in a letter home in December 1938 Hogg wrote to her that he too hoped that the relationship 'would grow into something more'.

By the end of that year a European war was clearly inevitable. Hogg's letters over Christmas echo his parents' concerns about London's lack of anti-aircraft defences. He also told his mother he was short of money. It was a source of great pride that he had earned enough to pay his hospital fees, but in fact the costs of his illness took all the bonus he had just received. With Christmas coming, he wrote home to say that if anyone wanted to give him a present, 'let it be cash'. And on Christmas Day, while at breakfast with the Millicans, he received a cheque for £10 from his parents.

He was incensed that the *Manchester Guardian* chose to publish his reflections on the fall of Hankow as a lead letter, thus avoiding payment. This was a cheap trick, and he urged his parents to claim payment from the paper at the rate of £3.3s. per thousand words. Echoing the sentiments of many a freelance journalist over the years, he described the paper's actions as 'absolute robbery', and wrote: 'All big papers are absolutely unscrupulous and the MG [*Manchester Guardian*] is the lowest paying paper in England.'

Their son's letters home at this point gave Kathleen and Robert further evidence of his hardening political attitudes. While urging them to take on the *Manchester Guardian,* he also vented his views about the Munich agreement in terms that would have won the approval of that paper's editor: 'It seems to me that someone should put Chamberlain in an Italian or German concentration camp for a few weeks, just to give him a taste. Maybe he did the right thing at Munich but he did it so obviously from the wrong motives, in the wrong way and at the wrong time.'

The Munich Agreement of September 1938, in which Czecho-slovakia was sacrificed by England and France in a vain effort to secure peace with Hitler, dashed hopes in China that foreign intervention might halt Japanese aggression. Tokyo had in fact sustained heavy losses in men and materiel in the long campaign to take Hankow, but Canton had fallen into its hands without resistance. Since all the major coastal cities and ports were in their hands, Japanese commanders assumed that Chinese capitulation would naturally follow. Indeed, several senior figures in the KMT pressed for a negotiated settlement.

Chiang Kai-shek put a brave face on the loss of Hankow and its sister cities. He moved his headquarters five hundred miles inland to Chongqing, and ordered his forces to retreat into the moun-tainous areas of central and western China, beyond the reach of the mechanised forces of the invader.

All sides now prepared for a long war. The communists and the KMT began drawing up plans for a ten-to-twenty-year struggle with the Japanese – and a final conflict with each other.

FIVE

Gung Ho!

'Why wasn't I at home fire fighting or somewhere
over Germany in a bomber?'

In February 1939, having recovered from paratyphoid, Hogg was
summoned by the Japanese authorities in Shanghai. He had sent a
number of articles home by post for forwarding to the *Manchester
Guardian* and the *New Statesman*. The censors routinely intercepted all mail, and they disliked the tone of the articles. More
damagingly, the Japanese knew that he had visited the communist
headquarters at Yenan. He was 'advised' to leave the country.
Although he had not formally been expelled, the Japanese made it
clear that they did not expect him to come back.

Hogg took the boat to Japan, where he tried to find the answer
to a question that had posed itself repeatedly during his year in
China. What was it in the Japanese culture and character that
endowed its military and most of its people with a sense of sacred
mission in its drive to subjugate China? The *realpolitik* of Japan's
China policy was clear. In April 1934 the Foreign Ministry in
Tokyo had effectively declared China a Japanese protectorate, in
a statement that also arrogated to Japan the right to act as the
'guardian of peace and order' in eastern Asia.

The myths of racial superiority and imperial divinity that underpinned the quest to dominate the Pacific region were rooted deep in Japanese history. Hogg believed that the press corps in China, and indeed most diplomats, had paid scant attention to the origins of the conflict they were reporting.

From his earlier visit to Japan, and from talks with captured Japanese soldiers, Hogg had heard and learnt much of the mystical origins of Japanese religious faith. To find out more, he decided to join pilgrims to Ise, home of two of the most sacred Shinto shrines since the fourth century BC. He put the idea to the *Manchester Guardian*, received agreement, and boarded the train from Tokyo. The train left at 10.30 p.m., stopping throughout the night to pick up more pilgrims until it rolled into the plain of Ise, on the Shima peninsula 290 miles south-west of Tokyo, the following morning.

The *Manchester Guardian* gave prominence to the article on 27 March, under the title 'Modern Pilgrimage'. Hogg found that the two main Ise shrines were simple wooden buildings in the Japanese style, with steep reed-thatched roofs, standing several miles apart at the foot of densely wooded hills. The outer shrine was in the suburbs of Ise town, surrounded by sweeping cedars which shielded it from the noise of traffic by day and the glare of the street lighting by night. Extraordinary efforts had gone into creating a feeling of peace and harmony for the worshippers. Swept gravel paths, carefully planted trees and streams of crystal water had all been designed to create a sense of order and well-being. Even the timber used in the wooden buildings was unknotted, to provide a smooth surface without unsightly marks.

At the outer shrine worshippers could enter the complex of buildings to pay their respects. The inner Imperial Shrine, dedicated to Amaterasu, the Sun Goddess, was more sacred, and was reputed to contain the Emperor's sacred mirror. Here too running water, groomed trees and gravel paths had been laid out to enhance the sanctity of the setting. At both shrines vacant plots had been left next to the main building to allow for the traditional reconstruction every twenty years, when the existing shrines were torn down in recognition of the impermanence of worldly goods and the immortality of the spirits they enshrined.

Hogg was struck by the sheer number of people who saw as it as their duty to worship ancient relics they could not even see. The two main shrines had attracted, by his estimate, 960,000 people in the first three months of the year. This meant that almost four million people, out of a population of seventy-three million, made the pilgrimage each year. Every Japanese is supposed to visit the Ise shrine once in his or her lifetime, but clearly they were doing so much more often in the wartime years of the late 1930s.

The pilgrims came to seek the blessing of ancient divinities for themselves, for loved ones, for a marriage or a business venture. Weddings were held at or near the shrines, and newborn babies were brought to be blessed. In the gardens schoolchildren purified themselves by dipping their hands into the sacred stream. A mother knelt with a baby on her back, old men briefly prayed. Many of the thousands who came to worship, including whole schools of children, had travelled for twenty-four hours just for a few minutes' silent ceremony.

Hogg asked a friendly guard the obvious questions. Why do they come? What do they think about silently there? 'He seemed surprised, as if it was the first time he had thought about such a thing. "Before the war," he answered, "it was generally to pray for the success of some new venture, a business, a baby, a new wife or a new husband. But now it is to pray for the war or for a son or husband at the front."'

Throughout his visit to the shrines, Hogg could hear the sound of aircraft taking off and landing at a nearby airbase: 'To me in this place of ancient trees, running water, peeping sky, deified nature it seemed like the sound of distant thunder ... to the Japanese who come here it must unconsciously have the same effect, consciously it must remind them of the power and might of their country.'

But nowhere did he find any answer to his next question: If ancient deities sanctified Japan's imperial conquests, what drove its troops to commit such acts of barbarism in their divinely ordained campaigns in China? Even the good Dr Kagawa could not help. But an answer of sorts emerged on the next stage of his travels.

Hogg left Japan by boat in February 1939 for Korea, then a Japanese-occupied territory. He made his way north by train through Manchuria, which was also under Japanese control. He did not declare himself to be a journalist, but he talked his way through several checkpoints by flourishing his English passport, and reached Beijing in March.

The ancient imperial capital was a timeless and enchanting city, half ringed by a crescent of hills to the west. In 1939 her four great gatehouses rose from the castellated city walls, within which square miles of streets and avenues were laid out on a grid formation. The city gates and much of the walls would be destroyed after the communist takeover in 1949.

Although Beijing had been the first city to be taken by the Japanese in 1937, not a shot had been fired within the city walls. The suburbs and outer villages had been bombarded, but the city itself remained untouched. But the war was never far away. Units of the communists' Eighth Route Army were active within a few miles of the city walls. The American writer Joy Homer records having tea in the Dowager Empress's summer palace a few miles from the city centre when a battle began behind a hill several hundred yards away. The tea party continued to the sound of mortar and machine-gun fire, without any of the guests remarking on it.

After the horrors of Shanghai and Hankow, Beijing was a revelation. Hogg found a city with a vibrant street life that seemed untouched by foreign occupation. Hawkers thronged the streets, noisily promoting their wares with a distinctive cry and a hand gong or trumpet. There were travelling puppet shows for children, performing animals and itinerant barbers on every street. Water was supplied to every household on single-wheeled barrows which fought for street space with rickshaws. Along the main avenues stallholders competed with hawkers selling everything from caged birds to tin bathtubs. Hooded hawks, usually goshawks, were sold in the weekly markets, along with cameras, radios and old European books. On public holidays the residents would indulge a passion for kite-flying. Animals, mythical characters and abstract designs were created from strips of coloured paper and sticks of bamboo and sent aloft over the city.

One of the first Japanese edicts after taking Beijing was to allow opium dens to reopen in certain areas. Sometimes European men would join the Chinese in these long, windowless rooms, lined on each side by benches on which the smokers lay with pipes of pure opium. George Hogg was either too busy or too cautious to write a feature that his editors in Washington or Manchester would have snapped up.

The Japanese exercised discreet but tight control of the old imperial capital. There were checkpoints on all the city gates by day, and they were closed at night. Feeling that he was being watched, Hogg reported his presence to the British consulate, and was invited to dinner by one of the diplomats. An American journalist based in Beijing, the Associated Press correspondent

Haldore Hanson, was a fellow guest. The conversation turned to the savagery of the invading army, and what the Japanese would do next. In particular, everyone wanted to know what had roused the Japanese army to such homicidal frenzy and sexual aberration at Nanjing.

In his book *Humane Endeavor* (1939), Hanson reported that the most obvious explanation was that the Japanese troops had been brutalised by the ninety-day battle for Shanghai, and had cracked under the strain. Certainly on the 180-mile march from Shanghai to Nanjing the invading forces committed casual atrocities against civilians on a scale that had not been witnessed before.

However, the grim conclusion among the expatriate community in Beijing at the time, and one which Hogg was to reach later, was that the atrocities were the result of an official but unstated Japanese policy of total warfare. The tactical imperative was not only to destroy the Chinese army, but to cripple the morale of the nation by mass murder of civilians and the destruction of their homes as well as of industrial plant, religious and educational institutions and hospitals. The Japanese view seemed to be that a nation traumatised by atrocities was a nation beaten. A strand of this policy was the indoctrination of Japanese troops in the belief that the Chinese were backward semi-savages who could never rise to their own civilised standards. Dehumanising the Chinese people in this way was certainly one reason for the continued atrocities inflicted upon the civilian population.

The dinner party opened up further employment for Hogg, as Haldore Hanson offered him a job as an AP stringer. The job with UPI seemed to have lapsed, and he happily accepted.

Hogg did not spend long in Beijing. The Japanese secret police had discovered that the Englishman they had politely expelled from Shanghai had turned up again. Within days of arriving he left the city, travelling alone and on foot. As a general rule the Japanese controlled the cities and main lines of communications while, in north China at least, the communist guerrillas controlled the countryside and most villages. It was while seeking contact with those guerrillas that Hogg fell ill again. He spent his first night in a small village inn not far from Beijing and woke with a splitting headache, shivering uncontrollably and with a high fever. Incredibly, having survived paratyphoid three months earlier, Hogg now had typhus. He had picked up the disease, which is transmitted by lice, despite having had all the right inoculations.

Once again his luck held. As in Shanghai, where the Millicans had been on hand to nurse him back to health, so now he found another lifeline. By extraordinary coincidence a New Zealand missionary nurse called Kathleen Hall had been staying in the same inn while on her way from Beijing to her clinic in the village of Songjiazhuang in western Hupei. She had been in China since 1923, and regularly crossed the lines seeking to recruit new staff and buy medicines. She took huge risks in doing so. At the very least she faced interrogation and deportation if the Japanese caught her.

Hall was travelling by mule cart with two Chinese staff. Between them they wrapped the hefty Englishman in blankets, lifted him onto the cart and set off on the four-day journey to her small mission. She had no idea who the stranger was, and had neither the opportunity nor the inclination to find out. Hogg was seriously ill, and was unable to talk; in any case, it was best not to ask questions of travellers in the no man's land between the Japanese and the communist forces.

Hogg's condition worsened as the mule cart slowly made its way deeper into communist territory. Fearing that he would die, Kathleen Hall opened his wallet and discovered the identity of the stranger. When the group reached the mountains Hogg was offloaded from the cart and placed astride the packsaddle of a spare mule, which was piled high with bedding. He later recalled the 'almost insurmountable problem' of not falling off the mule as the cart and outriders lurched up the mountain trails. His final memory before lapsing into unconsciousness was of a white-washed gateway and someone shouting '*Taola*' – 'Arrived!'

It was three weeks before Hogg was well enough to observe his surroundings. He found himself lying comfortably on a rustling straw mattress, and looking out at a large elm tree. In that time Kathleen Hall had nursed him without any of the standard drugs of the time. She washed him, fed him with millet soup and milk from the clinic's two goats, and used cold compresses to bring his temperature down.

Hogg awoke to a new and very different China. Songjiazhuang was then a small village of about 350 people, 250 miles south-west of Beijing, on the outskirts of the town of Xingtai. This was territory held by the communists, but its people were still largely loyal to Chiang Kai-shek's Kuomintang government. The first sounds he heard in the morning were the whistle summoning the local defence corps to drill and the reveille of a unit of regular troops stationed across a small river from the clinic.

Unable to leave his sickbed, Hogg could only listen and record the sounds as the village came to life and its people moved through their daily routines. In his book he wrote:

The chirping of magpies and sparrows took up the . . . [early] hours until the village was fully awake and then throughout the day came the full throated cry of the itinerant food sellers, the tricky tapping of the pedlar's conch and the touring tinsmith's whinnying gong. At about five o'clock the school children came out onto the village threshing floor to practise their songs and drill and from that time until ten at night there were constant whistlings, muffled tramping of

118

many cloth shoes running past in the dust, slogans shouted hoarsely
from men's throats and the singsong of modern China as women and
girls went to night school.

Throughout the war years famine was never far away from the
village communities of northern China. Songjiazhuang was
poorer than most, which is why Kathleen Hall had based herself
there. Everyone, young and old, was on the verge of starvation,
subsisting on one meal a day, usually a watery millet gruel. Their
clothes were worn thin, and offered little protection against the
cold. The children, usually cheerful in the morning, were miser-
ably hungry and cold by evening. Hogg's answer, as so often, was
to sing. He had a fine voice, and by now he knew Mandarin well
enough to sing Chinese guerrilla songs – one way of making the
children think of something other than their hunger pangs.

As he recovered, Hogg began to understand the political
nature of village life. There were farmers' associations, women's
associations, young men's associations and children's associations. The groups met every week amid fluttering paper pennants
of various colours which identified them. For several hours the
villagers sat through speeches and slogans exhorting the people
to victory in the war against the enemy. At meetings the local
hsien, or magistrate, explained that peace offers from Japan were
meaningless. 'The answer given by Chiang Kai-shek is that Japan's
peace is not a peace between equals but a peace between master
and slave,' he shouted at the crowd, and they roared back their
agreement. At this stage co-operation between communists and
nationalists was still effective on the ground. Guerrilla presses
would roll out statements from Chiang Kai-shek's new headquarters at Chongqing, just as local officials would stick to the
line that unity between the two sides was essential in the war
against Japan.

Kathleen Hall's clinic provided the rest that Hogg needed in order to recuperate, but once he was better he became restless. He had no room for books on his travels. His only reading matter was a collection of O. Henry's short stories about the people of New York, which he had read and reread.

It was time to move on.

A clatter of horses' hooves one morning changed his life again. The heavily armed riders, corseted in hand grenades, were from Mao's Eighth Route Army, and they had come for the foreigner. They explained that one of Mao's commanders, General Nieh Rong Zhen, wished to see the English journalist.

It didn't take Hogg long to pack his typewriter, camera and a small case of clothes. He was given a horse, and although he had never been in the saddle before, apart from a few days swaying around on a mule, he kept up with his escort and in a few hours found himself climbing the steps of an old temple to a guerrilla command post.

Nieh Rong Zhen was then forty years old and, unusually among Mao's military commanders, he was well educated, cosmopolitan, and came from a wealthy family. He had studied engineering in Paris and Brussels, and had met and formed a friendship with another young Chinese student in Europe, Chou En-lai. Nieh joined the Chinese Communist Party in 1923, underwent military training in Moscow and returned to China to pursue an army career at Chiang Kai-shek's Whampoa military academy. When the Kuomintang split from the communists he sided with Mao and made the Long March from Jiangxi to Shanxi in 1934–35. By the time he met Hogg he had been given field command of a large area close to the old imperial capital.

Nieh was to rise to become a marshal in the People's Liberation Army, and was ultimately given command of China's nuclear weapons programme. During the Cultural Revolution he was purged and isolated from his colleagues and family for years in a remote part of China. In September 1977, on the first anniversary of Mao's death, while tens of thousands gathered solemnly around the newly opened marble and granite mausoleum in Beijing's Tiananmen square, Marshal Nieh was among the first to publicly criticise his former leader. In an article for the *Red Flag* magazine, broadcast on Peking radio, he said that Mao's thoughts should not be followed slavishly: 'All correct ideas are subject to changes on the basis of time, location and condition.' In the context of the time this was unprecedented criticism, and set the tone for the change that Deng Xiaoping was to usher in.

Hogg had mastered Mandarin well enough to sing some of the guerrilla songs, but he was by no means fluent in the language; and while Nieh's French was excellent, his English was limited. Using interpreters, the two men spent hours in conversation talking about their very different lives, their plans for the future and how to beat Japan. In his letters home and his book, Hogg was careful not to mention where he met the guerrilla commander, or how long he stayed at the camp. He was aware that his mail was being intercepted.

On one occasion Nieh took Hogg to one of the two remaining hot springs in the north-west not to have fallen into Japanese hands. Warm water poured into a large rock pool in which the two men, with various local officials, sat discussing the region's tourist prospects after the war. Through clouds of steam the naked group agreed that with its hot springs, horse riding and mountain beauty spots, all within easy reach of the capital, this was the place for a large hotel. Special suites would be reserved for Captain Evans Carlson and the AP correspondent Haldore Hanson, who were among the earliest Western visitors to the region. Hogg knew Carlson from Hankow, where he had moved in Smedley's circle of friends. It was a surreal conversation. There were armed guards outside, and horses ready for a swift departure in the event of a Japanese advance.

At Nieh's invitation, Hogg agreed to go on an extended horseback tour of the region accompanied by an interpreter, four guards and six horses. As the party left on a trail winding into the mountains, Hogg wrote a brief note in his diary:

Along the lower slopes on either side cherry and pear trees were in bloom. Brown hills lay behind and purple razor-edge peaks stood up, like stage scenery in the distance. This was the second day of my life on horseback.

His tour brought home the success of communist tactics to control the countryside, leaving the Japanese to defend their base camps and lines of communication. Everywhere, even deep in famine country, the group of horsemen were welcomed by villagers with offers of food and drink. They passed through village after village of charred, roofless buildings with no sign of people. Every Buddhist temple had been reduced to rubble by Japanese gunfire.

There was method in this wanton destruction. If the peasants had to rebuild their homes, they would have less time to plant crops, and would thus have little food for themselves or the guerrillas. The repeated bombing of even small villages was to be a hallmark of the Japanese occupation until the end of the war in 1945.

In several weeks of travel Hogg and his small party crossed and recrossed Japanese lines of communication, almost always at night. Whenever the Japanese attacked targets in their area they melted away into the mountains. Various groups would attach themselves to the party. Sometimes these were students from Yenan who had formed a 'Resist Japan' academy. A troupe of singers and actors joined them to hold propaganda plays among the villagers. More than once Hogg looked up to see the Japanese flag, a red rising sun on a white background, hanging limply from a flagpole in the moonlight as they passed silently past a strongpoint.

Not surprisingly, Hogg found little time to write home. A postal service of sorts did work, as did a rural telephone service. Airmail letters were marked with a chicken feather stuck under the flap, and were carried from hand to hand, night and day, from north China to the Kuomintang-controlled areas in the south-west and then, somehow, to Hong Kong.

He may not have written many letters home, but Hogg certainly wrote. In the evening he would sit at his typewriter by the light of a kerosene lamp writing short stories based on his experiences for American and English magazines. He used his main contact in the United States, Ida Pruitt, who had been born in China to American missionary parents, to place the articles, and urged his Aunt Muriel to use what influence she had with editors on either coast. He even asked missionary societies to contact magazines and periodicals in the Bible belt in an effort to have his stories published.

They all turned him down. American magazines were not interested in stories, however well written, about the triumphs and tragedies of everyday life in wartime China. They wanted first-hand, blood-and-guts reportage from their correspondents – and they got it. Hogg's parents did, however, manage to place some stories with that reliable, if not very lucrative, standby the *Manchester Guardian*.

Throughout the weeks of travel Hogg everywhere met educated Chinese with professional qualifications who had fled the Japanese assault on the coastal cities. They were working in the countryside as doctors, teachers, magistrates and local government officials.

And everywhere he heard about the planned deployment, which he and Nieh had discussed, of small, mobile co-operatives throughout the rural areas to replace light industry that had been lost in the fighting for Shanghai, Nanjing and Hankow.

The Chinese industrial co-operatives (CIC) were the brain-child of a group of foreigners and Chinese intellectuals headed by Edgar Snow and the New Zealander Rewi Alley.* Chiang Kai-shek's wife Soong Meiling was an enthusiastic supporter, as was her sister, Madame Soong Ching Ling, widow of Sun Yat-sen. This heavyweight group of backers planned to create small industrial units in villages, employing refugees and war orphans to provide basic materials for both nationalist and communist forces throughout north and central China. Although industrial co-ops were to play an important part in the supply of basics to Mao's Eighth Route Army, the movement began very much as a bipartisan response to war needs in the struggle against Japan.

At first sight this was a well-meaning project born of wishful thinking. The Chinese government had evacuated heavy industry and military arsenals in the face of the Japanese advance, but had abandoned smaller industrial plant such as textile factories. Where was the equipment, the money and the organisation going to come from to recreate the country's lost light industrial base in the remote western regions of the country? One thing was clear: funding for the co-operative movement would have to come from the United States.

Edgar Snow invited Ida Pruitt to join the small group that was to launch CIC. Ida had been born and brought up in a small

---

* The CIC movement was launched in Shanghai in April 1938. As well as Snow and Alley, its committee included a prominent banker, Xu Xinliu, and several other senior Chinese figures from the city.

Chinese village, and knew the language and understood the rural culture. She had been educated in America, and this bi-cultural background brought a unique perspective to her work as a teacher, social worker and author in China.

She was well placed to help in another way. Her birthplace was Penglai, a small coastal town in Shandung province. In 1898, ten years after she was born, another child was born to a missionary family in the same town. His name was Henry Luce, and he was to become the proprietor of *Time*, *Life* and *Fortune* magazines. Using their shared family background as an entrée, Ida would approach him years later to help publicise the co-operatives.

While Rewi Alley set about organising the co-operative movement inside China, Ida faced the challenge of raising funds in America for Indusco, CIC's fund-raising arm.* Her intense lobbying in Washington, New York and Los Angeles paid off, and she created support committees in Hollywood involving senior executives from Warner Bros and Paramount studios. The President's wife Eleanor Roosevelt warmly praised the work of the co-operatives in her syndicated newspaper column 'My Day', and agreed to become a member of the CIC advisory board. The real breakthrough came when Ida lobbied Sam Goldwyn in Hollywood. The studio boss, already a legend in the movie industry, agreed to include China in his general war relief committee, and suggested that she also ask the media mogul Henry Luce to become involved.

Luce's passionate interest in China had deep roots. He had

---

* Indusco was established by Ida Pruitt in 1939. After the communist victory in 1949 it and other aid agencies were accused of 'philanthropic imperialism' by communist officials. It was also attacked from the right in America as a communist front organisation, and investigated by the FBI. It closed down in 1952.

been born in 1898 to a Presbyterian missionary family in the same mission station as Ida Pruitt, and educated in various mission schools in China. At fourteen he was sent to school in Europe, and at Yale he was voted 'most brilliant in his class', before returning across the Atlantic to spend a year at Oxford.

This eclectic education had given Luce distinguished qualifications, but he decided to join the *Chicago Daily News* as a junior member of staff. At the age of only twenty-four, with money borrowed from family and friends, he and his friend Brit Haddon invented the concept of the weekly news magazine with the launch of *Time* in 1923. The business magazine *Fortune* followed in 1930, and the illustrated *Life* in 1936.

Luce's admiration for Chiang Kai-shek and his wife was reflected in the coverage that both *Time* and *Life* had given to the war since the Japanese attack on Shanghai in 1937. That year, *Time* named Chiang Kai-shek and his wife Meiling as its People of the Year – the first of several covers the magazine would devote to the couple. Pruitt knew Luce had been working to bring together the scattered and often competing agencies providing financial support for relief projects in China, and that he was heavily involved in raising money for Christian colleges in China. He readily agreed to extend his fundraising to cover the industrial co-operatives.

Luce proposed a merger of the various relief organisations under the umbrella of a new body called United China Relief (UCR), and a publicity campaign was launched to promote the image of China fighting back against the Japanese. Luce offered to contribute $25,000 to the fund, provided other sources matched the sum. He also co-opted great names to join himself on the board of UCR, including Eleanor Roosevelt, Paul G. Hoffman, head of the Studebaker motor company, John D. Rockefeller III and senior movie-industry figures such as David O. Selznick and Louis B. Mayer. The idealism of the board members was matched in some instances by their old-fashioned business interests. Selznick, for instance, was well aware that *Life* magazine could make or break a new Hollywood film.

Luce had long been attracted by the idea of helping to found what he called 'a guerrilla industry' in China. *Time*'s correspondent in Chongqing, Theodore White, knew of this enthusiasm, and reported regularly on the development of CIC. The story had immediate appeal both to the reporters in China and to their readers, because it was a rare example of good news from the war zone.

Luce and his second wife Clare Booth Luce, whom he married in 1935, travelled to China several times. On their first visit to Chongqing, in 1941, Chiang Kai-shek received them with due regard to the publisher's role as the nationalists' most influential supporter in the United States. Luce reciprocated, placing the Generalissimo on the cover of *Time* magazine eight times in the space of four years.

At a time of hyper-inflation in China, the key to the success of the co-operative movement lay in its funding. Hogg noted: 'Most of the co-ops had invested nearly everything in equipment at the beginning before money depreciated so that the problem later on was how to get enough circulating capital to keep the machines running.' When the co-op movement was born in 1938 the price of wheat, the staple food in the north-west, was 43.50 Chinese dollars a bag, the equivalent then of £2.10s; by the spring of 1942 it had risen to $100 a bag. Cotton yarn had gone from $350 a bale to $8,000 in the same period. Hogg estimated that production costs for the co-ops had risen twenty-fold in under four years. In the spring of 1938 a co-op needed on average $2,000 start-up capital, about £125 at the official rate.* By 1942 that had risen to almost $12,000.

In 1940 there were 362 co-ops in the north-west of China, making shoes, clothing, cooking utensils and basic tools. This was well below the much-trumpeted figure of tens of thousands that Rewi Alley had talked about. They had outstanding loans of $4 million between them, and the banks were reluctant to lend further sums. Money lenders in cities such as Xian and Lanzhou were charging 8 per cent interest a month, and the orders that co-ops won from the army and other government contractors were held down to margin-squeezing rates. The army knew that the co-ops would find it hard to sack their staff, and would opt to take loss-making contracts rather than have nothing at all to pay wages and the food bills.

While the outside world, especially Luce's magazines and the US press, applauded the co-operative movement as the advance guard of democracy in China, the reality was that the army, the banks and above all the nationalist government were throttling the fledgling movement. Hogg complained about the effects of this publicity: 'The support of the American people is absolutely essential to our progress and even to our survival at this time . . . Yet every article in popular United States magazines and news-papers seems to add fuel to the fire of those in Chongqing who are labelling the CIC as "un-chinese".' The truth was that, like the missionary movement, the co-operatives were seen by many Chinese as another example of foreign interference backed by

---

* The official exchange rate for the Chinese dollar in 1938 was $17 to £1 ster-ling. Throughout George Hogg's time in China the government printed money to fund the war. This led to hyper-inflation. By 1940 the rate was $70 to the pound, although a flourishing black market meant the official rate rarely applied.

foreign funds. Worse still, many in the nationalist government regarded the movement as a communist front.

The early success of Indusco's fundraising was to prove as illusory as the ambitious plans for the spread of tens of thousands of co-ops. By 1940 the Nazi onslaught had left Britain alone and imperilled in Europe. The focus of public opinion and of the news desks in the United States changed. The German blitzkrieg through Belgium, Holland and northern France provided better copy than the Japanese bombing of unpronounceable Chinese cities.

The triumph of German arms in 1940 had also aroused isolationist sentiment in an American election year. China moved off the front pages, and the fundraising effort turned in on itself, with bitter infighting over priorities and control of the money.

Part of the problem was that the Chinese-based American correspondents had seized on the co-operative story and hailed the project as a triumph for democracy in the face of a fascist Japanese invasion without checking the facts on the ground. The coverage given to the movement both by Luce's magazines and by the American media as a whole was so coloured by wishful thinking that it verged on outright propaganda, and George Hogg knew it. He became embarrassed at getting letters from family and friends at home congratulating him on being 'at the heart of one of the most fruitful and constructive experiments in the world today', and his comments on the glowing descriptions of CIC in the US press were blunt: 'I felt quite angry with magazine articles sent me from America written by people who had never seen our co-ops and so could easily compose variations on the theme "the amazing success of thousands of little democracies that are now spreading invisibly across the countryside has proved beyond doubt that the Chinese are born co-operators". The Chinese are just as much and just as little "born co-operators" as any other people.'

Hogg knew that while journalists and some politicians saw the co-op movement as a force for democracy, and in some cases revolutionary idealism, the peasants took an altogether different and more pragmatic attitude: 'If these people can once be convinced that the movement means something to them in terms of the rice bowl they will throw their weight into the balance and will absorb all the educational and democratic ideas that the intellectuals care to suggest to them.'

Despite Soong Meiling's backing for the movement, the very strong suspicion in 1940 that the CIC's demand for democratic control on the ground was simply a figleaf for communist manipulation had hardened by 1942 into outright accusations. Rewi Alley was a known communist sympathiser; the articles praising the CIC in the United States had all been written by supposedly left-wing journalists such as Jack Belden and Edgar Snow. And the main cheerleaders of the CIC, Ida Pruitt and Peg Snow, were self-proclaimed supporters of the model for a new China that Mao and his Eighth Route Army were promoting.

Hogg and Rewi Alley were trapped. If the CIC was to be directly funded from voluntary contributions in the US and elsewhere, they would lay themselves open to charges of imposing an arbitrary and foreign system of management upon a purely Chinese organisation. This would, in the hands of critics, revive fresh and raw memories of the hundred years of Western imperialism in the country. But if the funding was routed through the banks in China, control of the money would effectively pass to a corrupt government that was already holding an axe over the whole movement.

The tensions came to a head in 1942, when Rewi Alley, the hero of many an admiring press interview in the United States, was fired by the CIC management in Chongqing. He left the co-op headquarters at Baoji uncertain of his fate and not knowing whether he was to be arrested. The US backers of the CIC guaranteed his safety by offering him the job as Indusco's field secretary in China.

Several thousand co-ops continued to function, but the movement never came close to the aims of its founders. Writing in New York in 1944, Emily Hahn observed:

> *I haven't anything but praise for the Co-operatives – I mean Indusco. But it was over advertised. The people who sponsored it wanted you to know what a good thing it was and they wanted you to help it with money. So they wrote a lot of articles about it, published a lot of glowing photographs in pamphlets and as a result Indusco over here in America has been blown up to amazing and quite false proportions.*

One enduring legacy of the co-operative movement was a slogan which was to enter the English language. The phrase which Rewi Alley claimed to have thought up to describe the movement and its ethos was '*Gung Ho*', which roughly translates as 'working together'. The Chinese name for the co-ops was '*Zhongguo Gongye Hezhoushe*', which abbreviated to '*Gung Ho*'. Edgar Snow designed CIC's insignia, a red triangle (derived from the YMCA logo) enclosing the Chinese characters for the phrase.

The man who projected '*Gung Ho*' into the dictionaries – and gave it a new, more aggressive meaning – was Captain Evans Carlson, a friend of Edgar Snow and an honorary member of the Hankow gang. Carlson had had a colourful career in the US military before being appointed, with the rank of Marine Corps captain, to be an observer with Chinese forces in 1937. He spent months with the guerrilla forces, studying their tactics carefully, and would adapt much of what he learnt to operations in the Pacific war, where he led a battalion of marines known as Carlson's Raiders. It was there that he used and popularised the 'Gung Ho' slogan, which the marines took home with them at the end of the war.

Depressed by the outcome of the funding battle, George Hogg began to wonder just what he was doing in China. He was lonely, he missed female company, and worst of all he was assailed by a nagging doubt: did he, could he, ever really belong to anything in China? He would later write:

Maybe it was want of a wife, maybe it was indigestion or the fact that the coffee supply was finished, maybe it was an overdose of sulphanilamide tablets, which our New York office has sent to cure my trachoma . . . anyway during the following weeks the usefulness of my existence . . . seemed very doubtful. Why wasn't I at home fire fighting or somewhere over Germany in a bomber? What had the CIC got to do with the battles for North Africa, the Solomon islands or the Don that were being fought at this time? I felt I simply must have an Old School Tie to wear.

Following long discussions with Nieh about the co-operative movement, Hogg was summoned to Eighth Route Army mobile headquarters in September to meet Nieh's superior, General Zhu De. Finding a man who moved positions almost nightly was not easy. The first task was to cross the Yellow River, known as 'China's Sorrow' because of its frequent flooding.

The Yellow River rose on the Tibetan plateau in the west, and flowed 3,750 miles through nine provinces to the sea at the Bohai Gulf. Its waters annually carried hundreds of millions of tons of silt from the highlands to the flood plains raising the level of the riverbed and causing cyclical floods. But Hogg's first sight of one of the world's great rivers did not impress him. He saw only a thick mass of muddy water oozing through embanked pastureland. He confided to the diary that would become his book: 'It seemed unbelievable that such a narrow strip of water should have kept back the Japanese all the way from Kaifeng to Mongolia.'

The Yellow River was not the only barrier to the meeting with the man who was to lead the communist forces to ultimate victory against the nationalists in 1949. Guided by General Hou, a Long Marcher with impeccable communist credentials who had studied with Nieh and Chou En-lai in Paris, Hogg had to cross a heavily fortified and patrolled road which the Japanese had turned into a blockade line separating the iron- and coal-producing regions to the north from the rich grain-producing districts further south. To stop the natural flow of trade and people between the two regions, garrisons had been stationed at close intervals along the road, and fortified villages constructed on either side. Beyond the villages a wide belt of territory had been turned into a free fire zone.

Hogg was travelling in a group of fifteen guerrillas, forty students, an engineer and General Hou. A complicated system of passwords was devised. The group filed silently through gutted villages, along stony riverbeds and across pastureland empty of livestock, with rests every half-hour for men and pack animals. Whispered commands were passed up and down the line: 'Don't cough . . . tell the mule man not to light his pipe . . . tell the animals not to make so much noise.'

Somewhere in the darkness Hogg lost the lead rein of the mule carrying his bedding, typewriter and camera. The group halted while the guerrilla escorts searched under the guns of Japanese sentries for the missing animal. Above them a Japanese flag flew in the moonlight over a roadside garrison. Discovery of the mule, or even the sound of its bray, would have brought searchlights and machine-gun fire. After half an hour the troops returned with the mule, and the bonus of a roll of Japanese telephone wire. The group reached the road, made a brief fifty-yard dash along its macadam surface, and then struck out into the countryside on the far side.

Zhu De was another of Mao's commanders who had studied in Europe, in his case at Göttingen University in Germany. Like Nieh he became a protégé of Chou En-lai and trained at a Russian military academy. There was one big difference which set him apart from other communist commanders: for a communist he had a remarkably corrupt and capitalist past. He had been a successful warlord in the south, where he had enjoyed the pleasures of opium and concubines bought with the wealth he extracted from the local peasantry. Quite where and how he took the road to Damascus is not known, but by the time he arrived in Germany he was a convinced communist.

Zhu was initially a commander in the Kuomintang army under Chiang Kai-shek. He secretly joined the Communist Party in 1926, and defected to Mao with ten thousand of his men two years later. As a reward he became Mao's most trusted military commander, and the architect of what would be called the Red Army. So close was his relationship with Mao that the two men were frequently referred to as 'Mao Zhu'. However, Zhu lacked Mao's gifts for intrigue and infighting, and he was consistently undermined and outmanoeuvred by his political master.

Hogg spent several months in guerrilla areas talking to soldiers and commanders. The access he was given was probably due to the fact that he had taken considerable risks in returning to China and crossing the lines into guerrilla territory. It may be that the commanders also saw in him a useful foreign journalist to exploit for propaganda. Mao was brilliant at manipulating the foreign media, and paid careful attention to the subsequent coverage. But the communist leadership was also genuinely curious about thinking and policy in the West, and would spend hours discussing overseas reactions to the war with journalist visitors. Both Nieh and Zhu seem to have understood that Hogg had more to offer than favourable reports for Associated Press or the *Manchester Guardian*. They steered him towards the co-operative movement, which at this stage in 1939 was growing rapidly in the north-west and within the communist-controlled areas.

Hogg spent long hours with Zhu talking about his Oxford days, his travels in America and Japan and the co-operative movements there. Dressed always in a plain blue padded uniform and a blue cloth cap without gold braid or other military insignia, Zhu looked more like a footsoldier in a peasants' army than its leader; but this short, unprepossessing man was the tactical driving force behind the guerrilla war. His only other interest was sport, for which he and Hogg discovered a shared passion. Basketball was their favourite, and whenever possible Zhu spent two hours a day on a makeshift pitch. Hogg would join him, and spent much of his weeks at the base camp playing basketball, listening to speeches, and occasionally accompanying patrols.

He was once asked to address one of the nightly meetings on the subject of England's role in the European war. His speech surprised his audience, because it was delivered in Mandarin and only lasted an hour. When Zhu De or Nieh addressed a crowd, three hours was the minimum. The long set-piece speeches proved an embarrassment, because Zhu tended to clamp his hand around Hogg's and hold it tightly for the entire evening.

Hogg had a certain rarity value for the guerrillas. Physically imposing, and by now with rapidly improving spoken Mandarin (he never properly learned to write the language), the young Englishman would have been an unusual sight anywhere in China at the time. There was no question of a military role for him – the

Eighth Route Army did not accept foreigners in its ranks, except for doctors, surgeons and nurses. In any case, Hogg wanted to report on the co-ops, and to do that he needed to get involved with them. The guerrilla commanders advised him to leave the front-line areas and go to the north-west headquarters of the CIC in Baoji.

Hogg arrived in Baoji in September 1939, as war broke out in Europe. Like everyone else, he tried to work out what the hostilities would mean for China. After two years of fighting, Japan controlled the wealthiest and most populated regions of the country, except for Sichuan province. The successive defeats had not, however, forced the nationalist government to capitulate; indeed, they had seemed to stiffen Chinese resistance.

Japan was also suffering a degree of economic strain and war-weariness. The military command in Tokyo now felt that China could be brought to its knees by economic blockade and isolation, and turned their attention to the opportunity thrown up by the outbreak of war in Europe to gain control of the rich mineral resources to be found in the British, Dutch and French colonies of South-East Asia. The chief obstacle to an aggressive South-East Asian strategy lay in US naval power in the Pacific, and specifically with the American battle fleet based at Pearl Harbor.

Chiang Kai-shek's government was isolated, and the Chinese economy weakened by corrosive inflation. The months of tension in Europe which led to the outbreak of war had brought about a sharp reduction in Russian aid. Britain and France had closed overland trade links from Burma and Vietnam respectively under Japanese pressure. Internally the communists were still contained in their stronghold around Yenan, but Mao was using the time to build up his forces.

Chiang's strategy was to avoid costly large-scales battles with the Japanese, and to embroil the US in the China conflict if possible. As ever, he was concentrating on the final showdown with the communists.

Mao Tse-tung also wished to avoid costly encounters with the Japanese, and bided his time while strengthening his political and military control in the expanding area of communist influence in the north-west.

SIX

Ocean Secretary

'I knew what I loved about her alright.'

Baoji was a small railway town 140 miles west of Xian at the beginning of the old caravan route to Europe. Here in October 1939 George Hogg was offered the job of publicity secretary to the north-west headquarters of the Chinese Industrial Co-operative movement. He was given a metal badge with the CIC motto 'Gung Ho' on it, and use of a twelve-by-six-foot bedroom in a hostel attached to the offices. He pinned photos from home on the wall of his room, and squeezed in a table for his typewriter. The Remington was so noisy compared to the quiet clicking of the only other equipment in the office, an abacus, that he was told to type outside. The job required him to travel throughout the north-west, writing reports on the progress and problems of the co-operatives. He received no salary, but expenses were paid. By way of celebration he bought himself a tie, a teapot and a bedspread.

George Hogg was a happy man. He was proud of his official title, 'Ocean Secretary'. 'Ocean devil' was the traditional Chinese name for foreigners: 'east ocean devil' meant Japanese. 'Ocean carts' were rickshaws, which had replaced the traditional Chinese wheelbarrows when smooth tar macadam roads were laid in the cities at the turn of the century. Hogg, who delighted in this terminology, insisted that he had heard bicycles referred to as 'ocean donkeys'. Certainly imported paraffin wax candles were called 'ocean candles', as opposed to the native tallow variety.

Just before Christmas 1939 he wrote home about the new job, partly it seems to reassure his parents that he was doing something worthwhile and not, as his mother seems to have suspected, just travelling around China looking at antiquities. Aware of the rationing and shortages at home, he was concerned to show that he too had to make do with a meagre diet.

> *This is really a good job. It combines the best of 'going into industry' and being a 'social worker'; and gives a good opportunity for writing too. And travelling. I have been to quite a lot of places in the last two months, Lanzhou to the North west and Hanchung to the west ... Did I ever tell you how we eat? Rice gruel and peanuts for breakfast [that makes] a good lunch and not a bad supper. If anyone feels like extra dishes there is a sort of lottery performed by throwing out a certain number of fingers and then counting the total around the table to see who will pay for it.*

He was also happy because he had a Chinese girlfriend. He was by now fluent in the Henanese dialect of north China, and had fallen in love with a woman he had first seen in Luoyang, a Yellow River city famous for its connection to Confucius, who was said to have studied there as a young man. He had been waiting at the railway station when he saw a girl of around eighteen years old trying to catch a train, while her small brother was doing his best to stop her: 'He was tugging silently at her hand with pleading and adoration in his face. And she was laughing into his eyes, half wanting to go back, wholly wanting not to disappoint him. They had not noticed me or anything else around them, standing there like that.'

Her name was Chiang Chi-hsia, a 'red faced healthy looking girl' who wrote plays for a student theatre group which visited villages and army centres throughout the war zone dramatising recent events: military successes or defeats, a good harvest or a raid by bandits. The plays were crude wartime propaganda, but they worked. After their tours the students would return to their base at the CIC centre in Baoji and teach in local schools. Hogg fell for the young playwright, and although he could hardly write Mandarin script, managed to get someone to pen love letters for him. He tried to keep the relationship secret, a forlorn hope in a town where tall Englishmen were not a common sight, and it was soon common knowledge. Hogg and Chi chi, as she was known, regularly stayed up late working on reports of recent tours and writing scripts.

The student drama group conducted themselves openly, in line with a 'no secrets from anybody' policy, and held monthly 'truth' sessions at which all problems within the community were aired. These sessions included romantic problems, and Hogg was persuaded to attend one of them to discuss his feelings.

*The room was packed with strange but sympathetic looking people, including three roguish 'little devils'.**

I wanted to rush out or cover myself up with a newspaper like a certain gorilla in the London zoo but everyone was very kind. Chiang Chih-hsia introduced the subject by quoting in full a love letter which

---

* 'Little devils' were tough urchins from the big cities, many of them orphans aged between eight and fifteen, who ran away from home to join the army. From the moment of enlisting the army made them attend literacy classes, and often sent them to work in the co-ops.

somebody had discovered among somebody else's belongings and bruited around in that happy 'no secrets from anybody' spirit for which the CIC is famed.

When the young girl had finished a tall and motherly woman got up and asked 'Ho Ke' to explain what it was that he loved about Chiang Chi-hsia. Hogg knew what he wanted to say, but somehow could not quite get the words out.

I knew what I loved about her alright – the way she laughed right out like a boy; the way she looked me straight in the eyes and said just what she meant; somehow I loved the way she rang the school bell for the kids to come out into the playground and the way she wiped their snotty noses for them. I loved the conspiratorial squeeze she had given my hand as we patched up a quarrel between a rickshaw coolie and his wife, and the way she had looked when . . . yes but how could I say all that to them and in Chinese. Needless to say the meeting was a hopeless flop.

The affair lasted several months before Chiang fell ill and had to undergo a minor operation. Although she and her fellow students had faced innumerable dangers in the front-line areas, she did not survive the rough-and-ready methods of rural surgery. She died of blood poisoning a week after the operation. Hogg spent that night going through the stories she had told him, and the scripts they had written together.

His depression deepened with the news of the German blitzkrieg through the Low Countries and France. Until the spring of 1940 he had never seriously thought about leaving China. The threat of German invasion and news of the Battle of Britain caused him agonies of indecision as to whether to return and fight. Such a move was clearly on his mind, and he mentioned it more than once in his letters home. He also missed his family, and asked constantly for news. He admired photos of his sister Barbara's children, and chided his mother for pressing upon him the charms of a local Harpenden girl with whom he had grown up, Ruth Thomas.

Hogg soon fell in love again. For some time he had been asking his parents to help raise funds for the CIC's women's department in Baoji, which was run by a woman called Da Ren. The department was staffed by young women refugees who worked in local orphanages and organised spinning and weaving classes in and around the town. One of these was Da Ren's niece, Xiao Ren, who had arrived after the burning of her home town, Changsha. She was small, intelligent and had 'glowing eyes and a wonderful smile', according to the English Ocean Secretary.

George Hogg was twenty-five and Ren twenty-two when they met in early 1940. Their affair lasted eighteen months, until the war parted them. They worked side by side in the CIC office in Baoji, which Hogg used as a base for his tours across the north-west. This time he was more open about the affair, although such a relationship was highly unusual, even in wartime China. European men did not consort with Chinese women, or if they did the affair was conducted with great secrecy.

But Hogg didn't care who knew, and neither did Xiao Ren. Years later she recalled the moment she realised she had fallen for the tall young Englishman who had blown into her life 'like a leaf on the wind': 'It was after a bombing raid on Baoji. George and I went to a CIC office that had been hit and found the body of a young co-op woman who had been killed by the blast; her clothes had been ripped off. George took off his jacket, knelt down, and wrapped her in it. Then he picked her up and carried the body outside town. He dug her grave with his own hands and together we buried her.'

Apart from the ill-fated Chiang Chi-hsia, Hogg already had several Chinese girlfriends in Baoji and elsewhere. But the more time he spent with the young refugee from Changsha, the more he realised this was the woman he wished to marry, a fact he later alluded to in a letter home.

George and Xiao Ren walked the mountains talking of their future and how he was going to take her back home to Harpenden to meet his family. There were 'cloudbursts of kisses' on their mountain walks, as Xiao Ren put it, and a stream of love letters, but the affair seems to have remained chaste.

Nevertheless, in a town packed with refugees, co-op workers and troops, the relationship attracted plenty of attention. To get away from the gossip, Hogg took Xiao Ren on a weekend visit to what was one of the famous tourist sites of China, the Hua Qing Chi pool, in a palace a Chinese emperor had built for his concubine in Xian. Years later Xiao Ren described how she and George discussed marriage during the long weekend away from the prying eyes and sharp ears of Baoji:

> *He never actually formally asked me to marry him but he wanted to marry me and I wanted to marry him. It was understood that we would when the war was over. He was different from all the other foreigners. The Americans whenever I met them always wanted to sleep with me but I never did. George was different, maybe that was why I was attracted to him.*

But, just as the war had thrown them together, so it parted them. Xiao Ren was fiercely patriotic, and wanted to work more closely with the guerrilla forces further north. This meant she had to cross the nationalist army blockade lines around communist-held territory. Hogg undertook the dangerous mission of escorting her from Baoji across KMT-held territory to Luoyang, three hundred miles east by road, in the middle reaches of the Yellow River valley. He had become an expert at talking his way through police and military roadblocks, but there were considerable risks in the journey. Luoyang was not a communist-held city, but it was close enough to guerrilla territory for the police to interrogate and arrest suspicious travellers. While Xiao Ren spent some weeks in the town awaiting word from her contact, Hogg made the risky journey to visit her three times. On the third, in the summer of 1941, he found she had gone. The guerrilla underground had spirited her out of the city to a training camp further north. He never saw her again. In November he wrote home to tell his mother he had nearly been married, 'but at the wrong time the Japs staged a big attack and she got left on the wrong side. Pity.'

Xiao Ren spent a year training with the guerrilla forces, and was allowed to join the Eighth Route Army as a front-line fighter in 1944 – a tribute to her military skills, since only 2 per cent of the guerrillas were women.

Hogg never forgot Xiao Ren, and they stayed in touch by letter until he died. When her letters arrived, he would literally jump for joy. Rewi Alley remembers that 'His face would light up and he would laugh the whole day pulling the letter out a hundred times and reading it until eventually it fell to pieces through too much handling. She was always on his mind.'

On 12 January 1940 Hogg heard the surprising news that Kathleen Hall had defied Japanese expulsion orders and arrived back in the war zone. She was forty-three years old, an upright Christian missionary whose years in China had inured her to death, disease and the atrocities of war. Shortly after she had nursed Hogg through typhus, her mission had been burnt down by the Japanese. She had finally been caught smuggling large quantities of drugs out of Beijing across the lines to the guerrillas, and was taken to Beijing and interrogated. She was threatened

The young George Hogg (always known as 'Aylwin' to his family) in the garden at Red Gables in Harpenden.

George takes tea with his father Robert and brother Stephen.

George's mother Kathleen in front of Red Gables with his brothers Daniel and Stephen.

Left to right: Rosemary ('Roke', the sibling to whom George would remain closest throughout his life), Daniel, Stephen, Barbara and George in 1922, when George was seven.

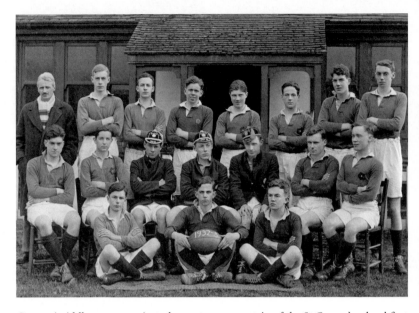

George (middle row, centre) aged seventeen, as captain of the St George's school first rugby XV.

George in 1934, during his first term at Wadham College, Oxford.

The Wadham rugby XV, 1936–37. George (second row, centre) captained the team.

George's aunt Muriel Lester, the 'Mother of World Peace', photographed a few years before her death in 1968. A lifelong pacifist campaigner, she set off with George in September 1937 on the journey that would lead him to China.

Left: Agnes Smedley, a leading member of the foreign press corps Hogg encountered in Hankow. He described her as 'tall, rather grim and Eton cropped, about forty, an ardent communist of the Chinese not the Russian variety'. Controversy was to follow her throughout her life, from her conviction for gun-running in 1918 to her death in 1950, while she was under investigation as a suspected Soviet spy.

Above: Rewi Alley, a New Zealander who was to play a crucial role in Hogg's life in China, He was one of the founders of the industrial co-operative movement, and was instrumental in securing Hogg's appointment as headmaster of the Bailie school in Shuangshipu.

Kathleen Hall, the New Zealand missionary nurse who restored Hogg to health after he contracted typhus in 1939. She came to China in 1923, and would spend nearly thirty years there.

Top: George Hogg with commander Nieh Rong Zhen (left) of Mao Tse-tung's Eighth Route Army. Hogg accompanied Nieh and his guerrillas on an extended tour of north-west China in 1939.

Middle: Hogg, accompanied by Nieh Rong Zhen, addresses troops of the Eighth Route Army.

Left: Ocean Secretary. George in Xian in 1940, wearing the 'Gung Ho' badge of the Chinese Industrial Co-operative movement.

Hogg photographed in Baoji in 1941 by his friend Carl Mydans. The portrait was intended to accompany a piece in Henry Luce's *Life* magazine on the co-operative movement, but the article never appeared.

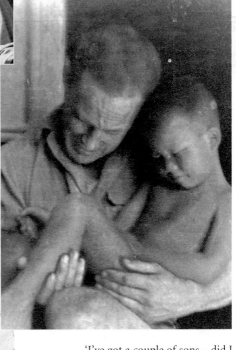

'I've got a couple of sons – did I tell you?' George in 1942, cradling Nieh Guangpei, the youngest of his four adopted sons.

The convoy carrying the school struggles across the Wu Ling Pass, on the last stage of the arduous seven-hundred-mile journey from Shuangshipu to Shandan in the winter of 1944–45.

Above: Xiao Ren and three of George Hogg's adopted sons standing by Hogg's grave in Shandan. Xiao Ren met Hogg in Baoji in early 1940, when she was a refugee working for the CIC. They spent eighteen months together before the war parted them, and Hogg wrote to his family that they planned to marry. The grave was desecrated in the 1960s during the Cultural Revolution, and restored in 1984. The co-operative movement's 'Gung Ho' insignia is carved at the top of the headstone, above the first verse of the First World War poet Julian Grenfell's 'Into Battle', one of Hogg's favourite poems. Left to right: Nieh Guangtao, Nieh Guanghan, Xiao Ren, Nieh Guangchun. The photograph was taken in 1985 by Hogg's fourth adopted son, Nieh Guangpei.

Left: The watercolour of George Hogg that hangs in the small museum near his grave in Shandan.

Above: Six of Hogg's 'old boys' photographed in spring 2007 in the city of Xian Yang, near Xian. Back row, left to to right: Qi Ranmei, Liu Shizhong, Yu Jinzhong; front row: Yang Chunlin, Chen Faxing, Liang Boran.

Left: The bust erected in Shandan to commemorate Hogg's memory.

Below Jonathan Rhys Meyers as George Hogg in a scene from the 2008 film *The Children of Huang Shi*, based on Hogg's life. On the right is the actress Radha Mitchell; her character is loosely based on Kathleen Hall.

with death and placed on a ship bound for New Zealand. In Hong Kong she jumped ship, joined the Chinese Red Cross and helped organise two large truckloads of medical supplies which were to be driven eight hundred miles north.

The destination of the supplies was a hospital run for the Eighth Route Army by one of the most extraordinary figures to emerge from the chaos of China at the time, Dr Norman Bethune. A hard-drinking forty-nine-year-old Canadian communist, a womaniser and a man of fierce views and a high temper, Bethune was a veteran of the Spanish Civil War. After Franco's victory he was determined to resume the war against fascism, and offered his services to Mao and his commanders in 1938. The guerrilla forces had primitive medical treatment for their wounded, and only crude field surgery available for combat casualties. Working as close as he could to the operational areas, Bethune performed prodigious feats of surgery with few drugs or anaesthetics. In his short life with the Red Army he became a legend, looked on with reverence by Mao, Chou En-lai and their commanders.

Hogg was intrigued that an upright missionary like Kathleen Hall should have developed a relationship with a man like Bethune. And it was, at the very least, a close friendship. Bethune admired Hall's professionalism, her courage, and the fact that she was prepared to take big risks to smuggle medicines across the lines. He also knew that she had occasionally smuggled students being hunted by the Japanese police out of Beijing hidden in her cart. For her part, Hall clearly rejoiced in Bethune's company, and admired his devil-take-the-hindmost character and the skill with which he could transform a dusty piece of ground under an old tree into a front-line operating theatre.

Bethune had plenty of lovers while working in the north-west, and whether Kathleen Hall was one is not known. But, as her biographer Rae McGregor has pointed out, the committed

Christian who had dedicated her life to her work and her faith, and the communist stalwart with a fierce loyalty to the Marxist cause, found a meeting of minds that became a deep friendship. They both wanted to develop a nationwide network of medical services in rural areas. Their ambition was to set up training in basic medicine for villagers, so that cottage hospitals could be staffed by local people. They shared a dream that one day treatment for the diseases that devastated the countryside – typhus, cholera, dysentery, malaria and beriberi – would be freely available.

Bethune operated from front-line guerrilla camps, using Mao's headquarters at Yenan as a base. Kathleen Hall was often working in the same area or camp, and would make sure that the surgeon had the basic supplies and equipment for his work. Bethune gave her long lists of supplies to be smuggled out of Beijing.

This odd couple were lonely, obsessed people living dangerous lives far from their homes and families. They could not have been more different. Bethune's support was the bottle, Kathleen's the Bible. After spending up to eighteen hours operating amid the blood, mud and screams of the wounded, he would find relief in alcohol – and women. She had her faith, her prayer book and her sanctity. Yet whenever they were together they would talk late into the night about their families, their lives and their ambitions.

The Chinese medical staff who worked for both of them speculated about a romance between the two foreigners. Bethune had married and divorced the same woman twice. Hall had never married and would never do so.

Bethune died in November 1939 of blood poisoning caused by an infection after he had operated without surgical gloves on a wounded soldier. Hall was on her way north by road, bringing him supplies from Hong Kong at the time, and she was devastated by the news, which caused her as much pain as the loss of two brothers in the First World War. Several months later she contracted beriberi, a disease caused by exhaustion and malnutrition, and to save her life she was forced to return to New Zealand.

Hogg's comment on Hall's remarkable fortitude in returning to China to deliver medical supplies to a man she clearly adored, and her despairing departure, was very much of its time and place. 'Plucky woman if ever there was one,' he noted in a letter home on 12 January 1940.

For his first job as Ocean Secretary, Hogg was sent 160 miles south of Baoji to a small co-operative in the village of Mien-hsien, near Hanchung. This was a desolate place, surrounded by barren mountains and redeemed only by the sparkling waters of the Han River. The Lord Mayor of London had raised £50,000 in an appeal for China. This was a huge sum, equivalent to £11 million today, and much of the money was supposed to have been given to the co-ops in the area. Among other things, CIC wanted Hogg to find out what had happened to it. In the shallows of the river he saw another reason why he had been sent.

A man stood lonely as a fishing bird in shallow water, blue smock opened at the chest, and pants rolled up to the knees with a rough sieve and a shallow pan beside him. The man's loneliness and the barrenness of his surroundings were only skin deep. Behind the mountain's bare sides was gold and behind the man were thousands of others.

Gold was rising rapidly in value as inflation reduced the purchasing power of the Chinese currency. Armed gangs were robbing the panners of their gold and receiving bounty payments for handing them over to the KMT as forced conscripts. Ironically, most of the bandits were themselves deserters. As the black-market gold price rose to three times the bank rate, bandits moved in to take over all the panning. Production around the town of Ankang, a hundred miles south of Xian in Shanxi province, dropped by 25 per cent.

Hogg had been given the Herculean task of reorganising the small groups of gold panners into larger co-ops for their protection. This would enable them to negotiate a better price from the bank representatives who travelled up from Chongqing to buy the gold. In two weeks the panners had reformed into a single large co-op, and gold was used to recruit armed guards. When Hogg left, a stronger co-operative was able to make greater returns for its several hundred members. But there never was any sign of the Lord Mayor's money.

The next mission followed immediately afterwards. Hogg fond himself clinging to the cargo of an open Russian truck that snorted over the mountains, fuelled by locally made alcohol, heading from Ankang to Hanchung, a market town at the centre of a sixty-mile basin of the Han River in the Tsingling mountains. Lying on the trade route running north–south through the western mountains, Hanchung had been a battleground for centuries. Imperial armies and warlords had continually fought to dominate the strategic area and draw on its wealth of iron, gold and copper in the hills and cotton, silk, hemp, bamboo and tea in the valleys.

The Hanchung co-operatives were bankrupt. Inflation threatened the workers with starvation, and the CIC had no funds available. It was a familiar story. Hogg deliberately took on the worst case he could find, a small oilcloth co-op whose nine workers had set it up after being sacked by a private factory for daring to ask for more wages. They bought their own looms with a grant from the CIC, and were joined by the wife of the factory manager, whose husband regularly beat her. The woman was called Ching Wen-shui, and she was chosen to lead the group.

Inflation and wartime uncertainties had then driven them to bankruptcy.

Hogg drew up a business plan for the co-op, and wrote in their looms as share capital. On this basis an advance of cotton yarn was secured, and turned into cloth. The proceeds from its sale allowed the co-op to buy wood oil and turn out higher-priced oilcloth.

This simple business success story did not quite end as planned. First, Ching Wen-shui's husband tried to close the co-op down, claiming that the members were using it for immoral purposes. He then invited her back home, to repair the marriage. When she failed to return, her mother found her hanging unconscious with a rope around her waist attached to the ceiling and her hands tied behind her back. Her naked body was black with bruises.

Wen-shui went to hospital, and her husband to prison. A few days later she was back at work, 'bringing all the dynamic force of an illiterate, embittered and intensely sympathetic woman to the job of making a successful family out of her co-op', as Hogg put it.

SEVEN

On the Road

'I've got a couple of sons – did I tell you?'

Hogg was now almost always on the road, criss-crossing north-west China writing lengthy reports on the co-operative movement for both the nationalist government in Chongqing and the communists based at Yenan. He travelled light, carrying a bedding quilt faced with blue indigo print and a grey army blanket. Both had been heavily patched over the years, but he refused to replace either, clinging to them like a child to a favourite teddy bear. The bedding would be wrapped in a piece of oilcloth as a form of waterproofing for the long trips, often spent on the top of over-loaded lorries. His wardrobe was equally minimal. He owned two pairs of shorts, two shirts, a light blue worker's overall, a woollen sweater, underwear and a suit of padded clothing for winter.

He travelled by horse, mule, donkey cart and what passed for buses: 'The so-called buses are just open trucks and everybody piles in his rolls of bedding and cases and babies and chickens and eggs and turnips and dried persimmon and tangerine oranges and sits on top of them . . . the buses run on charcoal because petrol is very expensive.' He turned his adventurous journeys by bus into a long feature article which was submitted to the

Manchester Guardian but later published by the *New Statesman* with the title 'China from a Bus Top'.

There was a crowd outside the great wooden door of the bus station. It stood dumb as a flock of cold sheep, as though there were something sub-humanly primeval about waiting for the dawn. The paper lanterns on the booths faintly lit men's faces as they merged and emerged with yellow bowls of peanut gravy. Babies cried sleepily and were fed. Soldiers, unhampered by belongings, stood aside, firm and erect. Country people anxiously counted their hampers.

Suddenly a chain clanked, a heavy bolt shot back, and a tiny wicket in the big door opened. We headed in for it like a football wedge. 'Where's 2177?' 'Where's 2466?' We ran to and fro searching for clues. A moment lost in finding the right bus might mean clinging round the edge of a swaying, hurtling mass for the rest of the day. How much more pleasant to be one of the first to dive in over the side (always supposing you didn't meet someone else doing the same thing from the opposite side) and to be wedged between a medley of babies, old gentlemen, peasant produce, camp beds, spare hats, oranges, pickles, and (if you were lucky enough) pretty girls with eyes as big as pumpkin seeds!

The plush, upholstered, high-backed monster that booms its way across a continent may exude exclusiveness, but the wartime bus of China at once puts its passengers on an equal footing. When everyone is cemented into position, and the out-clingers have arranged people to hang on to them while going round corners, the conversation begins by which every Chinese tries out new acquaintances and forms a background to his first impressions. Where is your home? What province's food is best? What province's dialect is most difficult to understand? These are the first essentials.

Our bus is a swan among geese. That is to say that we run on gas while the others are covered with ugly stove-pipes and charcoal burners. They do a kilometre per catty of charcoal (about seven dollars) and we do a hundred kilometres on ten gallons of gas, whatever that may cost these days. But that is not the only price we have to pay for our superiority; before we are allowed to start, we have to tow each goose along the road, until it is limbered up. The swan must do its bit in these days . . .

[Once the bus started] There was snow in the sky and the wind whistled by uncomfortably, lifting up the corners of coats and blankets as fast as the passengers tucked them back again.

Perched precariously round the edge of the truck were some soldiers going home on leave from the Shansi front. They hadn't been home for two years, and were picking out old landmarks excitedly to each other. Admiring civilians asked them questions about their exploits at the front, and were answered in a soldierly off-hand way, bespeaking the ease with which Japanese Devils are repelled or tied up in their own knots.

Miscellaneously dotted here and there were small merchants and their wares, country people on their way to show off the latest baby in the next town; and up in the front off-side corner was a theatrical singer who must surely have been a prima donna. Her music case was clasped against her as lovingly as ever a peasant woman clasped her baby, and she was humming snatches of Carmen from under her blanket. She was on her way from Lanchow to Chungking (she told the woman next to her) to fulfil an engagement there. If only she wouldn't so provokingly hide her head under a blanket!

All along the road were fleets of carts . . . hand carts and mule carts, private carts and government carts, carrying flour and cotton southwards and bringing back tea, rice, tobacco and paper money from Sechuan. Towards evening, winding down the well-engineered mountain road into the Han River valley, we passed a whole fleet of hand carts flying a co-operative pennant. And then, as it grew dark, there was a long line of camels on their way back to Lanchow with wood, oil and tea that would make its way right up through the neck of Kansu, across the sandy deserts, over the barren mountain passes and up the verdant sea-level valleys of Sinkiang, into Soviet Russia.

Just before we got into Hanchung we saw a very old man, who must have been stone deaf as well as blind. He waddled along in the middle of the road with a great load of firewood piled up over the back of his head. We hooted along for a while within six feet of his tail, in bottom gear, but it was no good. The assistant driver leapt down and angrily cuffed the old man, who fell over into the ditch, either with surprise or the force of the blow. Old China with the camel and the wood carrier must give way to the new; but we wished that the new could find a way of being more polite about it!

Hanchung was twinkling proudly under its new electric lighting system, and there were lots of good things to eat on the streets. The old women who sat beside the booths of Sechuan oranges, fat dried persimmon, beef-cake-sandwiches, were comfortable in the fashion of the place, with little baskets of charcoal sending a draught of warm air up their skirts, and others on their laps to warm their hands. Just time for a movie (the kind that gives you a headache in five minutes), and so to bed. Early to bed and early to rise is the rule of the road, providing you want a better place tomorrow than you had today.

Long before dawn next morning the inmates were up and calling for 'wash-face-water', 'rinse-mouth-water' and 'washed rice'. And while it was still dark they were packing themselves into the truck again.

So the bus charged on through this new-old part of China. Chicken feathers flew, pigs scattered around like black bullets or chased along head down behind us for the simple reason that they had forgotten to stop running now that we were past; bright red bales of paprika shone in the sunlight, and tattered rags tied to the sacred trees flapped in our wake. Dogs chased us and birds raced us. Cows lumbered swiftly away with tails flying, little boys ran down to meet us and little girls tried to look as if they weren't really afraid. Old men shook their heads ever-wonderingly, and old women nudged each other and cackled obscenely behind their hands at the comfortless passengers piled in on each other like so many sheep for the market.

On one occasion, to escape a Japanese advance and to save a vital piece of machinery, Hogg swallowed his principles and hired a rickshaw. The combined weight of a hefty Englishman and a big machine part proved too much for the puller, 'the most rabbity, most freckled, most weedy, most bandy-legged little man that ever ran between shafts. A missionary I met on the road said that he was an opium addict.'

Thus began a three-day journey in which the odd couple struggled to preserve their precious cargo and stay ahead of the enemy troops and out of sight of their planes. Despite the desperate nature of their journey, Hogg turned it into a rare comic interlude in his book. With enemy troops close behind and occasionally visible on their flank, Hogg decided to take turns with his rabbit-faced rickshaw-puller, whom he named Bunny.

From his point of view the arrangement was physically all that could be desired but he feared above all the jeers and sneers of his peers along the road. For this reason he gave me his big wide hat to pull down over my face as I ran and spread a filthy towel over his own so that for a time we got on fine as a mystery craft paying no attention to friendly calls or invitations to pull up and drink a cup of tea. Catching site of an old crony sitting in front of a teashop, Bunny's faith in his disguise suddenly vanished: 'Let me pull now let me pull you must be tired, rest a little,' he shouted, struggling frantically up the cart. Immediately the whole village turned to stare and covered us both with confusion by their ribaldry.

On the Road

We kept on, threading our way magically past all other vehicles on the highway. Bunny would never voluntarily relinquish his place, but after pulling what he considered to be a fair distance he wandered discreetly off the road to make water, and always feigned great surprise when he found me waiting between the shafts on his return.

It was amazing how easily the cart moved on its rubber tyres. The load is arranged so that the shafts press slightly upwards. As soon as the coolie puts his weight on them it moves forward and at the same time takes his own weight off his feet, so that on a level road he can average faster than walking pace with very little effort.

Out on the road it was sunny and devil-may-care. Mule-men cracked their whips, and the teams of great mules – the one animal in creation that really likes to work – snorted majestically along.

Lines of handcarts with furniture and rickshas with city evacuees trotted by in single file. Donkeys tripped from village to village taking country misses, dressed all in spotted silk trousers and cart wheeled silk smocks, to visit their relations.

For a few moments a wide flight of bombers cast its shadow over us; then we emerged from the ditch like rabbits, to forget them. Five hours later we found Nanyang still in flames. No hotel was left standing and the inn at which my luggage had been stored was a blackened shell.

Bunny and I went on through the night without stopping, for the Japanese were only a few miles away. Only those with relatives to bury stayed behind, picking out charred sticks by candlelight from the ruins and placing them carefully in coffins while the rest of the city poured out past them onto the road going north.

We could no longer take the main highway, for patrolling planes were machine-gunning all signs of life. We could no longer take turns at pulling each other on the cart, but together tugged it over hills and streams.

On the third day of travelling the pair made it to the safety of Lushan in the Fu Niu mountains, about two hundred miles south of the Yellow River. Hogg paid Bunny off and began to remove the large family of lice his driver had passed on to him.

He rarely stayed anywhere for more than a few nights, and seems to have delighted in his peripatetic existence. Travel may well have helped blot out worries about his girlfriend Xiao Ren, his family at home and his friends. But home was never far from his thoughts or his dreams: 'The other night I had a dream that St George's rugger team was playing out on the field and everyone was clapping and yelling "schoooo-oo-ool" like mad while I was being kept in and given a jaw in the head's study.'

In the summer of 1940 Hogg made the second of several trips to Chongqing, which proudly called itself the most heavily bombed city on earth. The Blitz on London was about to begin, but the Chinese capital had endured almost two years of constant air raids since Chiang Kai-shek had moved his headquarters there in October 1938.

Hogg found life in the city frightening and depressing. The bombing was far more intense and less discriminate than that he had endured at Hankow. The air raid warnings, the rush to shelter and the bloody aftermath were a daily reminder of the London Blitz, which was being widely reported in the Chinese press. Of Hogg's immediate family, only his father worked in London, but that was not the point. He knew first-hand what bombing could do to civilians in crowded cities. Added to that, the idealism which had carried him through his first three years in China was beginning to fray. In September 1940 he wrote home, as always to 'dear mother and daddy':

Today being Friday and about 11 o'clock at night dear old Hitler may
at this moment be launching his death attacks on Britain. And there

my thought ends. As I walk about the wreckage of a once beautiful city [Chongqing] I imagine that London may soon be worse than this plus every other city in that incredibly small place (much smaller than one province of China) ... Things are not too encouraging here either. If you remember all the stuff I wrote about progress within-war (from warlordism to democracy, the power of youthful energy etc?), wash it out because it is increasingly untrue of today.

The corruption of the nationalist government, the failure of the Western powers to stand up to Japan and the fact that both communists and nationalists were clearly preparing for an ultimate civil war were reason enough to be depressed. Life under daily bombardment from the air did not help.

But if London could take it, so could Chongqing. In many ways China's wartime capital was better placed to survive the long years of air raids. The city was built on a steep hill jutting out on a whale-like hump of rock at the confluence of the Yangtse and Chialing Rivers. Its history stretched back some 4,200 years, and it rightly claimed to have been an important trading centre when Rome was a mere village and London no more than marsh and woodland. An imposing rather than beautiful city, Chongqing was obscured during the long rainy season by fog, mist and a roof of gunmetal-grey clouds which slumped over the housetops, regularly delivering prolonged rains. An old saying about the city has it that 'When the sun shines even the dogs bark in fear.'

During the war years the population had trebled to just under a million, and people did indeed learn to fear the good weather. When the clouds cleared the bombing began. The population quickly learnt that the only safe place during air raids was in the deep tunnels that the government had dug into the sides of the mountains, creating about a thousand public shelters. Hogg found these dark, slimy and highly attractive to the city's rapidly expanding population of rats, which were just as anxious to get out of the way of Japanese bombs as anyone else.

Government offices, banks and the wealthier citizens constructed their own deep dugouts, which were well furnished and equipped with cooking facilities. Invitations to join the privileged in these shelters were much sought-after. The Australian journalist Rhodes Farmer described how the YMCA even turned the raids into a business opportunity, by investing heavily in deep shelters and then offering members fifty-dollar season tickets to cover the bombing months.

The government officials, foreign correspondents and diplomats who arrived from December 1938 onwards found a city whose main streets were slimy with sewage and alive with outsize rats by day and by night. The city centre had been destroyed in the early stages of the Japanese campaign, and beyond it lay what Rhodes Farmer called 'a medieval morass of dingy alleyways and almost vertical stone stairways which the water carriers' splashes turned into death traps for the unwary'. The riverfront was as crowded as the city streets. British, American and French gunboats that had sailed upriver from Hankow jostled for space with sailing junks and sampans.

Chongqing lay 1,500 miles from the Pacific coast, and was closer to India than to Shanghai. Over the centuries the city had spread from the waterfront up the sheltering mountain, where homes clung improbably to the cliff face. Houses on the river were built on fifty-foot stilts, a graphic illustration of the annual surge of the Yangtse when the 'River of Life' became swollen with melting snows from the Tibetan mountains.

Hogg, like other newsmen, arrived long after the best accommodation had either been taken or destroyed. As well as his job for CIC he was now an AP correspondent, and was still writing for, and accredited by, the *Manchester Guardian*. He managed to scrounge shared rooms with the rest of the press corps in a jerry-built government building called the Press Hostel.

The hostel soon succumbed to the bombing, and a bamboo-and-mud building was erected in its place, with oiled paper for windows and a plywood floor that was no defence against rats. The press hated it, but morale was high. A heroic atmosphere pervaded the city, echoing the defiant Blitz spirit in London. Journalists, diplomats, nationalist and communist officials found themselves sharing the same objectives and risks as the office workers, watermen, rickshaw pullers and slum dwellers. The bombing forged a communal hatred of Japan, and a shared confidence that the enemy would be defeated.

Although he was still a journalist, Hogg's job with the co-operatives had taken him far from the action. Associated Press was not interested in stories about the rural peasantry. But the major correspondents such as *Time* magazine's Theodore White were, and they used Hogg as a source for optimistic features about the success of the co-op movement. Many of the old Hankow gang were in town, and Hogg worked closely with them on CIC stories.

The American journalist Annalee Jacoby was a new press corps member who had arrived in 1940, fresh from Hollywood, where she had been writing film scripts. She worked with Theodore White in the *Time* bureau, and caught the mood well in her description of Chongqing's miserable conditions and its defiant spirit:

Living conditions were terrible, the city was filled with rats, the food was dreadful, bomb craters everywhere. Everything was slimy, cold, wet and mildewed. In the summer the humidity was high and the bugs flourished. There were spiders four inches across on the walls of your room. All the water [for the Press Hostel] had to be carried up from the Yangtse river in wooden buckets and we had one tin basin a day to bathe in, that's all. The rats chewed our boots and through the telephone wires at night. They ate our soap. But though it was most uncomfortable physically, it was absolutely inspiring mentally, it was a great year!

Jacoby and others who arrived in the city in 1940 were lucky. The worst of the bombing had taken place the previous May, when the Japanese air force had deployed the greatest concentration of bombers on a single mission during the war. The aim was to create a firestorm that would destroy the nationalist capital and force its government to seek surrender terms. Hogg's first visit to the city took place later that month, and he filed extensive despatches on the destruction and carnage for AP.

The armada of Japanese bombers had launched their raid from the captured airbase at Hankow, requiring a 1,200-mile round trip. The planes flew five abreast as they attacked the city at dusk from a height of ten thousand feet, the range limit of the ancient anti-aircraft batteries. A journalist who watched the raid from the hilltop overlooking the city estimated that 250 planes took part. The mix of incendiaries and five-hundred-pound high-explosive bombs created a mile-wide wall of flame which roared through the matchwood city.

As ever, there was cruel purpose behind the deployment of the new armaments. The hundreds of buildings that had recently been erected to accommodate the influx of population in Chongqing were, by government order, designed with stone-walled basements as bomb shelters. They proved death traps. A first wave of bombers rained high explosive on the city, collapsing the flimsy mud-and-timber frames. A second wave then dropped incendiaries, creating a firestorm which carbonised the sheltering families in their basements. A quarter of the city was gutted by the flames; the death toll ran to countless thousands.

Chiang Kai-shek's staff concluded, almost certainly correctly, that Japan's new German advisers had been involved in the planning of the raid. The tactics looked very much like those used in Spain, most notably at Guernica, and foreshadowed those to be used against London. Hitler's regime in fact operated on both sides in the Sino–Japanese conflict: German advisers had been working with the nationalists until early 1939. Berlin and Tokyo had signed an anti-communist pact in 1936, but a German military mission had been working with Chiang for a number of years. Hitler closed the mission as the war in China intensified, but several of the German staff stayed on.

At this stage the great-power contest in China was chiefly waged between Japan and the Soviet Union. Until the outbreak of the war in Europe, Moscow was lavish in its aid to China, providing over a two-year period some thousand planes, two thousand pilots and five hundred military advisers. From September 1939 the aid was sharply reduced.

The great Japanese raid on Chongqing was designed to break civilian morale and turn people against both the nationalist government and its communist rivals. Neither the Japanese nor their German advisers seemed to realise that the aerial bombardment which slaughtered the civilian population of Chongqing, and which was repeated throughout the war elsewhere on a smaller scale, had the opposite effect. Hogg reported both in his agency despatches and in his letters home that the bombing of civilian targets merely reinforced the feeling of *Kang chan tao ti* – War of Resistance to the Finish.

The diplomats and journalists in Chongqing drew the answers to important questions from the city's defiant response to the bombing. Would the refugees who had fled from the coast yet again put up with life under fire? Could they be bombed into supporting the Japanese puppet regime set up in Nanjing, or would they stay loyal to the nationalist government? Would people really work to revive the shattered industrial base of the country in small mobile units scattered far and wide? Would the peasant communities of Shansi accept the level of death and destruction brought upon them by the retreat of the nationalist government to their ancient capital?

The answer in all cases was a resounding yes. The government invited a number of well-known Americans to the beleaguered capital to amplify the message. The most famous of the celebrity writers and journalists who arrived in the war years was Ernest Hemingway. He and his wife Martha Gellhorn had been touring front-line areas with KMT commanders for two weeks. They flew in to Chongqing on a DC3 in April 1941, landing on the makeshift airstrip on a sandbar in the Yangtse river. There were no other passengers, but the plane carried several hundred million newly-minted banknotes denominated in Chinese dollars. The government was printing money in Hong Kong to meet wartime expenditure without having to raise taxes. It would do so throughout the war, leading to the hyper-inflation that destroyed the national economy and contributed to the fall of Chiang Kai-shek's government in 1949.

Chongqing's sandbar airport was a suitable introduction to life in the city. The Hemingways spent three weeks amid the rubble and the rats, being given VIP treatment by government officials. It was not a happy experience for either of them. Gellhorn, although a famous war correspondent, was fastidious. She was appalled by the sanitary arrangements – or lack of them – wherever she went. She did write six long features for *Collier's* magazine, including a glowing profile of Soong Meiling that she would later regret. Hemingway, who would later tell the author and critic Malcolm Cowley that he 'finally recovered from his fear of death in China', wrote little about his visit. His main concern was to get a decent drink. Every bar he had been to, and he included the US embassy in the list, had served what he called 'snake liquor'. He finally discovered that a US naval lieutenant based on a gunboat in the river had won two cases of whisky in a blind auction. Hemingway offered a huge sum in cash for both cases. After much negotiation Lieutenant William J. Lederer sold him six bottles in return for six writing lessons. Peter Moreira, in his book *Ernest Hemingway on the China Front* (2006), claims that Hemingway was in fact on an espionage mission for the US Treasury, which wanted an independent assessment of government corruption and communist threat.

The Japanese never understood the futility of their bombing campaign. Well after Pearl Harbor and the start of the Pacific war, Japanese planes would repeatedly bomb insignificant targets in the rural west and north-west of China. The cost in manpower and munitions was totally out of proportion to the results. And the results were often farcical. The clockwork planning behind the raids often meant that in good weather the same planes would appear over the same target at the same time of day.

Hogg often worked in the small town of Chenping, twenty-five miles west of Nanyang in central Honan province. The town was a crossroads, with highways leading north to Luoyang, west to Xian and south to the Han River valley. East lay the Japanese lines. It had been bombed so often and on such a regular timetable that Hogg had portable desks made, which were moved out under a clump of willow trees at 5.30 each morning when the skies were clear.

One morning while Hogg and his colleagues were hard at work under the trees, a single plane came over at the usual time. They sat back and watched what had become almost a ritual:

> *. . . it came down in a low dive with a terrific roar and stutter of machine gun fire. On a second swoop the pilot landed a small bomb in front of us and we could see him leaning out to get a good look at what he had done. In the old days before the Nazis were the enemies the RAF fighters used to demonstrate on 'native huts' of brushwood in the airfield at Hendon. I suppose we were just natives to the Japanese too. By the time he had come down once more and finished machine gunning, a peasant's farmhouse was in flames, a lot of cotton had been destroyed and three mules and four mule men had been killed.*

After the devastation of the May 1939 raids the Chinese developed an elaborate early-warning system which successfully limited casualties. Chinese agents near Japanese positions and airbases used field radios to flash the strength and bearing of attacking aircraft to the headquarters in Chongqing via a network of radio relay stations. Likely targets would be identified by the control room, and messages relayed to the cities and villages in the path of the bombers. Most of the raids on the Chinese capital took off from Hankow, some three hours' flying time away by bomber. Large poles were erected on the mountains around the city, with enormous paper lanterns hanging from them. The lanterns shone a white light, which together with a siren in the city signalled that the planes were an hour away. The lanterns turned to red when the raid was imminent. When the lanterns went out, the populace knew to take to their dugouts. Loudspeakers would relay warnings in the larger cities, and in small villages temple drums and bells would be used to sound the alarm.

The foreign business and diplomatic community in Chongqing, which had increased hugely with the arrival of the nationalist government, survived the air raids largely unscathed. Their once-elegant houses lined the broad streets of the old treaty port section across the river on the south bank. Since the American embassy was on the south bank, and the British, American and French gunboats were moored alongside it, the Japanese had indicated that it was neutral territory and would not be bombed. The British embassy under the redoubtable Sir Archibald Clark-Kerr remained proudly in harm's way on the north bank.

About half the foreign community of some three thousand lived in fading colonial splendour on the south bank, and during the raids they would be joined by the rest of the expatriates. But they were not all spectators during the big attacks. Great acts of heroism were performed by Western medical and nursing staff, and by the diplomats. The British ambassador and his staff were prominent in the rescue work, and Clark-Kerr did not hide his feelings about the perpetrators of the horror. After one raid he was seen walking through the debris of the British consulate, white-faced, bare-headed, wearing baggy old flannels and swinging a stick viciously at imaginary Japanese airmen. 'On no other man's face have I seen such a mixture of hate and horror as was borne by Sir Archibald Clark-Kerr,' said one eyewitness.

The repeated bombing did not change the foreign community's attachment to that unique colonial institution, the club. With its long teak bar, crumbling tennis court and scuffed billiard tables, the club was the hub of expatriate social life in Chongqing. Ancient staff delivered the drinks, and equally ancient magazines lay on the tables of the library. One writer described it as 'a melancholy relic of the semi colonial years in a minor treaty port. Chinese were still barred from the club as members and were not welcomed as guests.' Here, in between the bombing, Hogg played tennis with an improbable collection of missionaries, diplomats and fellow journalists. Old friends from Oxford turned up. Rather as Hankow had once been, Chongqing now became the place to visit in nationalist China.

In July 1940, Hogg gave a forty-minute talk to senior CIC officials in Chongqing in his capacity as the organisation's 'Ocean Secretary'. He reported on the progress of the co-op movement, its need for funds and plans to raise its profile with the American public. He spoke in Mandarin, with a strong northern accent. Although he was not completely fluent, his grasp of the language impressed his audience, among whom was the co-founder of the co-op movement, Rewi Alley.

Alley had gathered powerful allies behind his plan to develop rural co-ops. His communist sympathies were known to the government from his Shanghai days, but what mattered in 1940 was a united front against the Japanese. The KMT security organisation may have viewed Alley as an outright communist agent rather than just a 'foreign friend' of the party, but that hardly mattered when Chou En-lai was part of a unity government.

In any case, Soong Meiling and the British ambassador were among those who supported Alley's vision. He was not only one of the founders of the movement, but its driving force. He was a brilliant publicist, promoting the co-operatives as a great democratic experiment to any American correspondent who cared to listen. When Emily Hahn said that the publicity for the co-operatives got well ahead of the facts on the ground, she would have had Rewi Alley in mind.

Alley greatly influenced Hogg's later years in China, and regarded him as a protégé, although that definition of their relationship was not one Hogg ever recognised. Nor did he realise that Alley was a master myth-maker who always tailored his remarkable life story to suit his audience. It is clear from Hogg's correspondence, and from his book, that the story Alley told him was not the whole truth.

Born in 1897 in Springfield, a village near North Canterbury, New Zealand, Alley was christened Rewi after a Maori chief who had become a legend for his role in resisting the British forces during the land wars of the 1860s. He grew up on a farm but moved to Christchurch at the age of nine, when his father became headmaster of a school there. In 1916 the death of his elder brother Eric, who had been fighting with the New Zealand expeditionary force in France, persuaded Rewi to sign up. After training he spent from January to April 1918 in the Ypres salient. At the age of twenty-one he experienced the horrors of trench warfare, was twice wounded and was awarded the Military Medal, established in 1916 for individual acts of bravery that were regarded as insufficient to merit the award of a Distinguished Conduct Medal (DCM). In the carnage of trench war it was difficult to determine degrees of valour, but Alley must have displayed real courage.

Back in New Zealand, he spent six lonely years struggling to make a success of a small shared farm in the wilds of Taranaki in the North Island. In 1926 he left New Zealand for China. The papers in Auckland were full of reports of civil war between warlords, nationalists and the underground communist movement. Alley was weary of farming, and curious about China. But he was also homosexual, and he knew that China, or more specifically Shanghai, was famous for the liberal sexual attitudes of its expatriate population. In the 1920s and thirties many visitors were drawn to the city by the lure of sexual tourism. Dr Anne-Marie Brady, author of an illuminating book on Alley (*Friend of China: The Myth of Rewi Alley*, 2003), says: 'Shanghai was a city with an active homosexual scene. However it would be a mistake to view this as something separate from the heterosexual scene; homosexuality was simply another option for the sex consumer.'

Alley arrived in the city in April 1927, just as the first united front government between the KMT and the small Communist Party was ending in a bloodbath. Chiang Kai-shek had launched his 'white terror' to destroy the new party, and many thousands of communists were summarily executed. Within days of arriving, Alley witnessed the terror at first hand: 'I saw five lads being carried naked and hanging from poles. Right in front of me they were dumped on the ground and an officer got down from a horse and pumped a bullet into the head of each one of them. Next day I read in the newspaper that they were "young agitators trying to organise a trade union".' This was the moment of Alley's politicisation, although strangely he did not mention the incident in letters home, but merely recorded it years later in his memoirs.

The terror was largely conducted out of sight of European eyes, in the Chinese quarter, where a population crowded into shanty towns endured a harsh existence of poverty and disease. By contrast, in the international settlements life, even at Alley's relatively low level, was luxurious. He joined the municipal fire brigade, and began to study Mandarin and Marx. He fought the exploitation of child labour, especially that of country children sold into virtual slavery in the city's many thousands of workshops.

A short, stocky man with cropped ginger hair and a prominent nose, Alley became a familiar figure in Shanghai before the Japanese takeover. He rose to become Chief Factory Inspector for the municipal council, in which capacity he launched himself into a crusade for the city's poor. His humanitarian work extended to flood and famine relief in the wider Shanghai region. In the early thirties the press in New Zealand began to publicise his work, and he became something of a minor celebrity in Shanghai, with a circle of friends that included Edgar and Peg Snow, and prominent missionaries such as Ralph Lapwood. Auden and Isherwood looked him up on their visit, and persuaded him to take them on a tour of the hospitals and slum areas.

The Japanese destruction of Shanghai's industry in 1937 propelled Alley into what would become his mission for the next decade. He abandoned his life of relative ease in Shanghai, leaving behind his lover, an Englishman called Alec Camplin, who returned to Britain, and moved first to Hankow in pursuit of his co-operative ideal, then to Chongqing.

Alley was always highly discreet about his homosexuality. Although same-sex relationships were not the social taboo in Chinese society that they were in the West, the communists frowned on them. George Hogg seems to have been naïve in this respect, and it appears from passages in his book that it never occurred to him that Alley was a homosexual.

After he was fired from his position as technical adviser on the CIC executive, Alley concentrated on the development of technical training schools named after Joseph Bailie, an American Presbyterian missionary who arrived in China in 1890. Bailie had originally set up a programme to send young Chinese abroad for technical training. Given the difficulties of foreign travel, especially after Japan's entry into the world war, Alley's idea was to develop such schools in China. They would take in war orphans and turn them into trained workers for the co-ops. Bailie, who had become Alley's mentor and friend, worked closely with him in humanitarian relief work during the floods in the Yangtse valley in 1932, and died in China three years later.

By way of a tribute and in order to solicit missionary funds, Alley decided to establish a technical training school in Bailie's name. There was a political motive behind this move: it would be easier to prevent KMT action against the school if it carried the name of a prominent American missionary. The first school was established in 1941 in a small village, Shuangshipu, sixty miles south-west of Baoji in Shanxi province, with initially disastrous results.* Headmasters came and went. They were all locally

---

* The school survives to this day, and still carries Joseph Bailie's name.

recruited Chinese, and lacked the training, inspiration and character to deal with sixty-five unruly boys. Pupils were mistreated with severe punishments, and funds were stolen. Alley began to cast around for yet another headmaster – the eighth.

He had possibly seen George Hogg as a solution to the problem when they met in Chongqing. But Alley, as he was to demonstrate later in his life, was a political animal who moved with crablike caution in the minefield of China's politics. He did not wish to be seen to promote the young and inexperienced Englishman openly, fearing that his own reputation would damage Hogg's prospects. Instead he made sure that Hogg was brought to the attention of the British ambassador and Soong Meiling, and allowed them to advance his name. The manoeuvring worked all too well. The very people in the CIC who were to offer Hogg the headmastership fired Alley from his position in the organisation a year later.

Hogg remained unaware of Alley's machinations. He felt lonely and depressed as he left Chongqing in the autumn of 1940 to continue his travels. Whether it was because of the bombing, his disillusionment with the political deceit of the united front or the absence of his girlfriend Ren, the fact was that he was homesick, and desperate for news from Harpenden. He had written to his parents imploring them to send their news, and newspaper cuttings on almost any subject: 'I would love this more than anything.' There was also a word of reproach. An American acquaintance sent him clippings from the US press on the conflict in China; why could he not get something similar from home? He particularly craved news of his sister Rosemary:

How is Roke? Funny thing about our family, the way it doesn't write to itself. The other day a man in the train looked at my eyebrows and said 'your eyebrows are too much spread out. That means your relationships with your brothers are too far apart and that they will desert you when you need them.' It was with some dignity and cold British reserve in my voice (I hope) that I answered him that however it might be with people whose eyebrows were spread out in China this was not necessarily the case in England, my country, and that my three brothers were all very big and very reliable. Then he asked how old my father was. Fortunately I could remember within the nearest five years and [that] silenced all aspersions cast upon our name.

When the news did come, it was not good. Hogg was deeply upset to hear of the death in action of his old school friend Robert Nelson, and paid his tribute in a letter home: 'Robert was a real leader, he knew how to encourage the green beginners, discourage the smart alecs and keep his head in any given situation.' Hogg thought his friend personified the best of the public-school spirit, but he might have been describing himself when he talked of his 'fair play, common sense, scorn of too much theory and talk . . . with a good deal of idealism not too far under the surface'.

Hogg's family had scattered during the war. His three elder brothers went into reserved occupations, which meant they were not eligible for conscription into the armed forces. Gary and Stephen were teaching in different parts of Britain, while Daniel had used his language skills to secure a position as an interpreter for the League of Nations in Switzerland, where he remained throughout the war. Hogg's father Robert stayed in Harpenden and continued to run the business in Hanover Square. His mother Kathleen often travelled to see her daughter Barbara and her grandchildren Gillian and Judith at Bampton in the Lake District. Kathleen moved around during the war, and was often away from home for long periods. This strong, self-opinionated woman made for a difficult wife, but there is no doubting the love she bestowed on her children, and especially on her adored youngest son.

If Hogg wanted to provoke his family into correspondence, he probably succeeded with a throwaway paragraph at the end of his next letter:

I've got a couple of sons – did I tell you? . . . They were a bit weedy at first and needed rubber sheets in their bed more than anything. However they are growing up to be very tough now and will no doubt be a credit to my old age.

Hogg had adopted two boys, and in the next year he would adopt two more, making a family of four children, all brothers.

Since none of his parents' correspondence to Hogg has survived, we do not know their reaction to the news that their youngest son, now aged twenty-six, had started an adoptive family. In almost his next letter, a year later, he reported on his growing brood. He also sent the good news that his girlfriend Ren had surfaced behind Japanese lines.

March 8th 1942

My Dear Mother and daddy,

You might all have been dead since last August for all I know. A lot of people dying these days. No doubt some letters will arrive some day soon.

I've got four adopted sons now. I think I told you that after having been out of my loving care for some time I found 74 lice in one of their shirts, and there was a lot more, so I burnt it, and bought them two new shirts and two pants each. Last time I inspected them they had only three fleas between the lot of them. Proud father beamed. They love taking baths now, too. The fleas have taken root in our room. Such is life . . .

I have told you about my girl friend who got lost on the other side of the Jap lines, didn't I? Well, I've just had a letter from her . . . first in a year and she's okay, so I'm rather happy!

When the two eldest of the adopted boys recalled their wartime upbringing with their English father, they remembered Hogg telling them of letters from home expressing astonishment – and congratulations – at the additions to the family. Hogg spent hours with his 'children' telling them of his family, and life in England. In an effort to connect their world with his, he told them that he had been born on the night of the only bombing raid of the First World War over, or near, his home in Harpenden. This was perfectly true. The 'boys' can still remember him reading descriptions from his parents' letters of the London Blitz, and the comparison he drew with the bombing of Baoji.

Nieh Guanghan and Nieh Guangchung were aged seventy-five and seventy-nine respectively in the spring of 2007, when they described how they came to be adopted by an 'ocean devil'. Their brothers Nieh Gungtao, then seventy-one, and Nieh Guangpei, sixty-eight, were not able to attend the lunch, but were living happily in retirement outside Beijing.

The boys had been born in Manchuria, where in 1932 their father had been active in the communist underground. He was imprisoned by the KMT after refusing to serve with the national-ist forces. On release he moved to work as a teacher in Baoji with his wife and their four young sons. His communist activities forced him to flee the police, and this time he vanished and broke off all contact with his family. He was later thought to have died in combat, and when Hogg adopted the boys he did so in the belief, which they shared, that they were orphans. In fact their father survived the war, and was eventually reunited with his children.

While her husband was on the run, his wife, the boys' mother, had become seriously ill, and was taken to a hospital in Baoji. Her four sons were sent to the local orphanage, and it was there that they came under the care of Xiao Ren, Hogg's girlfriend at the time. Shortly afterwards, Hogg adopted the two older boys and transferred them to the Bailie school in Shuangshipu. The youngest two remained with their mother until she died in the summer of 1942. Hogg physically carried the dying woman the twelve miles to hospital when she became ill, and visited her every day until her death a few weeks later.

The brothers, who were aged fourteen, eleven, seven and three at the time of their adoption, were malnourished, covered in lice and fleas, and suffered in varying degrees from scabies, dysentery, trachoma, beriberi and body sores. One of them was also diagnosed as suffering from congenital venereal disease. Hogg took his new family to the clinic in Baoji, where they were treated for their ailments. They went to school 'fat and happy', leaving their new-found father with scabies, a minor irritation compared to what he had been through. He worked out that he had survived trachoma, dysentery, malaria, typhus, paratyphoid, anthrax 'and a few other funny things'.

The boys were to spend the next three years with the English-man who became their father, headmaster and doctor. They were given numbers for names: thus the eldest became Lao Da (No. 1), then Lao Er (No. 2), Lao San (No. 3) and Lao Si (No. 4). They first went to school in Baoji, and later transferred to the Bailie technical training school in Shuangshipu, sixty miles away. All except the youngest retain vivid memories of the 'high-nosed stranger' who entered their lives with sulphur, disinfectant and endless baths to rid them of lice and scabies. Their orphanage diet had consisted mainly of rice, and the introduction of vegetables and occasionally meat at the school improved their health and weight dramatically. Hogg's letters home from this point almost always include a reference to the prodigious appetites of his adopted sons:

Son No 3 has lost his two front teeth and looks rather intriguing as a result. No 4 gets rounder and rounder every day until we don't wonder if it is right that he should be so chubby. Is there any limit to chubbiness? They are both in the garden now helping ... put up a bamboo fence for the tomatoes. (Chinese name for tomato = ocean persimmon). Son No 4 has just found a very big bean and brings it to me for inspection suggesting that we buy some meat and fry them together for lunch. His greatest object in life is to achieve greater rotundity.

The adoption of the four boys was a perfect foil to Hogg's mother's repeated references to his need to find a wife, and helpful suggestions as to who might fill the role: 'So good of you and Barb [his sister] to find me these wives. Don't quite know when I will be able to come and fetch them away. How about my four sons?'

By 1942 it was clear that Kathleen wanted her youngest son to come home. He was twenty-seven years old, and had been away for five years. She played on the fact that his father, now seventy-five, was not well, and was desperate to see his son before he died. Hogg was having none of it, and replied flippantly:

July 24th 1942

It is nice to think of daddy trying hard to 'hang onto this terrestrial globe' in the hope of seeing me again. Surely 75 is quite young? I reckon I have another quarter century's grace yet.

Hogg did not appear to be close to his father, and rarely mentions him except to agree that he was the 'charming personification of an English gentleman'.

From 1941 to his appointment in May 1942 as headmaster of the Bailie school in Shuangshipu, Hogg worked as CIC inspector

175

based in Baoji. The town lay at the foot of a range of mountains 140 miles west of Xian, and was originally thought to have been beyond the range or interest of the Japanese air force. In the early years of the war refugee trains would arrive weekly from the east, carrying a freight of human cargo crammed into the carriages, clinging to the hot metal roofs or lashed to the girders beneath the coaches.

Confronted by the formidable Tsingling mountains, through which the track rose to the remote and inhospitable western regions, the refugees tumbled off at Baoji, seeking shelter in a mushrooming shanty town outside the eastern gates. On his first visit in 1939 Hogg watched them trying to build shacks and burrowing into the hillsides for shelter: 'Utterly played out some just sat down for days on the dusty plain by the railway track. There were no sanitary arrangements and no one came to bury the dead.'

On his return eighteen months later he found a different story. The old refugee camp had become a new suburb which was bigger than the city itself: 'Its houses were taller and better built, its main street was broader and better surfaced. It was six o'clock in the morning and bitterly cold but already the street was ringing with hammers and saws and the builders were grunting cheerily as they rammed down new mud walls into the frames.'

The man responsible for the transformation was the local magistrate, Wang Feng-jei. Hogg found him on the steps of the police station early one morning, 'a tough looking, thick set figure in a dressing gown, hair still tousled, beard unshaven'. He was watching his police drag a condemned man off to execution. The shackled prisoner dropped to his knees in the dust, pleading for pardon. Wang made no sign, and the man was dragged away to his death. 'He killed a man,' Wang said in reply to Hogg's horrified look.

Baoji did not turn out to be the hoped-for place of refuge, and nor were the new streets and houses in the eastern suburb to survive the war. By 1941 Tokyo's air force was bombing as far west as Lanzhou, a thousand miles from the coast. As a railway junction, and the first major centre on the silk road west of Xian, Baoji came under heavy attack.

Hogg was by now reporting for the Associated Press, using the terse, unembellished language required by the news agency. He changed style when he wrote home to his family and friends, but some of his descriptions of the grisly aftermath of the raids seem indifferent to the human suffering involved, probably because bombing and civilian casualties had by now become almost routine: 'Yesterday 27 very beautiful planes came to Baoji. They looked so nice and they sounded so nice and it was all quite like Hendon air show [until] the good old whistly noise such as cricket balls make when they get old, began to swoosh.'

Hogg dived into a hole in the city walls, but others were not so lucky:

> There were a hundred prostitutes in another hole, not so stout (the hole I mean) and they all got buried ... I wonder why I tell you all this, when you must hear almost exactly similar stories every week? Only on a grander scale. Maybe because when I went out to look afterwards at the fires and the collapsed mud and wood houses and the piles of wreckage all down one street of our little town I thought this must be 1/100th of what it is like in London town.

Although Hogg witnessed and wrote about many such scenes, and came close to death on a number of occasions, his luck held. He even caught anthrax in bizarre circumstances. He had visited a brush-making co-operative and bought a shaving brush made of pig's bristles, from which he contracted the disease. Anthrax was normally fatal without swift and advanced treatment, but Hogg as usual came through.

Carl Mydans was one of a series of *Life* photographers sent to China at about this time, and he would become one of the most famous. In 1941 he went to Baoji to photograph the co-operative movement in action, and took a series of shots of George Hogg. Hogg appears in one photograph smiling under a straw hat, and in another looking improbably well groomed, with his hair carefully brushed back. The accompanying article never appeared, but Carl and his wife Shelley became friends of Hogg's.*

Despite the constant travelling and his work for CIC in Baoji, Hogg spent much of 1941 working on the final chapters of his first book, and beginning the outline of a second. He worked on a typewriter in his small room, interrupted by daily air raid warnings and the constant need to find fresh typewriter ribbon and carbon paper, both of which were in short supply. His letters home at this time were almost illegible.

He had already sent the first chapters to Muriel Lester in New York, with the title 'All but a Yellow Skin'; he later changed this to 'Yellow River Watch' – both titles were eventually dropped in favour of his publisher's choice, *I See a New China*. All his letters home now tell of efforts to find a publisher, and to get the photographs and drawings he wanted as illustrations. He was well aware that the market for books about the war in China had become saturated. Many of the correspondents who had witnessed the battles for Shanghai, Nanjing and Hankow had produced their own accounts, while Auden and Isherwood's *Journey to a War* had created considerable interest when it was published in 1939.

---

* In 1944 the New York publishers Little, Brown provided only six complimentary copies of Hogg's book *I See a New China*, of which one went to the Mydanses.

Hogg did not intend his book to be just another account of the war. He told Aunt Muriel:

I think that this book, being an account of the way in which brave people struggle to survive and create while the world is being destroyed around them, will still be of fresh and universal interest. Though written while journeying for 18 months in the midst of war, it is in no sense an attempt at a newsy account of battle campaigns and bombings which are being repeated ad lib from London to Timbuktu. It is rather a story of the very human reactions to war, which differ, just as man differs, all the way from Timbuktu back to London.

Hogg wrote about what he saw and what he deeply believed in: the instinctive kindness and decency of people who had been shaken out of their 'well mannered aloofness' by the struggle to survive a savage war and who had become as a result 'real human beings'.

There were political risks in publishing any book which made heroes of the peasants of north-west China and criticised their distant masters in Chongqing. Hogg begged his aunt not to say anything about the fact that he was working for the CIC, but merely to say that he was an accredited correspondent for Associated Press.

Muriel Lester had already published an account of her own travels, and sent the manuscript to her publishers, Harper & Brothers in New York, but then the trail went cold. She returned to wartime London, and Hogg heard nothing for six months. In desperation he wrote to Ida Pruitt, who pursued the matter with Harpers. A polite rejection note came back in June.

By October the gloomy news arrived that several other publishers in New York had turned the book down. It was held to be too personal, and lacking in detail. Ida Pruitt enlisted Peg Snow to help find a publisher; ironically the success of Peg's book *Inside Red China*, published under her pen name Nym Wales, was cited by agents and publishers as a reason not to take on Hogg's book. There were already too many books on the American market, written by journalists such as Haldore Hanson, who turned gripping reportage into long narratives. Back in America these authors could make political judgements and give details of places and contacts that Hogg dared not do while he was still in China.

He began to rewrite the book, adding new chapters. He decided to challenge the censors by exposing much of the corruption and bureaucratic obstruction he encountered, especially within government-controlled areas. Rampant inflation and a collapsing currency had led to a thriving black market throughout China in the war years. The real corruption lay at the heart of Chiang Kai-shek's government, where everyone – from the Generalissimo down – took their cut from official revenue and foreign loans. The 'squeeze', as it was called, was commonplace throughout the civil administration and the army.

By mid-1942 Hogg had found a powerful new sponsor for the book. It appears that he pressed the draft upon Henry Luce, while taking him on a tour of co-operatives around Baoji. Luce read several chapters, took the draft back to New York, and passed it on to what would be the final publisher, Little, Brown & Co.

Peg Snow also wrote to her own publishers praising the book in December 1942. She had met Hogg in Hankow, and had heard of his decision to abandon journalism for life in the co-operative movement. She wanted to know what had happened to him, and found her answer in his book.

How long would he stick? How long would the Chinese tolerate him? Would he become disgusted and cynical as so many foreigners do? He had nothing to give the Chinese but himself, no relief or missionary money to make himself popular. Would this be enough to assure him a place in their movement?

This book tells what happened. After some four years George Hogg has become an institution among the Chinese . . . he has participated in the most heart breaking endeavour ever tried in China – helping build small co-operative industries among the interior villages, trying to find a middle way when political lines are drawn so tense that when young Indusco organisers work too hard and too late at night they are accused of being reds because of their exceptional zeal.

The book was finally published by Little, Brown in June 1944, as *I See a New China*. The publisher bowed to the author's third thoughts, and removed many of the exposés of graft. Hogg realised that criticism of the KMT government in Chongqing would rebound both on the CIC and on the school of which he had by then become headmaster. This, together with a certain lack of narrative structure, left the book deeply flawed, but it won enthusiastic reviews nonetheless. Hogg himself said that given the cuts he had to make it amounted to no more than a travel book and a string of personal experiences.* In fact it was much more than that. The *New York Times*'s reviewer Mark Gayne said:

I See a New China *is the story of the Chinese common man, hungry and oppressed, harried by the alien invader and his own army, by the tax collector and the pawnbroker, and yet ever patient, hardworking*

---

* In his Introduction to the book, Hogg wrote: 'What I wanted was to live among the people themselves to see what war was doing to their daily lives. How were the students, professors and businessmen, I wondered, getting along with the farmers and how were the peasant craftsmen surviving side by side with the skilled workers from Shanghai and Hankow? What actually happened to refugees once they got beyond sight of the city walls?'

and ingenious. He is the artisan who goes back into the Japanese held village to save his co-op equipment, the nonchalant mule driver who steals a roll of Japanese telephone wire, the farmer who reclaims a silted bank, knowing that the treacherous Yellow River would betray him, the young girl who escapes from Peiping to guerrilla territory to starve and be useful, the 'little devil' who will some day be a Chinese legend . . . For all versions of this common man Hogg has a compassion and respect. All of them he describes in detail until the reader can smell and feel this corner of China . . .

In late 1941 Hogg had been promoted, receiving what he called the 'magnificent' title of Chinese Industrial Co-operatives Inspector, with a pass signed by China's Finance Minister, H.H. Kung. This made travel easier, although by now he had become adept at talking his way past KMT checkpoints and dodging bandit blockades.

Hogg met, wrote about and made friends with a range of eccentric characters, foreigners and Chinese, on his travels, most of whom appear either by name or thinly disguised in his book. Some had good reason to be in China, others were drifters who washed around on the rough seas of the conflict through no choice of their own.

In Lanzhou there was a German Jew who had survived three years in Dachau concentration camp, but had managed to escape to Italy on the eve of the war in Europe. This unnamed hero crossed into the Balkans, entered Russia and, having been refused entry to India and Indo-China (Vietnam), made his way via a remote Chinese border post to Sinkiang. He liked China, he said, because it was the only country in the world that would have him.

Hogg had spent Christmas 1940 with English missionaries in Xian, feasting on home-made plum pudding and marvelling at the lifestyle of his hosts, who lived in a large house behind high walls with thick entry gates. The Oxford-educated husband had breakfast at 9 o'clock prompt every morning in dressing gown and slippers, with a months-old English newspaper propped up against the toast rack on a spotless tablecloth. His chief comment on almost everything was: 'This could never happen in England.'

Much more to Hogg's liking was a clearly mad Swedish missionary who roamed north-west China carrying an expensive accordion and accompanied by a dog called Trotsky. He had apparently been thrown out of his home in Stockholm after making a speech at his sister's wedding denouncing the evils of alcohol in general and of champagne in particular.

Grand American journalists, especially Art Steele and the legendary Haldore Hanson, both of whom he had already met in Hankow and Beijing, would drop in and out of Hogg's life, turning up at remote airstrips in private planes bearing golden gifts of typewriter ribbon and carbon paper.

An odd couple of Englishmen whom Hogg described as 'apple cheeked, straw haired and curry chinned' turned up and persuaded him to accompany them as a guide on a long cross-country trek to Xian. Ralph Lapwood was a missionary, and Michael Lindsay, later Lord Lindsay of Birker, an Oxford graduate who arrived in China in 1937 to take up a teaching post at the American-funded Yenching University, just outside Beijing. After Pearl Harbor the university lost its extra-territorial status and Lindsay fled to guerrilla-controlled areas. As a keen amateur radio technician he was welcomed, and became a senior radio communications expert for the communists in Yenan. After the communist victory in 1949 he became disillusioned with the excesses of Mao's China, and switched allegiance to Chiang Kai-shek's nationalist regime in Taiwan. He was one of the few former 'foreign friends' from the Yenan days to make such a break.

Lindsay, Hogg and Lapwood walked hundreds of miles

together through territory fought over by the Japanese and the guerrillas. They averaged twenty-three painful miles a day over rough terrain, thinking only of 'boils, constipation, lice, sleep and the distance to the next stop'. On their travels the trio reverted to the stereotype Englishmen abroad. Behaving with characteristic reserve, they did not talk to each other as they packed up their bedding each morning and slurped back their breakfast noodles. Plodding over the mountains, they found themselves exchanging inane remarks about the weather. Only in the evenings did the strange group relax and allow themselves a little conversation about school and university days.

In this company Hogg found himself, to his alarm, slipping back into the very English habit of viewing all foreigners, especially those of a different colour, as hopeless incompetents. The three Englishmen agreed that Chinese villagers – all Chinese villagers – lied when asked simple questions. Rather than distressing the travellers with the real distance to the next stop or the number of mules available when they got there, villagers would glibly give the answer that they thought they wanted to hear. Above all, the group were irritated by being constantly told by their village hosts to stop and rest.

They could not rest. They were bound for a meeting with the co-operative movement leadership, and had to cross Japanese-held road and rail links to get there. Hogg and his fellow travellers found little peace when they finally reached Xian, however: 'Overawed by such luxuries as running water and spring beds in our hotel bedroom we stacked our dirty clothes in the corner hoping that whatever was inside would not jump out, and crept between white sheets dreaming of buttered toast and coffee in the morning. Instead we woke to the sound of the anti-aircraft sirens.'

One day a young man who called himself Bong appeared in Baoji and demanded to meet the foreigner called Ho Ke. He wanted someone to listen to his story – someone who was not Chinese. Hogg agreed to give the young man a hearing. Bong's real name was S.H. Jeung. His father was a Chinese laundryman in California who had married an American girl. When Bong was fifteen and excelling in his class, his father had decided that he should be the link between the Chinese and American branches of the family. Accordingly he was sent to stay with his grandmother in Canton, and told to find a nice Cantonese girl as a wife.

Bong was unlucky in two respects. He intensely disliked the nice girl his grandmother found for him. And the Japanese had started their assault on Shanghai the moment that he arrived in the land of his father's birth. Fired both by the desire to fight for what he saw as an emerging democracy and by a desperate desire to avoid matrimony, Bong joined the Chinese army in the safest role he could think of: a driver. As the Japanese advanced up the Yangtse the Californian high-school boy found himself driving truckloads of ammunition through shellfire, ambushes and minefields. He was by now seventeen years old, and must have felt a long way from the John Muir school in Mercedes, California.

To complicate matters, Bong took it upon himself to denounce corruption in the army. He refused to take part in the 'squeeze' rackets, whereby drivers extorted the local populace and sold their own supplies on the black market; and he refused to take opium or to join his fellow drivers in brothels. This did not make him popular in his unit. He was denounced as a criminal half-breed and a spy, and thrown into jail. He escaped, stole his own truck and headed north, finally winding up in the Tsingling mountains. There he heard about the strange foreigner who was looking after Chinese orphans.

Bong explained his problem to Hogg in stark terms. He had been sent to China to discover his family roots and bond with his own people, only to discover that the Chinese were 'lying, boot sucking, swaggering, cruel and everything else that they were supposed to be in the days when opium and concessions were part of the white man's burden'.

Hogg, whose own youthful idealism had been tempered by the harsh realities of life in wartime China, felt considerable sympathy for the unfortunate Bong, although he still had hopes for the country's future:

> Each of us coming from the west with the same kind of outlook had been living alone among the Chinese, but while he had experienced the seamiest side of an ancient civilisation and with youth's intolerance had magnified it into something a great deal more important than it was, I had been living with people who were trying to build something new.

Nevertheless, Hogg shared Bong's view that behind the stirring political rhetoric and the press releases about the struggle for democracy in new China, the nationalist cause was mired in the violence and corruption of old China. While Bong received letters from his parents condemning him as a traitor to his country, Hogg was just as irritated by letters from home congratulating him on his part in building a true democracy.

Hogg took Bong under his wing, giving him a job in the CIC office and making plans to repatriate him with the help of the US consul in Chongqing. The two walked the mountains discussing China's struggle to free itself from a feudal past and the cultural obsession with 'face'.

But whatever advice Hogg gave the young fugitive did not work. Bong wrote a farewell letter in the early hours of one morning and took a truck down south. Hogg never saw or heard from him again. Months later he received a letter from Bong's old headmistress in California saying that plans were being made to repatriate him from Hong Kong.

Wherever he went on his travels Hogg was accompanied, or so it seemed to him, by at least three of the four horsemen of the apocalypse. By 1942 the war had caused several million deaths, and left many millions more refugees. As if that was not enough, plague and famine took a huge toll of the suffering populace, and added millions more to the death toll. Everywhere Hogg found that half of the populations of the villages and towns he passed through had died within the past few months of typhus, typhoid, relapsing fever and 'flu. At one large student college 'somewhere in the country' nearly half the students had TB and were suffering from malnutrition.

In August 1942 the great Yellow River burst its banks above Tongguan, and Hogg was sent to oversee a relief programme. The flooding had been caused by cloudbursts hundreds of miles upstream in Gansu province. But the real problem lay in centuries of deforestation, which had brought – and still brings – cyclical devastation and death to the great flood plains of China.

For millennia farmers working the banks of China's two great river systems, the Yellow River and the Yangtse, had considered timber to be an inexhaustible fuel supply. As the forests receded, the hills were stripped of cover, allowing summer downpours to flood unchecked into the valleys, stripping off topsoil and dumping it into riverbeds. River levels were raised, dykes were built and regularly overwhelmed by floodwaters that went on to change the course of the river.

Hogg witnessed this biblical cycle of destruction at first hand:

A huge wave of flood water the whole length of the river. There was no question of 'China's sorrow' changing her course. It was merely that there was enough water for two rivers so that whenever its banks

allowed it to do so the river spread out over them. P'ing M'ing county
which ordinarily lies a few feet above water level was covered for
fifteen hours by water 10–20 foot deep travelling with force enough
to wrench huge lumps of coal from a Shansi seam 70 miles further
north and strew hundreds of thousands of tons of them in the mud
all the way down . . .

The destruction was total. Every house in the region had been
built of earthen bricks, and 'dissolved into the component
particles of Yellow River mud and with their rafter poles floated
away downstream'. As the flood subsided, the survivors faced
fresh peril:

Then the Japs began to open up with their big guns across the river.
They were only covering their own retreat into the mountains
thinking that we might take advantage of a shift in the river to cross;
meanwhile we thought that they were making use of a shift in the
river to attack us. Actually of course both sides were flooded equally
badly but we didn't know that then.

Among the human debris left by the floods Hogg found an old
woman who had fled to the area after the strategic decision
to break the dykes to halt the Japanese advance in 1938. She
had crawled onto the roof of her house clutching her grandson,
and had finally been swept away. Somehow she kept afloat on
the turbulent waters, and managed to keep hold of the child. After
half an hour she was deposited on a riverbank ten miles downstream with a very wet, very angry but very alive child in her arms.

Hogg reported that she laughed at the Yellow River, saying,
'I've escaped him twice now, he won't get me again!' He quoted
her words in a piece for the *New Statesman* magazine.

This was a rare story of survival. Elsewhere Hogg found nothing but tales of death in the floodwater. He met Liu Teh-ch'ing, a woman who had saved herself by clinging to an oxcart:

'We tied the cart to a tree before the water came,' she said, 'but as ours is a new village the tree was small and the flood dragged the tree and the cart away together. I was holding my small baby but I swallowed so much water that I became unconscious and let him go. My father and husband and two children were all drowned.'

The villagers collected their surviving livestock, possessions and their windfall of coal and began to rebuild their lives. With characteristic optimism Hogg extracted a message of hope from the death and destruction around him:

Although I have seen enough concentrated starvation, misery and destruction to last me for weeks – it was as though the entire Luftwaffe had been diverted from the Russian front to bomb every village and hamlet in Ordinary People's country – I felt glad and exhilarated. Now I knew it. I knew that these were the real people of China, who would remain and rebuild whatever complicated muddle the round cheeked shiny-eye-lidded bureaucracy got itself into. I felt refreshed. For a long time I had been waiting ... and suddenly today I find that the people were infinitely more heroic, in a quite ordinary sort of way, than I or anyone else could ever make them out to be.

Although the war had reached a strategic stalemate, air raids had become so much a part of his life that his press reports and letters home refer to them only in laconic afterthoughts:

My diary continues to be fairly interesting. The other day there was an air raid. Luckily I was outside the little city [Baoji] and saw the whole thing at a safe distance. Two flights of beautiful silver birds and the hum of a brass stop of the organ in church . . . then spurts of flame from in amongst the houses, a fountain line of dirt and smoke shooting upwards and a terrific roar.

When we got back the place was wailing. Two bombs had landed right at the entrance to two caves in the mountainside where the poor people live. They can't afford houses but at least they thought they were safe in one respect . . . They were glad to shelter their neighbours during air raids. When we looked in . . . on the floor lay the remains of ten people. Two children were already coffined up in a small crater outside and another man was having his corpse washed and dressed while the women moaned and wailed mechanically around.

Hogg's travels took him as far west as Lanzhou, the capital of Gansu province, east to Luoyang and south to the provisional capital.

By 1942, most foreigners who had been caught up by the war had left. Many of those that remained, even missionaries, were planning to depart. Hogg had no such plans. It was clear to him that he had found his home. 'If I had to choose where to live, I think I would choose to stay here. I have many friends and we are doing good work, what more could you want?'

News from home had by now become very scarce. By May 1942 Hogg had not received a letter from anyone in England for eleven months. The last letter from home had told him that Muff Hunter had given birth to a baby girl, and that her by now estranged husband Andrew had won the DFC for his role in coastal command operations.

The letters he used to receive from his family and friends, including even one from his old French teacher, Miss Terry, whose car he had once commandeered, had stopped. The war at home left people little time to write to faraway friends in China, and the postal service via Hong Kong had stopped after the Japanese occupied the colony.

That left the link via the Burma road, which had been reopened in the south-east, and in the north the old silk route via Russia. Both routes were unreliable and subject to closure without warning. It was Japanese policy to choke off China's communications with the outside world.

The deterioration of the overseas postal service was the least of the government's problems. Tokyo's tightening grip on her trade routes posed a strategic crisis for China's united front government. It was one which the industrial co-operatives were in part designed to solve.

EIGHT

The Headmaster

'I am fat and robust and happy.'

In March 1942 Hogg received news that was to change his life. Acting on Rewi Alley's recommendation, the board organising the CIC in Chongqing had appointed him headmaster of the Bailie co-operative training school in Shuangshipu. This was little more than a village where the roads from Lanzhou and the south met in a valley of the Tsingling mountains. The school had been sited there in the belief that it was too small to warrant bombing and, given the mountainous terrain, too difficult for any ground attack.

The school that Hogg took over was in chaos. There had been seven headmasters in eighteen months. Six had been dismissed or left in the first year. He was to be the eighth. He took over a school that consisted of three brick-built classrooms standing on an open plot on a steep and bleak hillside. The only equipment in the school was a barely workable loom and a warp winder for threading the yarn onto it. There were no books or writing materials in the classrooms. The kitchen was bare. Outside the school a national flag bleached white by the sun hung in tatters. There were no beds, and the dozen boys who were left of the thirty-five supposed to be on the school register slept on the top of desks in one classroom. They were listless, covered in scabies, malnourished and lice-infested.

Little wonder that CIC officials in Baoji had laughed at Hogg when he told them of his new job. They immediately began planning to get their hands on the government money allocated to the school.

Most of the teachers and the majority of the pupils had left along with the seventh headmaster. When Hogg walked into the school he was met with a mixture of indifference and hostility by boys whose sole concern was their next meal. The first step was to find somewhere for the children to sleep and food for them to eat. Hogg borrowed a few local co-op workers, and within two days had turned a neighbouring cottage into a dormitory. Having little cash, he established credit in the town and managed to buy millet and vegetables.

The next step was to make the collection of buildings look like an organised institution. Mud walls were built around the classrooms and dormitory to create a compound. Within this area vegetable gardens and basketball courts were laid out. One of the two classrooms was turned into a workshop, and another workshop was built within the compound from mud bricks and timber. Two caves were excavated from the soft soil of the cliff against which the school abutted.

One cave was the sleeping quarters and office of the headmaster. The other made do as a spare room for visitors. Cave living on the dry loess plains of northern China had been common for centuries, and continues to this day. Excavated from the soft soil of the mountains, caves provided cheap, easily insulated accommodation that could be expanded to meet the needs of a growing family. George Hogg was considered mad by the people of Shuangshipu for many of the things he did, but making a home in a cave was not one of them.

The buildings lay six hundred yards from the upper reaches of the Jialing River, a distant tributary of the Yangtse. Hogg saw it as an ideal source of fish, drinking water and a possible power supply. He begged, borrowed and bartered equipment for the workshops, and the school soon owned a new loom for making textiles, truck engines which were laid out on benches, a lathe driven by a small diesel engine, a model steam engine, a printing press and other machinery for paper-making.

The boys were aged between six and eighteen.* All had been touched by the war in one way or another. Some were refugees who had moved from the coastal areas to Hunan province. Others came from the province itself, as overcrowding and shortage of food forced poor families to send their elder children further into the interior to fend for themselves. All had stories to tell. One boy lost his mother while on a crowded ferry evacuating Shanghai, and had never seen either her or the rest of his family again. He had simply been cast adrift, and had eventually ended up in an orphanage. Four or five came from Manchuria, where the Japanese occupation had created a flood of refugees. They were all refugees, and their stories were those of every refugee in China: enforced flight from bombed-out homes, hunger, destitution and the loss of friends and families.

The boys were a complete mixture, and spoke varying dialects of Mandarin. Their backgrounds were as varied as their ages. There were big ones, small ones, some with middle-school education, others illiterate. The most marked differences were between the sharp-witted city boys from Manchuria and the coast and the

* Co-education was a social taboo in rural China, where girls were expected to remain in the family home and await a suitable marriage. After the war the Bailie school, then in Shandan, began to admit girls and to recruit women teachers.

slower, peasant children from the north-west. Once again Hogg was known to his school as 'Ho Ke'.

Hogg already knew Shuangshipu, whose name means 'twin rock village', as he had visited it while inspecting local co-operative organisations in his role as Ocean Secretary. He had also inspected the very school he was to take over, and had a good idea of the problems ahead. These problems were compounded by destitution in the town. The local population was competing with an influx of refugees for meagre food supplies. Many were close to starvation. A familiar story of ruinous deforestation had unfolded on the hillsides, where farmers had stripped the cover of conifers as they pushed their smallholdings to the summits to eke out a living. Deforestation ruined farming on mountain and in valley as the brief but violent summer rains cascaded into the lowlands, sweeping away crops and topsoil.

The heights around Shuangshipu may have created a formidable barrier to any advance by the Japanese forces, but there was a darker world in the mountains which terrified villagers, refugees and the whole school that Hogg was to take over. That world was brought to light by the most engaging of the itinerants who crossed Hogg's path. The American author and artist Graham Peck had already published *Through China's Wall* (1940), a part travel book, part history of northern China, and was writing his second book when he heard about an Englishman living in a cave in the north-west mountains. Fascinated by the idea, Peck asked Hogg if he could try cave life himself, and was allowed to move in for a while. In return he made a signal contribution to the co-operative cause by designing an earthenware crock which first cooled boiled water, and then kept it cool. Hogg reported that this greatly improved relations with the local Chinese, since it showed that ocean visitors with their high noses could actually make things that worked.

Researching local history and folklore, Peck uncovered a world of ghosts and mysterious powers that shaped the lives of the people of Shuangshipu. He described the peasant community of the mountains in his second book, *Two Kinds of Time* (1951):

Apart from the grinding poverty which kept them in rags, unwashed except at birth, marriage and death they suffered an unknown multitude of ills. None could afford the refugee doctor and there has never been a public health service here. Some limped, some walked sideways, some winced at every step, many had peculiarities that approached lunacy. But they knew nothing of the broken bones, the traumas or obsessions which handicapped them. The insides of their bodies and minds were a dark world, walled off as completely as they hoped to seal away the outer universe of supernatural threat.

The reason for the range of mental and physical ailments afflicting the local people lay in their extreme poverty and the resultant high rate of goitre. Caused by a deficiency of iodine, goitre leads to enlargement of the thyroid below the neck, resulting in large bulbous swellings below the jawline, especially in women. The lack of iodine and severe malnourishment which affected two out of every three families in the region produced a high birthrate of cretins, dwarfs and children suffering from other abnormalities.

Shuangshipu stood at the junction of the single road leading north from Chengdu, 320 miles away. The road divided at the town, with one fork leading north-east to Baoji, Xian and the communist territory centred on Yenan, while the other turned west into the mountains towards the capital of Gansu province, Lanzhou. The village straddled the banks of Chialing River, which flowed south-west on its journey to join the Yangtse. The river, the six-to-eight-thousand-foot mountains which girdled Shuangshipu and the isolated setting in the Tsingling mountains all proved a magnet for the endless tides of refugees that flowed from the coastal cities of the north-east through Xian heading south and west in search of a safe refuge. When George Hogg first visited the area in late 1939 the population was hardly more than a thousand. The number had trebled by the time he became the headmaster of the local CIC school, and it was to increase further as government troops moved into the area.

The town had a main street of shops, one or two inns and even a bank. Local co-operatives had rigged up a water-powered generator to provide streetlights, and there was a traditional bath-house in which weary travellers could soak away the aches and pains of the road.

The refugees, mainly from Honan and Hubei provinces, turned the main street into a permanent all-day market, with stalls selling cigarettes, food – mainly in the form of vegetables – and an array of cheap cloth. Amid the refugees who thronged the village by day were barbers, garage mechanics, builders and carpenters. Ironically, the refugees were much better off than most of the local peasants, who barely scratched a living in the hills; everything they could force from the barren soil – logs, kindling, bark, roots and the occasional scraggy sheep or chicken – was brought into town for the weekly market.

As spring turned to summer in 1942 the school began to take shape. The boys who had fled the chaos started to drift back. Soon there were thirty-five, and Hogg drew up a routine and a curriculum.

The school had two aims. The first was to take in young male refugees and educate them to a standard that would allow them to work in the village co-ops. The second was to recruit promising young boys already in co-operatives and teach them to read and write, and to improve whatever technical skills they had. Once familiar with the workings of basic machinery such as looms and generators, the boys would then be sent back to the co-ops as what Hogg called 'shock workers'.

Hogg was not surprised by the state of anarchy he found on arrival. Two of his adopted sons had been pupils at the school, and he measured its decline by the number of lice he found on their shirts. One week he squashed ninety-six lice on one shirt alone, and decided that burning the clothes was probably the easier option.

What did surprise him was the boys' strong antipathy towards the 'ocean devil' who was their new headmaster. Hogg's Mandarin was by now perfect, and although he spoke with a strong accent all the boys easily understood him. But they did not understand the system that he began to put in place. And they fought it. Most of them were strongly nationalistic, and attributed their troubled lives to the evils of foreign imperialism, both Japanese and Western.

Just as Hogg was an 'ocean devil', so his new rules were regarded as 'ocean principles'. Hogg met his critics head on: 'We had a few stormy sessions about opium wars, Foreign Concessions and such like but it all calmed down when they realised that, in spite of the respective height of our noses, we really saw eye to eye on these subjects. The main trouble comes from their past environment and from the fact that their previous deans [headmasters] of whom there have been seven in two years, have not understood the real purpose of the school.'

Hogg organised his pupils along lines that would be recognised in any English public school. He split the boys into three teams. Each elected a captain, who was responsible for looking after his team and making sure they got enough to eat, and that their occasional medical needs were seen to. The captain led group discussions in the dormitory at night, and drew up resolutions for discussion at the school general meeting on Saturday mornings.

School tasks were apportioned to the team captains, who handed them out as punishments to those who had broken the rules or behaved badly. Discipline was enforced by praising those who dressed smartly or had done well at their lessons, and by making it clear to malefactors that failure to fall in with the new regime would result in the school returning to anarchy.

The boys were given responsibility for six school committees, including those for food, sport, the library and the wall newspaper (where boys stuck up messages and comments about the school, to which Hogg and his fellow teachers responded). They also ran their own shop, where they could spend their small monthly allowance on towels, soap, toothbrushes, straw sandals, pencils and paintbrushes. These items were all made by local co-ops, and were in good supply. Other things like toothpaste were prohibitively expensive: the boys used salt instead.

The boys were consulted on, and asked to agree, every step of the reorganisation. The initial arguments were endless. Democracy worked, Hogg said, but it was far more trouble than dictatorship.

The new headmaster's second task was to reinstate the school curriculum and timetable. This was done without democratic discussion. The pupils were required to do five hours of classwork a day, plus three and a half hours' practical work in the school workshops or in neighbouring co-operatives. Lessons included Chinese language for the younger and less-educated boys, many of whom were illiterate. The more educated boys received lessons in accountancy, economics and advanced geography. All studied current affairs and received instruction in hygiene and first aid. In preparation for the workshop classes there were lessons in motor mechanics, with particular reference to the workings of the internal combustion engine and mechanical design.

Hogg himself took on the task of instilling discipline. He also taught English, economics and geography. In the early months of his leadership he spent much time motivating the small group of Chinese teachers who had returned.

His first act in impressing his authority on the school was to stop the boys taking a shortcut to the river across a neighbouring farmer's field. The farmer had objected, but he was ignored, and the villagers soon followed the boys in tramping over his land to the water's edge. The new headmaster identified the key trouble-makers, those whom he 'deemed quarrelsome, disobedient, time wasting', and made them dig up the path and build a stone wall at either end where it crossed the farmer's property. The farmer was suitably grateful, and the boys who had sweated over the project made sure that they and the villagers took another route to the river – or else they knew they would have to do the work all over again.

After a few months Hogg decided that the successful working of the school depended on getting the mix of pupils right. When it came to selecting new entrants – and there were always more applicants than places – he was not shy about social engineering. He decided that the majority of the pupils should be working-class, with an even balance between 'stolid peasant natives and quicker witted city lads'. Only 10 per cent should be 'student class' boys who had received some form of higher education due to their wealthier backgrounds.

Hogg reckoned that boys from a more privileged back-ground – although that term was relative in China at the time, and by no means implied a comfortable life – would pass on their bad habits, a 'long-nailed' attitude to working with their hands, and a sneaking admiration for non-productive bureaucratic officialdom. Sometimes, however, it was the 'long-nailed-attitude' boys who bucked the trend and turned out to be good leaders. Hogg cited one student who was 'an absolute pest of haughty unco-operative ways for the first months and then made a complete switchover to being easily the best boy in the school'.

The system worked. The school quickly returned to what counted as normalcy, although one major problem remained. It was one Hogg would wrestle with for the rest of his life. Democracy may have worked, but it did nothing to alleviate the bitter feuding between the two regional groups – the north-easterners and the north-westerners. The clashes along regional and class lines had paralysed the school from the outset. Teachers and successive heads had been unable to cope with the fiery mix of city boys and less-educated peasant boys from the remote north-west Gansu province. Staff as well as pupils divided into sectarian groups, and both came to treat the school as little more than a strange foreign charity to be used as a convenient bolthole from the war.

The north-easterners came from the industrially developed Manchuria region, which had long been open to foreign influence, and which had fallen to the Japanese in 1931. These boys were independent, individualistic, and had learned the importance of standing together in difficult times.

The north-westerners came from the poorest parts of China, many from Gansu province. They were regarded as backward country bumpkins, and they knew it. Class distinctions overlaid the regional differences. Middle-class boys from the coast were being asked to mix with native peasant boys from the hinterland.

The undercurrent of tension between these two groups surfaced in surprising areas of school life, and not just in scuffles in the dormitory. During the singing of an old Gansu folksong into which the whole school was putting great choral energy, a boy from the north-west region jumped up and brought the performance to a halt with a shout: 'They think they're so clever, don't they, copying our accent like that!'

Hogg realised that most of the children were subconsciously looking for the parents they had lost one way or another in the war, which had also parted him from his own family. His aim was to turn the school into a replacement family for the orphans in his charge. It became a family replacement for him as well.

> It involved at first a tremendous amount of time spent in listening to woes, patching cut knees, towelling dirty backs and rubbing in sulphur ointment. It involved even expensive things like sulphanilamide tablets, fish liver extract and sending boys to Xian to have their eyes tested ... [and to receive] thorough treatment for scabies, malaria, sore eyes and dysentery. Most people thought we were crazy but as far as I could see there was nothing crazier than paying for boys to be trained and then letting them get unhealthy or go away from school with no particular sense of loyalty.

Hogg's desire to be headmaster, father and mother to his pupils was not readily understood by the local population. When two of the boys were found to need circumcision, a doctor and two nurses arrived from Baoji with a black bag filled with cotton wool and sharp instruments. In spite of a local anaesthetic, one of the boys began screaming during the operation. A local peasant peered through the window to find out what was going on, and immediately reported to the population of Shuangshipu that the foreigners were castrating the boys to make them fat. The resulting furore only ended when the smiling victim of the operation presented himself to the townsfolk.

As the school grew, new staff joined the teaching team. Among them was an extraordinary Scotsman who was entirely in character with the eccentrics that Hogg attracted on his travels. Andy Braid had travelled to China as a Quaker to drive ambulances in the war zone. He had been loaned by the Friends'

Ambulance service to the north-west CIC, who in turn had passed him on to George Hogg.

Braid spoke no Chinese, but he had a language of his own that soon proved popular with the boys and staff. As a good Scotsman, he always travelled with his bagpipes. Having conquered the school with the wailings of this instrument, he followed up with lessons on highland fling, tap dancing and Scottish folk songs; he also did a turn on his mouth organ, producing a sound he termed American jazz.

The Scotsman's more official contribution was to spend hours each day explaining – always through an interpreter – the mysteries of cost accounting and truck engines. But his greatest triumph came the day that the school needed someone to castrate its pigs. Braid volunteered: 'Used to keep pigs myself in Scotland,' he said. 'I suppose Chinese pigs are the same. Let me do the job.' The awe of the students, who had previously imagined foreigners as good for nothing but sitting in motor cars and eating with forks, knew no bounds.

Hogg described the strange Scotsman in a letter home, and evidently received an incredulous reply that led him to explain Braid's role further.

He is tall and handsome and a jack of all trades besides being a master of some. He is a good accountant, farmer, bagpipe player, dancer (ballroom and highland), truck mechanic and teacher. He is an experienced nurse and runs the CIC clinic besides keeping all our boys so fit that they are a legend all round the neighbourhood . . . He is now going to marry a Chinese Hawaiian born girl who at present teaches social science.

To instil order into the school, the new headmaster introduced a daily regime which came as a shock to boys who had been used to getting up and attending lessons when they wanted to. Sixty years later Nieh Guanghan, or adoptive son No. 2, can still recall every moment of the new and arduous routine. 'We were woken at 6 a.m. by a teacher – usually the head – ringing a bell. We then walked to the river, taking a towel and a small bar of soap. We were given the towel but bought the soap from the shop. We were given two yuan a week pocket money. We washed our faces and then did our exercises.'

Hogg's version of the early-morning regime was: 'Everyone had to get up early and swim in the river, rub sulphur ointment into his scabies if he had any and get rid of the lice. Put to the poll, it turned out that sixty per cent of the boys believed lice to be natural to the human body. Health talks and swimming soon put this right.'

After the morning ablutions in the river, Hogg put the boys through what was then the mandatory regime at any English prep school – open-air exercises with much arm-swinging and jumping up and down. Breakfast was at 7.30 a.m., always *congi* (a Chinese rice porridge) with steamed bread. Sometimes there would be vegetables: cabbages, hot peppers and tomatoes, depending on what was in the garden.

From Nieh's recollection, the regime appears a great deal more rigorous than that of the average English prep school: 'At the end of breakfast we all had to raise our heads and open our mouths and Hogg came round with a small syringe and squirted in drops of Vitamin A. After breakfast classes started at 8 a.m. We worked until twelve. I cannot remember a break, we just worked through the morning without stop, and then had lunch. It was usually the same food as breakfast – rice and vegetables.'

After lunch the lessons became practical, with boys working on the machinery in the workshops from 1 to 4 p.m. Then there was ninety minutes of sports, either volleyball or basketball. At 5.30

the evening meal was served – more rice and vegetables. The 7 to 9 period was for evening study, and at nine the boys were packed off to the dormitory. There was no electricity, and the evening homework was done by the light of gas lamps and candles. Kerosene was in short supply, so once the boys were in the dormitory, the candles and lamps were extinguished.

No variance from the school routine was allowed. Like his boys, Hogg became superbly fit. He rose at 5 o'clock every morning, joined the school for thirty minutes' exercise at 7 a.m., and throughout the day either walked or bicycled wherever he had to go. He thought nothing of cycling twenty or thirty miles to a meeting. By 10 p.m. the headmaster and his school would be asleep.

Above all else, the school sang. Every day in between lessons, or sometimes instead of evening homework, there would be choir practice. Hogg taught the school to sing as a choir, and personally coached the more talented boys.

Some sixty years later, when asked what it was they remembered most clearly about their adoptive father-cum-headmaster his sons unanimously agreed: it was his love of singing and the way in which he used songs as a communal language in the school. Son No. 1, Nieh Guangchun, said: 'Songs were the language we all spoke. There were many different dialects at the school, and sometimes it was hard to understand other boys, but when we were singing we all understood each other. We always sang together almost every day, everyone joined in. He taught us all the English nursery songs, revolutionary songs, anti-Japanese songs and Chinese traditional songs. He made up songs for us. He sang with us as much as he could. The first English we learnt was by singing the language. He taught us English songs but he also collected old folk songs from wherever he travelled, and he would bring them back to us and teach us how to sing them.' Almost the first question asked of a new boy was whether he knew any good songs.

The only instrument the school possessed was an *erhu*, a two-string fiddle played by hand rather than with a bow. Hogg became an accomplished *erhu* player, and built up a repertoire of folk songs, holding the tunes in his head – they were never written down, because he could not write music.

Hogg managed to squeeze a further duty for his pupils into this packed regime. Everyone had to help with improving the school grounds. Picks and spades were bought so that the boys could work competitively in gangs. No one was excused. The 'old boys' agreed that the hard work was a shock at first, and led to some muttering about the mad ways of the ocean devil, but that it gave them a sense of order and security.

This was a six-day-a-week regime. On Sundays there was little let-up, with either a hiking expedition into the mountains or swimming lessons in the river. The mountain hikes were an education for the city boys from the coast, although they took the boys from Gansu province into the familiar world of the spirits and supernatural powers that inhabited the high country. On their day-long walks the school party would find that the heaped graves of the dead and the shrines raised to appease the local spirits easily outnumbered the homes of the living they passed. The graves and shrines were always placed at a particular point on the mountainside, a strange rock or an indentation in the ground, where local people could infer some hidden meaning or some message from the spirits.

The boys from peasant families in Gansu province came from family backgrounds which gave credence to the world of the supernatural and ancestor worship. The weekend hikes would always include a lengthy break around a hillside tomb for a discussion of the traditions of the local people. In these talks the country boys from Gansu always outshone the city slickers from the coast.

Hogg won the trust of the boys because he joined in their activities. He sang with them, swam in the river with them, played sport with them and walked in the mountains with them. He was consciously creating a sense of family for children many of whom were orphans or had little hope of seeing their parents again; and he recognised that he too was in search of what he had left behind in England: family and friends, and the chance to marry and have children of his own. 'One way or another the family making process worked ... after all if the kids were subconsciously searching for their parents ... we were subconsciously searching for children too,' he wrote.

He described the school spirit and the sense of family on the last leg of a fifty-mile two-day hike back to the school across the Tsingling mountains one weekend:

Walking together, camping together, swimming together in new and exciting pools, sometimes going hungry together and often marching until we were hot and tired, arriving in a new place together, performing our songs in front of strange people and inspecting many new co-ops which were all part of our 'family', all this did something to the school. As, rounding a corner on the last stretch of our homeward journey, we caught sight of our own particular mountain with the school lying snug beneath it, a spontaneous cheer went up that afterwards made all of us feel very warm and proud. From that day I knew we would make something of the school.

The traditional punishment in the school was being made to kneel in front of the national flag, a white sun with twelve rays projected against a red background. In the heat of the midday sun this was a cruel trial. Hogg stopped the practice.

But there was no lack of discipline. Hogg was remembered for being strict during lessons. He insisted on good classroom behaviour, which he defined as paying attention and being polite to both the teacher and fellow pupils. Boys would be made to stand up and explain themselves if they transgressed. Hogg did not tolerate breaking of the rules outside the classroom, either. Of one incident he said:

One afternoon we had all been down to the river making a sand map of Asia with real seas and rivers. To finish things off we all took big stones and bombed Japan until it sank under the water. One of the pupils liked the idea so much that he took to bombing the peasants' ducks on the theory that they were Japanese submarines. This was strictly against orders and he soon found himself sitting with all his clothes on in the river. The howling was terrific and lasted nearly all day but it was a milestone.

The headmaster, his teaching staff, his adopted sons and all the children at the school regularly came down with malaria. This was regarded as an occupational hazard for anyone working in western China at the time, and the routine treatment was large doses of quinine. If a boy's temperature stayed above 106 for more than twenty-four hours he would be loaded onto a handcart and pushed over the Tsingling mountains to the hospital in Baoji, a journey that took between six and eight hours of backbreaking labour.

Unexpectedly, Hogg found that the staff posed bigger problems than the boys. The Bailie school was a break with educational tradition, both Chinese and Western. The biggest difference was that the boys were given responsibility for running their own committees, which gave them some control over the management of the school. The Chinese clung to their own traditions and those they had inherited from the West with tenacity. These called for a top-down approach to school management, and a punishment regime for pupils. They regarded Hogg's approach as heresy.

The problem was summed up by a conversation that Hogg recorded with a forty-one-year-old teacher called K'ang, who complained: 'The boys here are unruly. They don't understand correct school manners.'

Hogg replied, 'That's true. I hope that teacher K'ang will do his best to help them do so.'

'If they don't understand manners then there is no point in our trying to teach them. We need hardly be expected to sacrifice our own spiritual energy to that extent.' With that he turned on his heel and left the school.

In dealing with his staff, the new headmaster could on occasion prove ruthless. One Chinese teacher was asked to leave after going into the dormitory at night and beating boys who had not done their homework with a ruler. This was normal behaviour in Chinese schools at the time, and the boys expected and accepted such discipline. George Hogg did not. The matter was discussed at the weekly meeting, and the teacher was fired.

Hogg also sacked the school bursar, who had attempted to 'borrow' sixteen thousand yuan (about US$800) in the first year of his headmastership. The bursar was reduced 'into blubbing' by Hogg, and forced to admit his crime. The money had been recovered, and the bursar begged for his apologies to be accepted and the matter forgotten, but Hogg would have none of it. He questioned him until he finally confessed that he wanted to be a professional musician, and needed the money to buy instruments. Hogg fired the unfortunate man, casting him adrift in wartime China with little prospect of employment other than joining the army.

Hogg saw the bursar's light-fingered approach to the school

funds as symptomatic of a deep-rooted national malaise. Maybe it was, but his unforgiving reaction smacked of priggish intolerance. It was an unattractive side to his character, inherited from his mother, that occasionally emerged in his correspondence with her. He himself probably recognised this, because his letters home justifying his treatment of the bursar are decidedly defensive:

When everything is shifting, uncertain, people aren't the same day to day, money and prices aren't the same day to day – what happens to the mores? ... There is something to be said for making each man carry his own standards inside him and to hell with what other people say.

From then on he and the boys did the accounts themselves. There was much celebration when the school could show a small profit on the sale of blankets, shoes and paper to other co-ops.

While trying to improve the moral standards of his teachers and change their educational conservatism, Hogg faced criticism from government officials who attacked the whole concept of industrial co-operatives. He found it ironic that while US journalists were hailing the industrial revolution taking place in hundreds of Chinese villages as a blueprint for the future, Chinese officials were using the press to damn the transplantation of small-scale industries to the rural areas as an unfortunate wartime necessity. Hogg was blunt: 'If Indusco is really only a wartime expedient then a school to train co-operative leaders for the future is meaningless.'

For two and a half years, from March 1942 to December 1944, Hogg lived in a mountain cave overlooking Shuangshipu. It was, he explained to his mother, half cave and half house. The house extension was made of a wooden frame with large windows, with paper taking the place of glass. No one could actually see out, but at least some light could get in. After a year the ultimate luxury in cave furniture arrived from Xian: a pane of real glass, allowing a real window on the outside world.

The window made it easier to see the great problem of cave life: fleas. Fleas were a problem for the whole school. The boys had been taught how to delouse themselves by careful inspection after washing in the river, but fleas were a different matter. The war against them took a year of radical action: the floors of the caves were covered in lime, the school's two puppies were bathed and disinfected, and the chickens killed and eaten. Still the fleas thrived. Tins of Keating's insect powder were scrounged from friends in distant cities; the fleas lapped it up and came back for more. A university chemical expert was asked for advice, and said that fleas could not stand salt; bags of salt weighing hundreds of pounds were bought from the local market and mashed into the cave floors by foot. Local farmers who called at the school occasionally for medical treatment were horrified at the sight of so much waste. Most of them had to eat hot peppers as a substitute for salt, and suffered from goitre accordingly.

Finally the *kang*, or mudbrick bed, which half filled the cave, and which had proved a haven for rats, was broken up and the rubble spread over the garden. At the same time Hogg and his boys invented their own steam steriliser, into which clothes could be dropped before bathing. The plague of fleas began to die out.

But the rats did not. They developed a taste for the flour-based paste that had been used to glue paper to the ceiling of the caves, and at night they would scuttle up and gnaw through the paper roof. Ever the enthusiast for new ideas, Hogg decided to cut pretty shapes around the ceiling rat-holes, and to add to the effect by circling them with red paint. This highly artistic addition to the caves confirmed the general view in Shuangshipu that the ocean devil on their doorstep was more than a little mad.

The only other cave decorations were photographs pinned to the walls, mostly of famous visitors who had become Hogg's friends. Henry Luce and his fashionably tailored wife Clare Booth Luce were snapped in front of a towel-making co-operative in Baoji, and a head-and-shoulders shot of the beautiful Nym Wales, otherwise Mrs Peg Snow, and Ida Pruitt with a group of American-Chinese engineers she had bought out to work with the co-op movement also joined the gallery.

There was no such thing as a headmaster's study; the cave was where Hogg slept, lived, worked, wrote his letters and received visitors. The whitewashed walls were complemented by a wooden desk in front of the window and a Buddha statue placed on it to catch the light. Niches were dug into the walls of the cave in the shape of cathedral windows, and in each Hogg placed bearded statues of 'unknown contemporaries of Marco Polo' which had been unearthed when a new moat had been excavated around Luoyang. Whoever these unknown contemporaries were, they certainty attracted the attention of missionary visitors to the cave, many of whom left muttering about heathen idolatry.

Hogg had taken over a school of thirty-five pupils in the spring of 1942, and by autumn of that year the number had risen to sixty. News of the school's successful relaunch had reached co-operatives over a wide area, and they began volunteering to send their bright young members to Shuangshipu to learn industrial practice. As Hogg's boys honed their mechanical skills, so the Bailie school at Shuangshipu developed into both a school and a training centre.

In the summer of 1942 a number of the older boys were sent to Chengdu, the provincial capital of eastern Sichuan, to be trained on new machinery. They returned in the autumn, bringing with them the component parts of a new machine that was to become an obsession with Hogg for the rest of his life.

We are just beginning to get the important machinery set up here now and to get our boys back from Chengdu . . . It is quite a moment in the school's history. It meant a lot to us in the early days to send our best students to Chengdu just when we had got them licked into shape, and to take raw new ones on. Now we have got those trained up pretty well and the old ones are coming back so the school as a whole is feeling strong.

The important new equipment was a Ghosh cotton-milling machine, which was used to produce wool and cotton. It had originally been made in India and shipped in crates to China via the Burma road. Weighing over two tons, the huge contraption would not fit into the school's workshops, but was housed by the river, where Hogg planned to provide power from waterwheels. A group of refugees was put to work digging a channel branching off the main river to provide sufficient flow to turn the wheels. This was a complex technical exercise, but Hogg and his team ultimately got the machines working, drawing power from the river, and began turning out textiles that would equal anything produced by the city factories – or so he claimed. But no sooner had the machine clanked into action than flooding wrecked it. It was not until late 1944 that Hogg could finally report that the wheels were again turning out real power for the co-op.

Apart from sectarian feuding among the pupils and the constant search for new staff, the initial problems facing the new head were money and food. All funds allocated for the school were sent from CIC headquarters in Chongqing to the regional HQ at Baoji. Getting the money from there was always a nightmare. On occasions in the summer of 1942 Hogg would have to ride his bicycle sixty miles over the Qinling mountain pass down into Baoji, plead and argue for his money, and then cycle back the same day. He was able to do the round trip in a single day by hanging onto the back of lorries while riding up the pass between the two towns. The return journey was always by night. Twice he was ambushed by bandits, but outpaced them on his bike.

Money was so tight that the school often had to borrow cornmeal from local traders. They would advance him just enough for one meal for every pupil, so that for months the school lived hand to mouth. Famine was always close at hand. Not far from the school, price controls had been placed upon tree roots and bark, which were the only things the people had to sell or to eat.

Hogg operated on the basis that the school would only survive if it used every available resource. That included the human tide of refugees who flooded into the hinterland as the Japanese 'Three All' campaign – 'Kill all, burn all, destroy all' – made great swathes of rural areas uninhabitable. The campaign had been launched in 1942 against the communist base area, and had reduced the population under communist control from forty million to an estimated twenty-five million in twelve months. The Japanese tactics had been a major cause of famine in the neighbouring Honan province, and throughout 1942 several thousand refugees camped on the far side of the river from the school.

Having recruited labourers from among the refugees to dig out the river channels for his waterwheels, Hogg also set them to work in the mountains rebuilding a disused lime kiln, felling what little timber was left, and planting more vegetable patches along the riverbanks. Some of the refugees turned out to be masons, and their skills were used to make stone hammers for pounding out bricks from dried mud.

Hogg had become headmaster, at the age of twenty-seven, of a school that even by the chaotic standards of China at that time presented huge problems. But he relished the challenges, and he rose to them. It was as if everything he had experienced before in his life had prepared him for the task of disciplining, schooling and nurturing a group of unruly Chinese war orphans.

Quite apart from his enthusiasm and his ability to mix in with the boys, he possessed one supreme attribute that his surviving old boys remembered many years later: he took huge pleasure in what he was doing. He was happy, he was enjoying himself, and he communicated that sense of joy to all around him. A letter in 1942 sums up his mood.

> *Dear mother*
>
> *Today is happy. Which, apart from the fine weather, the noise of the river where it swirls around the new concrete piles of the about-to-be bridge, the corn getting tall but not yet yellow, our peach tree covered with spherical green objects about 2" in diameter – apart from all this – probably means that I am happy. Which may or may not be due to the state of the moon ... Coffee may also have something to do with it as I had some for breakfast mixed with bean milk. Absence of indigestion – for the first time since a bout of malaria three weeks ago – certainly has a lot to do with it; the indigestion suddenly announced its absence quite surprisingly last night, after I had dragged my unwilling, gurgling, wind begetting stomach a couple of miles upstream to the Ghosh place and arrived there just in time to sit down to an outdoor supper of home caught fish, home grown potatoes and 'squash' or 'kua' of some kind.*

Food is a constant theme in his letters. It must have been tantalising for his family in England, where rationing had reduced the diet of all but the very rich and the very young (the latter doing well on cod liver oil and orange juice), to read how the school's kitchen was developing such a varied diet for the boys and their masters.

Eating is good these days. Tomatoes in the garden still going strong. Corned beef presented by embassy friend still unfinished. Waffle machine just bought from retiring missionary went into action today using whites of eggs separately beaten as a leavening agent. Potatoes in season. Bean milk always a good stand-by. Honey from the Tibetan border district is very pure and white – much better than the local brand which is largely frustrated with malt, adulterated I mean, how stupid of me.

In June 1942 Hogg's observations in a letter home about the problems of wet feet show just how at home he was in his remote corner of China.

I am fat and robust and happy. It is a noteworthy and memorable fact that only people who try and live like foreigners ... find life difficult here. Take wet feet for example, wet roads, slushy paths, no taxis, buses etc. no good shoes, no galoshes nowhere to dry your shoes when you get home. What would you do? Try and make the best of things and worry about 'it wouldn't be like this in England'? No ... Buy yourself a pair of cloth sandals that grip the mud, don't wear any socks, go out and frankly splash through all the puddles you can see. Cover your feet in lovely squelchy mud. Have a good time ... nothing could be healthier or nicer.

Later that month his family in Harpenden received a description of life in wartime China that must have seemed idyllic compared to that in Britain.

The gramophone alternately playing Ave Maria, Chevalier and some piece by HM Coldstream guards ... our hen now nearing her 21st day of sitting on eggs clacking deprecatingly at food placed before her ... a mass of little boys learning to do the highland fling to the tune of a Chinese folk song, two puppies rolling around and barking at each other's fleas, somebody digging the vegetables ... altogether quite like home. Not very like Wayfarings but still a home. No women so everything in a bit of a mess.

The recurring problem was malaria. But Hogg found the disease's cyclical attacks fascinating, and described them in detail:

First an ache in the finger joints and an inclination to eat more than usual. Then the first spinal shivers. I always feel particularly adventurous around this time like waiting for a great friend on a railway station ... Once I was down at the machine shop when it came – a boiling hot summer's day and they were smelting iron. I stood as close to the furnace as I could get with the sun on my back and was I cold! But of course when it's really got going there is nothing fascinating any more. That's when one begins to feel homesick.

China's not really much of a place. After all I've been here seven years now. It's been very interesting but I can't hope to do anything. They never really trust us.

At the height of his malaria attacks Hogg's feverish dreams would turn to fantasies about being back in England surrounded by the comforts of home: 'choc ices, shredded wheat on Sunday evenings, reading in front of the radio, eclipse of the moon seen from mother's bedroom ... a longing to be at home. And never coming back to China.' But once he was better he decided that 'perhaps there is no need to be going home just yet'. And to reassure his parents he added: 'You must not get the idea that I am malaria ridden. I only have it about once a year and can always stop it pretty quick. It is of the every-other-day variety which gives one time to recuperate and counterattack.'

In the background, Rewi Alley was working to support the school and keep Hogg in touch with the complex and hostile politics between the two partners in the united front government. He often stayed in one of the school caves at Shuangshipu and spent time with the boys, although he did not teach them.

Alley was careful to disguise his homosexuality both at the time and later in his writings, and even promoted the idea that he had been engaged to a woman back home in New Zealand. Hogg's ignorance of Alley's sexuality and the issue it raised in the environment of a boys' school emerges in an uncomfortable passage in his book, where he describes a typical scene in Alley's cave:

Boys looking at picture magazines and asking millions of questions. Boys playing the gramophone and singing out of tune. Boys doing gymnastics off Rewi's shoulders or being held upside down. Boys being given enemas, or rubbing sulphur ointment into each other's scabies. Boys standing in brass washbasins and splashing soapy water about. Boys toasting bare bottoms against the stove (the scar across Rewi's own nether portions testifies to his own indulgence in this form of amusement). Boys pulling the hairs on Rewi's legs, or fingering the generous proportions of the foreigner's nose. 'Boys are just the same anywhere,' says Rewi. 'Wouldn't these kids have a swell time in New Zealand!'

That could not have been written by anyone who had an inkling that Alley was homosexual. Hogg was naturally generous and open, but also in many ways naïve.

Years later, when I discussed the issue of Alley's homosexuality with the old boys, there was much shaking of heads at questions about whether this might have led to sexual abuse. Hogg's old girlfriend Xiao Ren, who knew Alley and the school well, was also adamant that he had not abused the boys in any way. She pointed out that in the closed environment of the school it would quickly have become apparent to Hogg.

NINE

Journey Over the Mountains

'Oh boy! Oh boy! Oh boy!'

From March 1942 Hogg immersed himself in rebuilding his school, recruiting new staff and increasing the number of pupils. He still travelled, but not as widely as before, and almost always in search of supplies or funds. But he yearned for news of the world beyond the boundaries of school life. Such news, even news of what was happening in China, was hard to come by.

He had been able to listen in to the BBC while in Baoji, but he found that the service contained just as much boring propaganda as did most sources in China: 'The British radio news is now obtainable here through a co-op radio set but it consists of nothing but bombs and spitfires. For some reason the Philippines radio station has also taken to [broadcasting] British Reuters service so nothing from there either. Of course propaganda is all very well and proper but I would like to get other kinds of propaganda, interpretive propaganda for a change.'

His source of information about what was going on in China was limited to local papers, which merely repeated wholly fictitious government handouts issued from Chongqing. News from passing travellers proved unreliable. Letters from home were full of family gossip and news about life in wartime Britain, but they sometimes took a year to arrive.

Hogg's own letters reflect his obsessive interest in the school. The articles he continued to submit to the *Manchester Guardian* either concerned the CIC movement, or were human interest stories based on the lives of ordinary Chinese people.

The huge shift in the strategic balance in both Asia and Europe created by the Japanese attack on Pearl Harbor on 7 December 1941, and the US entry into the war, went, if not unnoticed by Hogg, certainly unremarked. In his book he never refers to the political struggle taking place within China, or the strategic conflict beyond its shores. The world he described was that of the ordinary Chinese caught up in a catastrophic war. Yet Pearl Harbor was to be one of the deciding factors in shaping the outcome of the Sino–Japanese war and, as importantly, of the conflict between nationalists and communists.

From the start of the war with Japan in the summer of 1937 until Pearl Harbor, China had fought alone. Chiang Kai-shek's united front government, formed in the aftermath of the Japanese attack on Shanghai, had received expressions of support and limited loans from Western powers, and coverage in the Western press had been consistently hostile to Japan. But the only practical aid had come from the Soviet Union.

Stalin was anxious to keep the war going. Japanese involvement in a long-term conflict in China removed its threat to Russian borders. As Moscow realised early on, Japanese action in China also provided a strategic opportunity for Mao's Communist Party.

Pearl Harbor changed everything. The war in China was suddenly seen in Washington and London as part of the global struggle against the Axis powers. The Allied powers set up a new theatre of war embracing China, Burma and India, and placed

Chiang Kai-shek as supreme commander of the Chinese front.

The Generalissimo drew two lessons from the strategic importance the Allies now attached to the Far East. Firstly, he could count on hugely increased US aid. Secondly, he could now afford to let the Allies take on the burden of the war against Japan. This would allow the nationalist leadership to concentrate on its real enemy – the communists. Chiang Kai-shek had never hidden his view that Mao's CCP was always the more dangerous enemy: 'The Japanese are a disease of the skin, the communists a disease of the heart,' he said.

The KMT forces had deployed at various times between 150,000 and 500,000 of its best troops in blockading Mao's Eighth Route Army in its northern base at Yenan. This was to become a major source of friction with the man Washington sent as Chiang's chief of staff, General Joseph Stilwell. 'Vinegar Joe', so called because of his brusque manner, had been well known and liked by Agnes Smedley and her 'gang' in Hankow, where he had been US military attaché. He would certainly have heard their revulsion at the corruption of the nationalist government, and probably shared it.

The relationship between Chiang and his senior American adviser started in bitterness and ended in hatred. Chiang refused to allow the US military to train his officers, or to strengthen his army in the fight against the invaders. He feared a coup if his command was strengthened with freshly trained officers, and preferred to stick to the corrupt military elite who were bound to him by feudal loyalties and business deals. His reluctance to wage all-out war against the Japanese was grounded in his belief that the real threat lay elsewhere. Let America take on Japan, let barbarian fight barbarian, was very much Chiang's tactic after Pearl Harbor. He would wait for the final confrontation with the CCP.

Throughout 1942 the sham of the united front government became more apparent as the government organised fresh purges of known communist supporters. Chiang Kai-shek's strategy was to seek increased US aid while avoiding a showdown with the Japanese. Mao's communists played the same game, manoeuvring for US support and avoiding costly confrontations with the invader.

Both nationalists and communists were strengthening their positions while they awaited the inevitable conflict. On the face of it Chiang's situation was far stronger. He was the internationally recognised leader of a sovereign government. His army of several million was receiving American equipment and support. His communist enemies were blockaded in an impoverished area of north China. And as Chinese leader he had a seat at the negotiating table, even if well below the salt, at which Roosevelt, Churchill and Stalin plotted the course of the war and its aftermath.

The deteriorating relations within the united front government, and the increasing and fully justified paranoia among Chiang's top commanders about the growing strength of the communists, were to have consequences for the school in the remote Tsingling mountains. George Hogg's role in the CIC, his connection with Rewi Alley and the liberal sympathies that surfaced in his journalism, led him too to become a suspect.

In the spring of 1944 the Japanese returned to large-scale ground operations, launching half a million men from north China across the Yellow River. Armoured and infantry divisions rolled south to cross the Yangtse and drive on to Changsha, the burnt-out capital of Hunan province. From there the Japanese fought a bitter battle for the city of Hengyang, with its major US airbase. By July the city had fallen, and the Japanese had driven a north–south wedge through China.

Relations between Chiang and Stilwell collapsed in acrimony.

In an angry letter to the Generalissimo, Roosevelt demanded that Stilwell be placed in charge of Chinese forces. Chiang, equally angered, fought back. In October the American officer was recalled to Washington.

The success of the Japanese offensive forced the government troops to retreat west. It seemed natural that after their success the Japanese would turn west and north to attack both nationalists and communists. Xian, Baoji and even George Hogg's remote base in Shuangshipu were now threatened.

From the end of 1943 the pressure on Hogg from local KMT commanders had intensified. The Bailie school at Luoyang had closed following the arrest and imprisonment of its directors. Half the students fled to join the Eighth Route Army, while the remainder were taken to Shuangshipu and placed in Hogg's school. Much the same happened to the CIC-run school in Baoji, which in any case had been bombed to a virtual standstill.

In retrospect it is surprising that George Hogg managed to keep his school going as long as he did. The Japanese were within striking distance, the local KMT commanders were determined to conscript any boy over the age of sixteen, and Hogg himself was politically suspect in the eyes of the government.

Recruiting was a major problem for the nationalists. The inhumane treatment of new recruits meant that many more died from malnutrition and disease than in action against the enemy. It was a standard KMT tactic to deploy recruits as far from their home areas as possible, to avoid desertion. Despite this, thousands of nationalist troops could be found on the roads near any front line, heading away from the fighting and towards their homes.

KMT officers had already raided schools in Baoji and Luoyang. Clearly Shuangshipu would be next. In the past eighteen months there had been a number of visits to the Bailie school by KMT officers trying to persuade the older boys to join the nationalists' youth wing. They were only interested in boys over the age of sixteen, and at that stage there were only a handful of the sixty pupils old enough.

Hogg always turned these visits around by arguing that the cause of the anti-Japanese war was better served by training boys to make the co-operatives work more efficiently. At this time the co-ops were turning out basic weapons and ammunition for the military, so the argument had some force. But with each visit the message became clearer: sooner or later the older boys would be taken away to the war.

The showdown came early in the summer of 1944, when ten of the most senior boys were ordered to leave and join the local army unit. Hogg refused to let them go. He was arrested, and taken first to the KMT garrison at Shuangshipu, and then to a military compound in Baoji.

Rewi Alley worked hard to secure Hogg's release, making use of the facts that the school was internationally funded and carried the name of a prominent American missionary. He also pointed out that Hogg was a British passport-holder, and the Chinese government was a wartime ally of Britain and America.

Hogg was released after a week, but from then on he secretly began to plan the school's flight to safety. The reason was not just KMT pressure. In the summer of 1944, as the Allies opened a second front against Nazi Germany following the D-Day landings in Normandy, Japanese troops struck deeper into northwest China. The area around Luoyang was overrun, threatening scores of co-operatives in the region. Ida Pruitt raised funds in the United States to help evacuate the co-operatives' staff and machinery, but as usual the money got no further than CIC headquarters in Chongqing. A Japanese advance on Xian now seemed likely. If that ancient city fell, life at Shuangshipu would be untenable. Apart from the safety of the school's staff and boys, the KMT had made it clear that they would need all the buildings in and around the town for barracks.

The question was, where to go? One course of action would be to take the whole school and its equipment into Eighth Route Army territory. This meant crossing the KMT lines, which would be extremely difficult given the number of pupils and the amount of equipment involved. The possibility of moving the school to Yenan in the event of a Japanese breakthrough had been considered as early as 1942. Rewi Alley had mooted the move with Chou En-lai, who was then in Chongqing. He was not enthusiastic. Evacuating the school to the communist capital would confirm the suspicions of the government, and put an end to foreign funding for the whole co-operative movement.

By chance the British biochemist Dr Joseph Needham was heading to the Yumen oilfield in the north-west of Gansu in mid-1944, and passed through Shuangshipu. Needham was director of a Sino-British organisation for scientific co-operation in Chongqing, and was researching his pioneering work on Chinese science.* He joined Hogg and Alley for supper in the cave; in honour of their distinguished guest, corncob, bread and honey were served. Afterwards they examined the map together. Western Gansu seemed as far away from the war as they were likely to

---

* Needham's research sought to resolve a question that has long puzzled historians. Why was it that despite immense Chinese scientific achievements in the past, the industrial and scientific revolutions took place in Europe, and not in China? The resulting multi-volume work was published by Cambridge University Press from 1954 onwards. Needham's project won international acclaim, and he was hailed by the scientific community as the greatest Sinologist of the twentieth century. Throughout his academic life he worked at Gonville and Caius College, Cambridge; he was Master there from 1966 to 1976. He died in 1995, aged ninety-five.

get. KMT control of the region was weak, and the area was mostly under the control of a Muslim warlord, Ma Bufang.

In the late summer of 1944 Alley left to reconnoitre the region while Hogg quietly began to plan the move. He never doubted the boys' willingness to accompany him, even though it was obvious that the seven-hundred-mile journey would have to be made in the winter months. His letters home reveal that he always intended to give them the choice of whether or not to go with him, as indeed he did when the time came.

Kathleen Hogg at home in Harpenden could never contain her worries about her youngest son. The rest of the family was safe, although scattered around England in various teaching jobs. The war in Europe had entered its final stage, but the conflict in the Far East seemed to be getting worse. Her letter in the summer of 1944 raises all her old questions: Was he happy working with a school full of orphans in the Chinese mountains? Why was he living in a cave? And was he eating properly?

He tried to reassure her:

Yes I like the boys. They stop me getting too cynical! Tell Dorothy [his former sister-in-law] that one has to be cynical or blind to be here just now, but that I am fully aware of the danger. I have a very strong fundamental belief in boys. You say why live in a cave? well you come and try. It's cheaper to build, stronger, cooler in summer, warmer in winter, more rat proof, and more adaptable (you can dig a shelf whenever you want, add an extra cubby-hole or cupboard etc etc) . . . Don't worry. I am healthier than ever I was . . . the sons, grandsons to you, are all here in S'pu now. They are all good guys and coming along fast. The two in school are really first class guys and will do a lot of 'good-in-the-world' later. No 3 suffers from his upbringing and apt to tell a lot of fibs, but he is getting to be very good too, and is enormously healthy now. He goes to school every day and sleeps in the cave with me. We both get up at 5am. No 4 lives with some people in the village below ... today it is quite hot here and I went for my first swim although the boys have been in three times already. After swimming they all went off and caught a lot of shrimps and three crabs then I was called upon to supply the cash for 2 lbs of flour and they made shrimp and crab fritters for supper. This went down well. It is awful to have to live off rice all the time but flour is very expensive here. The boys are all northerners and just as used to eating flour as I am – they don't like eating rice all the time either. But it can't be helped. War, you know, war. But don't worry about me, I eat a lot of stuff, [Needham] is here and I take a good foreign breakfast with him every day including porridge etc. The orange season is on so I am revelling in oranges. Actually we all live a lot better than you people do I should think.

He was probably right. With a diet based on vegetables, rice and fruit, the pupils and staff at his school ate better than most in Britain. The school kitchen even made dim sum on occasion: Hogg went in to lunch one day and 'found all the boys in the kitchen making the best beloved dishes of all Chinese home cooking – sort of baby suet puddings, each one consisting of three or four bites, with meat, vegetables and spices wrapped up inside and steamed. My no 2 son beats all records for the quantity of these puddings he can make at one sitting.'

Mealtimes were now being used to accustom the boys to the idea that their idyllic life was coming to an end. 'Eat up, we shall not be here much longer,' was the way the headmaster began to prepare the ground. He wrote home to warn his parents that Rewi Alley was pushing for a move as well: 'He isn't exactly a pessimist but he is taking a firmly prophetic view that the nips are coming and soon.'

Questions began to be asked as to how and whether the school could take their newly planted apple trees, and whether the goats would stand up to the trip. In any case, where were they going? No one knew.

Alley's constant warnings about the need to move began to irritate Hogg:

> *The trouble is we have about 15 tons of essential machinery apart from other things and no trucks – only two carts and not enough mules to go around. So I sometimes feel like bashing him [Alley]. But of course it won't do any good, his mind just works that way. It is an accommodating mind when it hits a rock, like 'no trucks'; it flows around it and goes on to apple trees and goats . . . eventually it will spring a surprise and say 'we don't need trucks anyway I have got six army transport planes coming along tomorrow.'*

After breakfast one day at the end of August, Hogg summoned a meeting of all pupils and staff. He told them that the KMT local commanders were determined to recruit any boy over the age of sixteen. That and the threat of a Japanese advance meant the school would have to move. The boys listened in silence. When it was explained, with the aid of a rough map, where it was planned to move the school, there was uproar. Some of the pupils argued that it was too far – a journey to the edge of the world, as one put it. Zhi Fu Zhang, aged sixteen at the time, remembers Hogg writing three words in English on a blackboard: 'Where?' 'Why?' 'How?'. He said: 'Hogg answered these questions for us, and we understood why we had to go – but the older boys were a little unhappy.'

Hogg shared the general misgivings. Alley had returned to describe the wonders of a small town he had discovered in the Gansu corridor, on the edge of the Gobi desert. It was called Shandan, and it had plenty of empty temples and only a small population. To Hogg it seemed a very long way to go to start all over again.

In his book *At 90: Memoirs of my Years in China* (1987), Alley reports that Hogg was ecstatic at the news of the move. In fact he wasn't. Like many other memoirs written at the end of a long and eventful life, Alley's are highly selective and self-serving. Besides, the school was in good shape, and the Ghosh machine was finally coming on stream after two years of hard work and false starts. Hogg dug his heels in. In September he complained: 'And now, just as we've built a nice new motor road up to the school, and got the waterwheel here running, it looks as if we will be moving away pretty soon; and have to start all over again, in more difficult surroundings! It is rather discouraging . . .'

The mood was very much the same in October: 'And have we got to leave all this now and go up to Shandan where there is nothing and begin all over again? Seems as if we have, but we will hold onto this place for as long as possible. It's too much a part of us all just to let it go like that before any little nippers have come very near.'

By this time, however, KMT harassment was becoming unbearable, and Alley was constantly encouraging Hogg to face the inevitable. Troops from the local garrison had set up road-blocks around the village, and were forcing peasants to offload supplies of valuable goods such as charcoal and to sell them at artificially low prices. Foraging KMT soldiers had stripped the mountain behind the school of its vegetation and its few remaining trees. Early winter rains had brought large mudslides. Local farmers had been forced to surrender supplies of logs and kindling to the growing garrison, and KMT officers were openly looking for new buildings to use as barracks. School numbers were falling as some of the older boys quietly slipped away to avoid conscription.

At the end of October, soldiers ransacked classrooms searching for boys to conscript. A teacher was arrested and taken away. It was the same story in the village, where troops abducted young men, terrorised shopkeepers and regularly robbed the inns. On a cold afternoon at about this time one of the boys saw Hogg climbing the mountain above the school, and followed him. At the summit he found his headmaster seated on a rock, looking down over the school, crying. It was definitely time to leave.

Finally, in November, the decision was taken. For all his misgivings, it must have been a relief to Hogg. The school would move in two stages to Shandan, seven hundred miles to the north-west. An old temple and other buildings had been secured, and the regional governor in Lanzhou had given his permission.

In preparation for the journey the boys began weaving blankets and packing up the machinery. The bagpipe-playing Scotsman Andy Braid had been reassigned to Baoji, and most of the staff had gone into hiding after the last raid. Rewi Alley was away. Hogg was on his own. He not only had all the school duties to cope with, but also had to negotiate the closure of the school with local officials without letting them know where and when he was going.

Just at the moment I am manager, technician and cashier of the Ghosh co-op as well as dean, cashier, business manager of the school, chief doctor at the clinic, head of the household, head of the refugee committee; also trying to write a book and fight a lot of narks [local officials] at the same time. Had one big awful time yesterday would have been enough to turn you into a raging pro violent non pacifist for life . . .

Hogg's obsession was the Ghosh machine. The waterwheels would have to stay, and would provide power for the village. But he insisted that the Ghosh, in spite of its weight, size and complexity, would travel with them. A joke went round the school that the headmaster would happily leave a few boys behind, but never his cotton-milling machine. There were only three such machines in north-west China, and a Japanese advance on Xian and Baoji would remove two of those.

The prime need was for transport. The school had one large cart with four decent truck tyres for its wheels, but the Ghosh machine alone would be broken down into fifteen crates, making at least three cartloads. Added to that was the other machinery, the school lathe, the spinning machine, four looms, two small diesel engines and a printing press. Either Hogg had to break the equipment down into small loads for distribution onto pack animals and human carriers, or to find more vehicles. Engineer Kuo in the machine shop set about making them from bits of steel tubing, old tyre rims and planking. Meanwhile, boys who came from the Hweihsien region north of the school were despatched to buy or borrow horses and mules from the local farmers.

It was Kuo who had masterminded the assembly of the Ghosh machine, and he, with the rest of the staff, had no intention of making the dangerous journey to the edge of the Gobi desert. Bandit activity in the mountains during the midwinter months held far greater terrors than a distant Japanese army. This posed the problem of how the machinery, especially the large and complex Ghosh, was to be reassembled if the school ever got to Shandan.

To solve the problem, fifteen boys under the school draughtsman, Tsing, were set to work to break down the machinery and make detailed drawings of all the parts. Only the Ghosh machine was to be kept working until the last minute. Like the waterwheels it had proved a mighty challenge, but finally, on the eve of departure, it had begun to work to full capacity.

The plan was to leave Shuangshipu without the local KMT garrison noticing. An advance party of thirty-three boys with bedding and light school equipment set off over the mountains to the regional capital of Lanzhou in November. Word was put around the town that the party was undertaking a lengthy geological expedition. Rewi Alley arranged two trucks to take them, which he promised to send back. The vehicles never returned.

The party reached Lanzhou after one major incident, when one of the trucks ran into an ammunition lorry on the outskirts of the city. Both trucks caught fire and exploded, but the boys managed to get clear in time. On 21 December they transferred to a large Russian truck which Alley had hired, and arrived in Shandan on Christmas Day 1944.

Hogg meanwhile was keeping up the pretence that the school was still operational, although with a greatly depleted teaching staff. The remaining boys attended lessons and manned the Ghosh machine, which was kept working until days before departure. The garrison commanders and the villagers all knew about the cotton-spinning machine. It had become something of a local attraction, and as long as it kept working everyone knew the school was still there.

Hogg seemed to be as excited about the fact that the machine was really working as that the school was about to leave. He began his letter home on 26 November in exclamatory style:

Oh boy! Oh boy! Oh boy! Day after tomorrow we are probably starting off to Lanzhou on the first half of the journey to the promised land (far from the madding bureaucrats maybe). And today our boys on the ghosh are actually producing good fine cotton yarn for the first time. It is a milestone, landmark, headland, memorial, fitting farewell achievement enough to give us heart and hope in whatever sandy, gravelly, foodless desert of winter we find ourselves in next.

We've done it! Alone we've done it! . . . tamed the river and got the machines going.

With half the school gone, Hogg worked hard on his second book. This was to be an autobiographical account of his headmastership and the rebuilding of the school; he had written four chapters, and he planned to make the great journey over the mountains to the north-west chapter five. It was now December, and winter had closed in early. The bad weather which was to pose such problems on the journey also made writing difficult. On 20 December, in his last letter before leaving, he wrote:

I forgot to tell you how cold it is here. The other day I had the brilliant idea of propping my typewriter up against the fire to warm it up before using. Unfortunately I put it too close and five letters dropped off. I have sent it to Chengdu for repairs. Luckily there is another here or I would be diddled. 'Sensible Aylwin' I hear you say

Hogg posted the first four chapters of the book, entitled *Beyond China's City Walls*, to Little, Brown in New York before he left for Shandan, and also told his parents he would send them a copy. Neither manuscript arrived, nor has any trace of them been seen since. It is more than likely that Kuomintang agents in the post office at Baoji, the main sorting centre in the region, confiscated and destroyed them.

Hogg delayed his departure until the New Year, waiting for motorised transport and better weather. His old boys remember him searching desperately for a truck of any kind, as heavy snow-falls in the mountains made the need for motorised transport more urgent. The list of equipment to be taken was also growing, although Hogg had been advised that at that time of year the journey with a group of boys would be difficult enough, but that taking machinery would doom the whole expedition. Apart from the weather, there was the question of bandits, who might well be attracted by the prospect of hijacking valuable machinery.

Rumours that the Ghosh machine was to be moved aroused fierce competition for the machine from neighbouring co-operatives, but all offers to buy it were turned down. In any case, Hogg had to keep it working until the last minute to avoid alerting the garrison to the school's final departure. He sent Engineer Kuo to Xian to buy raw cotton and spare parts, so as to ensure the swift resumption of operations in Shandan. A shortage of horses meant that mules had to be found, and they were given extra feed to prepare them for the long haul over the mountains.

The preparations for the journey, and the worsening conditions in Shuangshipu, began to change minds among those members of the school staff who had previously turned their backs on the idea. On 17 January 1945 Hogg wrote to Rewi Alley, saying that now everybody wanted to come: 'Everyone praising [the planned journey]. Music master Chow wants to go. All sorts of people want to go . . . Engineer fatty Yang very enthusiastic.'

In his final message to Alley he said: 'Will be ready to go quite soon. Will bring you milling and planing machines in running order . . . our school lathe, some shafting and pulleys, 1 diesel engine. The card cloth that Bob Newell brought back from Chengdu, 1 sewing machine. I think we can get all this on, not quite sure.' The boys were given a last inspection. Two out of the thirty were found to have lice – one louse each, Hogg noted. This was a triumph for hygiene standards, and two new shirts were issued all round. In the days leading up to departure, messages had been sent to the older boys who had gone into hiding in the area, offering them a final chance to join the expedition. Several did so.

On or around 20 January, a convoy of five large carts drawn by a mix of mules and horses, one truck, thirty boys, three staff and the headmaster left the Bailie industrial co-operative school at Shuangshipu before daybreak and headed into the hills. They travelled on a road that became little more than a mud and gravel track as it climbed towards its highest elevation of ten thousand feet, between mountains rising to seventeen thousand feet. The higher they got, the heavier the snow fell. They hoped to arrive at their destination ten weeks later, at the end of March.

Although Hogg had commandeered hand-drawn barrows, what made the movement of the school and all its equipment possible was the hire of large carts with pneumatic tyres. These could carry up to two tons of equipment each. The smallest children travelled in the truck, sheltering under a tarpaulin slung over the cargo. The others walked, taking turns to hitch lifts on the carts.

Apart from the severity of the weather and the fact that the convoy would have to look to impoverished farmers to buy what little food was available, the biggest worry was bandits. This was bandit season, when slow-moving convoys in bad weather were likely to be ambushed by heavily armed gangs. It was another risk Hogg was prepared to take.

The troops and local people in the town would quickly have discovered the flight of the school. The first day took the convoy of vehicles only twelve miles into the mountains, but the weather and the terrain secured them from pursuit. The track rose and dipped as the foothills gave way to mountain country, but everywhere it was snowing hard. Arriving at a small village on the second night, Hogg distributed woollen leggings, which many of his pupils rejected on the grounds that they looked strange and ugly. At this point one or two of the older boys turned back, leaving Hogg with a group of twenty-seven pupils plus his precious equipment.

Hogg described the struggle to make progress in a letter home: 'In five days we made only 57 kilometres over the mountains and two carts overturned! It was the worst time of year over the high mountains in the coldest winter for 20 years (I see from your letters you had it too) and the roads were covered in snow and ice.'

One cart toppled over the edge of the road into a ravine, taking its horse and its load of equipment with it. Boys walking beside the cart jumped clear just in time. Another cart overturned but was righted again, and its cargo saved. Those were the only accidents on the first stretch of the journey. There was no sign of bandits.

One of Hogg's old boys recalled the experience years later. Fan Wenhai was fourteen when he went to the Shuangshipu school in 1942, and remembers meeting the headmaster and being given a blanket and quilt. He was one of the older boys on the journey. Now aged eighty, he lives in retirement in Meng Xian county, Henan province.

He said: 'It was very difficult for all of us, including the horses, which kept slipping. We rode on the truck under cover but sometimes we had to walk. We were all very tired early in the journey, but we never slept in the open. We were always given food and shelter by farmers along the way. We usually slept in their outbuildings.'

After twelve days the convoy arrived at the mountain town of Tianshui, which Hogg had visited a year earlier when he inspected a number of small co-operative workshops in the area. He reported that the town and its residents existed in a time warp.

Once within the gates the traveller is taken back a thousand years.
A long dusty main street squeezes itself through ten narrow gateways
and down it pad lordly camel trains bearing salt from Kokonor [the

traditional name for Qinhai province in the north-west], wool from Mongolia or dried fruits from Xiankiang [present-day Xining, capital of Qinghai province]. Bazaars line the street on either side. A black bearded son of Allah dressed in sheepskin gown sits toasting his feet on a platter of charcoal, his walls hung thick with the skins of tiger, leopard, wolf and fox smeared with ancient poison in the forests. Next door to the furrier the sun glints in over the polished tops of black lacquer furniture while farther on again sits the herbist doctor beside his weird potion of mountain roots, crabs, tusks, tortoises and unmentionable anatomical portions of rare beasts.

Hogg and his boys did not stay long. Even here, far from the areas of combat, the war had left its mark. An old temple which marked the birthplace of an early emperor had been turned into a home for crippled war veterans.

The convoy pressed on to the next settlement on the road north, the little town of Chingan, famous for its textiles. Their path lay through barren hills blanketed with snow. The truck led the way, pausing at the top of each ridge to allow the mule carts and foot travellers to catch up. All of them skidded, plodded and slogged their way through thick ice and snow for mile after mile of lifeless terrain.

Occasionally the track would pass a farmhouse made of mud bricks and timber, where small children could be seen sweeping the snow, searching for dead grass and roots to use as fuel. Even in midwinter they had only short jackets, and rags for trousers. For almost everyone in the mountains of western China, famine and disease were the real enemies.

Hogg had seen the results: 'In the scattered villages even the young men and women seemed somehow brow beaten by the enormity of the mountains around them. Superfluous flesh hung in great breasts from the goitrous necks of the old and middle

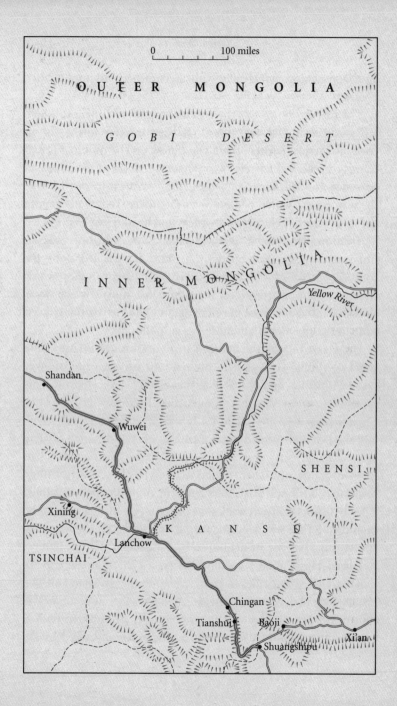

aged contrasting pathetically with their meagre undernourished bodies.'

The halfway point was the regional capital of Lanzhou, which Hogg had visited several times. He used to refer to the city in code, as the place where there was 'Snow on the mountains and Camels on the Main Street'. Government censors were unlikely to have been fooled, especially since Hogg went on to the describe the way camels would pad out over the frozen Yellow River until the ice cracked, then spread their legs and bend down to drink.

Traditionally known as the Golden City, Lanzhou was an important staging post on the silk route. It sprawled along the southern banks of the Yellow River in a narrow valley which trapped pollution from local industry. Dust storms which occasionally blew down from the Gobi desert added to the smog. Even in 1945 the city was infamous for its air pollution.

Hogg and his party rested in Lanzhou for several days. There was one special attraction in the city. An American missionary had a Frigidaire, and was able to make and keep ice cream. This novel luxury proved highly popular with the boys.

According to some accounts, it was here that one boy fell ill and died of a suspected heart attack. Over the distance of sixty years the old boys found it hard to agree exactly what had happened, but somewhere on the second half of the journey Hogg lost one of his boys. His letters never mention the fact, but Rewi Alley in his memoirs, as well as the old boys, recalls that one of the boys died on the way to Shandan. Other boys became ill, but only Fan Wenhai had to stay behind and recuperate.

It had taken almost a month to get to the regional capital, and there were 250 miles to go over high terrain to Shandan. The single truck they had used had returned over the mountains. The mules and horses were not fit to continue. Hogg again had to search for transport. A local official, Zhang Xinyi, looked kindly on the venture, and allowed him to hire six vintage Mercedes diesel trucks and a Dodge petrol bowser. Only the bowser had a starter that worked: the trucks' were all broken. So every morning the Dodge had to tow the first truck until it snorted into life, and then the first truck towed the second, and so forth. The morning starts, in temperatures that dropped to minus 20 overnight, were a lengthy and exhausting process, but getting the trucks at all had been an extraordinary piece of luck. Fuel was scarce, and most motorised transport was forced to use carbon fuel. But here too, Hogg's luck held, and he was able to persuade local officials to fill the bowser with diesel.

Sometime in February, the headmaster, his boys and all their equipment drove in their convoy of old trucks out of Lanzhou and into the foothills of the snowy Qilian mountains. They took the badly potholed, broken road through the Gansu corridor, a long panhandle that led past the Gobi desert to the north-east and a rumpled rug of chocolate coloured hills to the west. Disaster was never far away, as the trucks slipped and slithered through ice and snow. Windscreens cracked, tyres burst and vehicles left the road and had to be hauled back.

Only a few miles from their destination, the convoy passed the western end of the Great Wall. This was not the majestic stone wall that rose and fell for almost four thousand miles over the mountains of northern China. Here on the edge of the Gobi desert it was then, and remains now, a humbled mud rampart thirty feet high. Sandstorms, erosion and human activity had taken their toll of a wall largely built during the Ming dynasty (1368–1644).

Disappointing though it may have been on first sight, it was the wall that told Hogg that he was close to his destination. A day later, around 10 March 1945, the headmaster and his exhausted boys reached Shandan. They drove down a main street that was caked in ice and mud, and lined by double-storeyed wooden buildings. Most of them were empty. The population had fallen by over a third, to around twenty thousand. Many had fled south to Lanzhou, to escape fighting between Mao's guerrillas and the forces of the local warlord, Ma Bufang, years earlier. Bufang was unusual in that he had been governor of the neighbouring Qinghai province, and his family had dominated politics in the region for decades. He worked closely with local landlords, using traditionally brutal methods to extort taxes from the peasantry.

The first party of thirty-three boys had camped out and received lessons in some of the empty houses until accommodation had been found in a ruined temple. The temple of Fa Ta Si (temple of the hair) was so called because it was once said to have housed a box containing a single hair from the head of the great king Asoka of India, the first Buddhist leader of the sub-continent. It was now derelict, and was enclosed by a compound which contained other small temples. This compound had been used by the warlord's cavalry, and doors and windows had been ripped out for fuel, and the wooden supports chewed by hungry horses. There were innumerable images of Buddha in dusty alcoves. Pigeons clattered in and out of the buildings.

Around sixty boys aged from six to eighteen finally gathered in the ruined temple to rebuild their school and their lives. The youngest was Hogg's fourth adopted son, Nieh Guangpei, then aged six, who can remember little of the journey, but does recollect the temple he now had to call home: 'We were all very tired when we arrived and we were very disappointed – there was nothing in the temple, hardly even a roof. It was filthy. We had to clean it and then make our own furniture, but there was no wood. Everything in the area had been taken by the soldiers.'

TEN

Shandan

'Don't worry, I'll be back some day.'

Hogg used his emergency funds to buy three old houses in the town. They were empty, and the local landlords were happy to take cash. The houses were stripped of their wood, bricks and fittings, which were trundled by barrow to the old temple almost half a mile away on the town outskirts. The trucks that Hogg had hired mysteriously acquired drivers who took them back to Lanzhou, and school transport became the hand-pulled rubber-tyred barrows that had been taken with them on the carts.

In his first letter home after the journey, which was received with huge relief, Hogg described the task that now faced him.

Now that we are here the barrows are in full daily use on the job of clearing out the muck from the old . . . temple that is our school, and pushing in building materials from the houses that we have bought all around for wrecking purposes. The nearest timber available in any quantity is about 40 miles away so we have to be content with wrecking old houses and using the timber and bricks from them.

The local population had deep misgivings about the operation, not least because an ocean devil was in charge of moving the many statues of Buddha from the temple. In his first weeks in Shandan Hogg was shouted at in the streets. Locals yelled '*Yang gai zi*' ('Foreign enemy') as he cycled past. Delicate negotiations took place, and it was agreed that three of the largest gold-leafed Buddhas would remain in the temple, together with two baby pagodas and the traditional stone statues of watchmen which guarded the Buddhas (appropriately, the watchmen were placed at the entrance to the school store). This satisfied local opinion, but many remained puzzled by the school transport. 'The people here haven't got as far as inventing barrows yet. No barrows but plenty of buddhas,' reported Hogg. He and the children were amazed by the hundred-foot-high wooden Buddha in the town centre.

Throughout March, April and May 1945 Hogg and his boys worked at fitting out the school. The initial reservations of the Shandan population fell away as they realised that the new school would bring them business and money. Officials and local dignitaries paid regular visits. The first place the headmaster showed visitors was the main hall of the big temple, where three large Buddhas rising thirty to forty feet towered over boys working to assemble the Ghosh machine in what had become the spinning shop. This meeting place of thousand-year-old religious symbols and nineteenth-century industrial technology, with twentieth-century Chinese youth working in the shadow of both, must have been an impressive sight.

Using building material from the houses he had bought, Hogg fitted out workshops down one side of the compound. These housed carpentry benches, steam engines, an electric generator, lathes, a planer, milling machines and wool-spinning machines. Classrooms were built down another side, and along the third wall dormitories were constructed. The temple bell which hung high over the classrooms was found to be missing its clapper. A sledgehammer had been substituted, which had cracked the bell. This was replaced by a small hammer, and the bell was rung loud enough to be heard all over town.

Hogg was working with only two Chinese teachers at this stage, and Rewi Alley was away seeking recognition for the new school from the Chongqing government. Without the CIC stamp of approval the mafia of local officials and landlords would soon close in.

Hogg was in his element. He had turned thirty somewhere in the mountains between Lanzhou and Shandan on the last leg of his journey to the school's new refuge. He now knew the answer to the question he had often asked himself, and that others, especially his family, had asked him: What was he doing in China? The years of travel, the work in the co-operative movement, the writing of his books and journalism all made sense in Shandan. He had created a school from the chaos of war. He had moved it against odds to the rim of the remote Gobi desert. He had rebuilt it as a refuge and place of safety for some sixty pupils.

His old boys remember the extraordinary energy and the rollicking high spirits with which their headmaster worked alongside them to rebuild their school. Fan Wenhai said: 'Remember that in our society the man who was the head of the family, or of the school or of the company where you worked, was a figure of awe. You respected them sometimes because you were afraid of them. Hogg was so different. He spent so much time with us, and it didn't matter whether he was singing with us, playing sport with us or working in the classroom. He was always with us. That was very different. That was why we loved him so much.'

Hogg's letters home at this time reflect his optimism and the joy he took in what he was doing. He could clearly see the kind of school he was creating in this strange part of China. And he liked being in a place far – so he thought – from the tides or war and the interference of officialdom. He told his parents without much exaggeration that his back door opened onto mountains beyond which lay Mongolia, and his front door likewise looked out over mountains which descended on the far side into Kokonor, then claimed by Tibet. The appeal of such a remote location faded slightly when he found that a letter to Lanzhou took a week to get there. 'No newspapers nothing in this place,' he lamented.

The lifelines of the school were the boiler, generator and steam engine. With these working properly Hogg could power the machinery that lay at the heart of the educational programme, and provide light and heat for the bitter winter months. Twenty more boys were expected in the summer, and together with more teachers and support staff, school numbers were planned to rise to a hundred by the autumn. Many of the new entrants came from the town itself: parents would bring their sons to the school gates and ask for admission. The town had no electricity, but was a centre for crude open-cast coalmining. Hogg proposed to swap free coal from the town in return for electricity, but the plan did not come to fruition in his lifetime.

Shandan also provided the headmaster with a room rather than a cave as living quarters. Packing cases were turned into a bed and bookshelves. His little room directly overlooked a ruined pagoda, and beyond that the compound containing the whole school, classrooms, dining hall, workshops and dormitories. Having everything in one place was a huge advantage: 'I can do in an hour [at Shandan] what would have taken me a day at Shuangshipu and left me rather fagged.'

At about this time a British delegation arrived in Shandan led by the Reverend George Woods, a Labour Member of Parliament from the co-operative wing of the party. Although Woods was fifty-nine years old, he had decided to make the long journey from London after reading Hogg's book *I See a New China*. He wanted to see for himself the kind of school that had been created in the wilderness of north-west China. Such visits were time-consuming, since Hogg had to take his visitors into the mountains for a whole day; but they provided important political protection for the school. Woods brought with him a copy of *Picture Post* magazine, which contained an advertisement for shredded wheat, with a realistic and enticing picture of the cereal. This was a mouth-watering reminder for Hogg of one of the things he missed about home – the English breakfast, even in its limited wartime form.

In Shandan the school was forced to exist on a meagre diet. There were no vegetables, no fruit, no fish and no dairy food. The staple diet in the early days was steamed bread, millet soup and occasionally potatoes. Poor-quality meat, usually fatty beef and mutton, was on the menu twice a week. There were occasional treats; Hogg always looked forward to Sunday breakfast, when boys and masters ate eggs poached in beef soup. Eggs were rare enough for him to begin one letter home by announcing that he had eaten four fried eggs that morning for breakfast – small Chinese eggs, he explained.

Hogg always ate with his boys, all of whom lamented their reduced diet in Shandan. Visitors to the school in the spring of 1945 noticed that he looked thin and gaunt. The effort that went into planning the school move, taking the boys over the mountains and then starting from scratch had taken its toll even of a fit thirty-year-old man. Kathleen Hogg later said that she believed her son's resistance to infection had become dangerously low. She was almost certainly right. To supplement their diet the boys planted vegetables by the river, hoping for a harvest before the autumn. As at Shuangshipu, the river also offered the school a place for swimming and an early-morning wash.

Communications were difficult, but the occasional visitors brought news. Hogg knew that the war in Europe was coming to an end, 'but ours will last quite some time yet and may take some peculiar new turns I expect', he wrote on 5 May 1945.

By that month the school was coming together. The walls of the main temple had been whitewashed, the pillars had been painted red, and a huge wooden sign with golden dragons curling around the edges had been placed at the entrance, proudly proclaiming the Shandan Bailie school. A basketball court had been laid out and an area set aside for the headmaster's passion, daily PE exercises. The coal supply proved a problem, since the local mafia boss controlled the mines, but enough was found to power the generator and provide energy for the machinery.

Timber was the main requirement in the first months. Getting wood supplies for both fuel and building was very difficult. Shandan's historical importance as a staging post for caravans of camels on the silk route meant that the town had consumed the local forests as it increased in size and wealth. Hundreds of wooden temples had been constructed and then rebuilt on a grander scale to emphasise the growing prestige of the town. To keep wild animals away from their livestock the townspeople regularly set fire to the woods in the dry summer months to push the timberline back up the mountains. Overgrazing by goats and sheep had also stripped the hillsides bare.

To obtain wood, the school had to send parties thirty to forty miles to the northern side of the Qilian mountains, where the range descended to what is today Qinghai province, amid forests of fir trees. Here Hogg and his boys would spend days felling the tallest pines. The trunks were then hauled back across country on ox carts to the main highway, where they would be picked up by truck and taken to Shandan. There were plenty of wolves and bandits in the mountains, but the worst that the school suffered in its early months was a storm during one of these expeditions which swept away the tents, leaving the boys without shelter on a hillside for a night.

Ever the optimist, Hogg had initially thought that in Shandan he would be free from the corrupt and threatening politics that had engulfed the school at Shuangshipu. But as the school established itself and began to produce pottery from its kiln and textiles from its spinning machine, the local mafia began to pay attention. The school was receiving funds from the CIC, and was coming into competition with mafia-controlled businesses in the area. The nationalists were not strong enough to impose their rule in such a remote area, and Gansu province was run at regional level by a coalition of KMT officials working with warlords such as Ma Bufang. Local government, although supposedly in the hands of a magistrate, was in fact controlled by a mafia of local businessmen and landlords allied to bandits who lived in the mountains.

The threats to the school were crude. Hogg and Rewi Alley, on one of his regular visis to the town, were invited to dinner by the local magistrate, who pointedly told them that the previous day bandits had killed ten villagers with broadswords just three miles from the eastern gate of the town. This news was followed up with a request that the school provide English lessons for an hour a day in the local school. Hogg made a diplomatic counter-suggestion: why not invite some of the local schoolboys to join the Bailie school instead? The offer proved popular, and soon the people of Shandan were clamouring to get their children into the school.

The school also began to face the familiar pressure from KMT officials, who travelled from Lanzhou to argue that the older boys should be conscripted. These arguments were laced with the usual accusations that the school was a communist front. Hogg wearily fended off the charges, spending hours at local banquets –

something he complained about bitterly in his letters – pointing out that if the school was a communist organisation, why had it been set up almost a thousand miles from the CCP headquarters in Yenan? And why did it carry the name of a famous American missionary? And why was it backed and funded by the KMT government in Chongqing? Rewi Alley's efforts to get formal recognition for the school as a CIC institution had paid off, and this, together with a visit at the end of May 1945 by the CIC Secretary General and senior officials from the Chongqing government, ended the pressure.

The school seemed to have turned a corner. It was recognised by a distant government, and free from harassment by the local mafia. Thanks to the arrival of six skilled workmen, most of the workshop machinery was back in action, although the struggle to get the steam engine and boiler working properly continued. Hogg was able to write in May: 'We have a good staff, young fellows with a "now or never" attitude . . . together we are working things out and trying to set up a system that other people can work when necessary.'

He still found time to write, although the one day a week he set aside for work on his second book – Sunday – was occasionally wiped out: 'Last Sunday all wasted by a stupid feast at the bank. You have to attend such things or word gets round that you are proud, stand-offish etc and that is the end of everything.'

The book was now almost finished, and he had been sent reviews of the British edition of *I See a New China*, which had been published by Victor Gollancz in January, and was the Left Book Club's choice for that month. It was not just on the left that the book had won plaudits: both the *Times Literary Supplement* and the *Spectator* published positive notices. The reviewers were struck by the fact that an Englishman should have written a book from such a remote part of China at that time. News from the country was scarce. The final months of the war in Europe, and the intensifying war in the Pacific, consumed public attention. A book that described the conflict in China from the point of view of the ordinary people came as a refreshing surprise.

The anonymous reviewer in the *TLS* paid Hogg a back-handed compliment: 'It is an engaging record, full of humour but with no pretensions either to style or eloquence; and it reads as though it had been written rather for the author's own amusement than with any idea of publication.' He did however praise the book's projection of the co-operative ideal, and Hogg's down-to-earth dealings with the Chinese:

> *While it does not attempt to disguise the realities – and its frankness will shock many of those who love to idealise the Chinese character – the author's strong faith in what the co-operative movement can do for the country . . . lends something like a unity to what would otherwise be a serial of discursive, if picturesque, jottings. Like so many Englishmen he found no difficulty at all in working with the Chinese, whose salty humour and conservative common sense afforded him intense relish. The last words of the book are: thank God we are dirty, it's a comforting thought. One can see plainly what he means. The Chinese co-operative movement is grounded on the faith and work of people who are dirty. The enemies are the smooth bureaucrats and the civilised intellectuals who intercept the funds sent by sympathisers abroad and who raise the cry that China's independence is threatened by 'foreign interference'.*

The review in the *Spectator* was equally kind: 'George Hogg has no axe to grind, no propaganda to put across. This book is a straightforward, unpretentious but extremely interesting record of his travels.'

As May turned to June, the summer heat bore down on the

walled town and the new school in its midst. Drought threatened the harvest of wheat. Long processions of schoolchildren, officials and the old people of Shandan marched through the streets several times a day beating gongs. The marches always ended with prayers for rain at one of the many temples. Senior officials such as the local magistrate were expected to make obeisance to Buddhist deities by leading such processions on their knees. Hogg was delighted to discover that the magistrate had been rebuked by the townsfolk for having spent only three hours in this fashion.

Meanwhile he wrote a series of letters to CIC officials detailing the school's needs. He had not got enough staff, and he especially needed a maths teacher. The continuing problems with power, especially for the Ghosh, meant the school also needed a diesel generator. On 10 June Hogg wrote to Alley: 'Must have cash. Only $1.5 million* left here now and lots of important stuff waiting to be done ... if we don't do it soon winter will catch us all undone.'

At the end of June Hogg met a young British geologist from Cambridge University, who had been seconded to the West China university in Lanzhou. Brian Harland was making a survey of the Shandan area, and had heard about the new school and its colourful English headmaster. He was impressed by the school, but saw in it something that Hogg would probably have disclaimed:

They are succeeding in getting across what is of real value in the English Public School system minus the secondary things like academic specialisation and class snobbery. It is an expensive form of education because it means running full scale machine shops,

---

* The official exchange rate at the time was around five hundred Chinese dollars to the pound, but because of inflation $1.5 million would only have been worth a few hundred pounds in real terms.

textile machinery, leather tanning and what-not to train the boys practically.

Harland, who went on to have a distinguished academic career at Cambridge, was briefly tempted to throw his lot in with Hogg and teach at the school. He decided against, because 'It means giving up almost everything else as George Hogg has done.'

On 3 July Hogg wrote home reassuring his mother that he was well, 'thinner a bit, leaner and perhaps tougher'. He ended the letter with further reassurance: 'Much love and don't worry, I'll be back some day.' Five days later George Hogg wrote what would be his last letter to his parents. It was a long and joyful account of everything that was happening to him. He was working on the latest chapter of his book, and he sent news of his adoptive family, the school life in the cave, and how one boy had almost died of typhus.

He had just enjoyed a book of short stories by John Steinbeck called *The Long Valley*. He wished he could write like that. He mentioned the British reviews of his own book, including the *TLS*'s comment that he had no pretensions to style: 'I do try and develop a style of a kind. The review that said the book has an adolescent flavour was quite right. I am a case of arrested something or other . . . I don't quite know what at the moment.'

He had addressed a big meeting in town on a holiday to celebrate the birthday of the patron spirit of the local Buddhist temple. To general surprise he had only spoken for his usual forty minutes.

A new boy called Chang had joined the school. He and his family had been evicted from their home to make way for an airbase. He spoke in a dialect which only two boys in the school could understand.

The whole school of sixty-four boys had sung five songs as a choir. Afterwards they put on a long four-act play about resistance to the Japanese in Shanghai. Townspeople and peasants from miles about had crowded around the open-air stage until a sandstorm from the Gobi desert blew out the lamps lighting the action. There was almost a riot, and the police had been called. The magistrate and other local dignitaries had not arrived until the second act: 'But all in all it was quite a good show.'

No letter home was complete without a reference to food. He had eaten the top off a washbasin-ful of goat's milk that had stood for twenty-four hours. 'Thick creamy and slightly sour. Very refreshing and very nourishing.' He signed off with love, saying that he had to be up at 5 a.m. to practise Swedish drill with the boys by the river.

Sometime in the second week of July, George Hogg was playing basketball with his boys. They insisted he play with them, and there was always a scrum before the game as both teams vied to have the six-foot-two-inch headmaster on their side. He was wearing his usual shorts and open-toed sandals. During the game he stubbed and cut his toe. A few days later he complained that the toe had become sore and swollen, and dressed it with iodine. That day his jaw began to hurt and stiffen. The local doctor was summoned, and diagnosed 'flu. The next day Hogg was due to lead a party of boys on a hike into the mountains, but he was unable to leave his bed. Rewi Alley took the boys instead, while Brian Harland stayed behind with Hogg.

Over the next few hours Hogg's condition worsened rapidly. He had a high fever, and was suffering spasms that shook his entire body. A worried Harland set off in pursuit of the party of boys, caught up with them and took charge while Alley came back to the school. It was now clear that Hogg had tetanus. The incubation period for the disease ranges from two to fifty days, but the onset usually takes place within a week. Years later Rewi

Alley said that in retrospect Hogg had developed the classic symptoms of tetanus days before he fell seriously ill. Only days after stubbing his toe he had complained of stiffness in his neck and arms, and appeared to have developed a slight fever. The moment the diagnosis was made, telegrams were sent to Lanzhou asking for a doctor and serum. Two boys set off by motorbike on the five-hundred-mile round trip.

It was far too late. For three days Hogg suffered the agonies of a disease that always ends in a cruel death if untreated. Despite the spasms that tighten the abdominal, neck and back muscles, the patient's mental ability is unimpaired. The victim remains both conscious and aware, but unable to speak or cry out due to the tightening of the muscles of the face – hence the name lock-jaw. At present tetanus is estimated to cause half a million deaths annually around the world, with a 50 per cent mortality rate. In wartime China the incidence of the disease and its mortality rate would have been far higher.

Those pupils who had not gone on the hike, including Fan Wenhai, did their best for their stricken headmaster, trying to force water through his clamped jaws. Wenhai, who was seventeen years old, remembered Hogg's final days: 'He lay on his back most of the time and was too weak to move. I turned him over with help from another boy. He was dripping with sweat from his chin to his forehead. Sometimes he would ask for water in a very weak voice. First I could feed him by spoon, but after a while his mouth would not open. I had to hold his lower jaw and pour water through gaps between his teeth. We all tried to help him. We tried to open his mouth for soup but we couldn't.'

Although in great pain and suffering regular spasms as the disease tightened its grip, Hogg was conscious for much of his ordeal. He well knew what was happening to him and why. Rewi Alley wrote in his autobiography:

I cursed myself for not having realised that old houses and earth floors
would be breeding places for this germ and for not having any vaccine
with which to combat it. We telephoned frantically to places near and
far but failed to find any. George was as angry as we were that we had
been caught.

A doctor who had the serum was finally found in Lanzhou. But delay followed delay, first to find a car, then a driver, and then fuel. In the end two doctors set out, sending a telegram ahead that if Hogg could hold on for the two days it would take them to get there, the serum might pull him round. But the rescue party had left too late, and was unable to travel through a nine-thousand-foot-high mountain pass by night. When they arrived in Shandan in the early afternoon of 23 July, Hogg's funeral procession was winding its way through the streets. He had died at 2 p.m. the previous day.

That morning Hogg had asked for paper and pen, and wrote out his will in five simple words: 'My all to the school.' The will was witnessed by two boys, Fan Wenhai and Fan Kouqiang. Earlier he had gestured weakly and murmured through clenched teeth: 'I think I will pull through but one has to be prepared . . . I have only a few pieces of clothes and a camera. You can sell them for the school finances.'

When a doctor arrived from Wuwei, the nearest town, he confirmed that Hogg was in the death throes of tetanus. There was nothing anyone could do. Surrounded by many of his pupils, George Hogg died on Sunday, 22 July 1945. He was thirty years old.

The boys skilled at carpentry spent that night making a wooden coffin. The next day Hogg was buried in a grave outside Shandan's south gate. The district magistrate had presented a plot of land running down to the tree-lined river, with a magnificent view of the snow-covered ranges to the south. All the pupils and teachers signed their names on a flag which was placed on the coffin. The whole school of about a hundred boys and staff, all wearing black armbands, followed the coffin, which was carried by six boys. Several hundred people from the town joined the procession from the school to the burial place. Everyone bowed three times as the coffin was lowered into the ground. The boys seized shovels and filled in the grave, then built a large mound over it. Later, boys and teachers built a mausoleum over the grave. They created a garden around it with a small *t'ing-tze*, or summer house, and a large rock on which they carved the initials GAH.

On the evening of the funeral, Rewi Alley took a swim in the river and, looking back at the grave, saw three small heads bowed over the freshly dug earth. Hogg's adopted children could not bear to leave their father. For weeks afterwards Lao San and Lao Si continued to take food and fruit to the grave. They ate breakfast there, and sang the songs their father had taught them. They talked to him for hours, asking questions to which there was no answer. Even sixty years later, talking of their headmaster and father was enough to bring tears to the eyes of his adoptive old boys, now old men.

It was clear that had Hogg's tetanus been diagnosed earlier, and the doctors with the serum arrived sooner from Lanzhou, he might have been saved. As Brian Harland said in a letter to Hogg's parents, whatever mistakes were made in his treatment, the school did its best to save him. All the emergency funds were spent paying for the truck to fetch the doctor from Wuwei and for the private car to bring two doctors from Lanzhou. The bill, together with the funeral expenses, was around $80,000, about £1,300 at today's value. Hogg would have been appalled.

Kathleen and Robert Hogg heard the news of their son's death three days later, in a brief but regretful telegram from the CIC offices in Lanzhou. Rewi Alley's letter, written on 25 July, three days after Hogg died, arrived at Harpenden in the first week of August.

> *I know you will be waiting for news about George. Yet I wonder what I can say that will in any way comfort you. Words are poor things, and, as I sit on his bed and stamp these letters out on his typewriter I feel that very much indeed. He had recently gotten a letter from you, so the boys say, and was very happy about it ... I know we should have had tetanus serum here as with other serums. I ordered them some time ago but we could not get them through somehow. In that I am to blame ... Since coming to Shandan he has been much happier than before. The challenge of the work, the surroundings and the possibilities I think caught hold of his imagination. One of our troubles with him, though, was his unwillingness ever to admit that he was in any way sick and I am afraid he must have been suffering with his last illness a good deal before letting us know about it ...*

In his letter to the Hoggs, which was the first coherent account they received of what had happened to their son, Brian Harland said:

> *I am not anxious to re-enact the story as you will not be anxious to reread it and ponder on what might have been. Poor Rewi keeps wondering 'If only ...' But the rules of life do not permit any 'ifs' and I think George would not wish such idle speculations. George took things as he found them, he took people with their sorrows and tragedies, he saw his friends die and their hopes shattered. This was the kind of world in which George lived and he was part of it in life and death.*

In accordance with his instructions, all Hogg's personal posses-sions were handed over to the school. The valuable items, in-cluding his Remington typewriter, Zeiss camera and watch, were auctioned, raising a substantial sum for the school.

Hogg's parents received many moving tributes to their son. On 24 August the *Manchester Guardian* published an obituary, which ran in part:

> *Within a short time he had achieved remarkable success, and made the Bailie School, as it was called, a lively modern Chinese equivalent of the Danish Folk High Schools in their pioneer days. He applied in a common-sense fashion the best he had learnt in his own English education to the Chinese problem. Tough, intelligent lads of all social classes and from all parts of China were the pupils of the school.*
>
> *Plans were already made for starting other schools of the same kind under Hogg's direction in various districts, when the advance of the Japanese farther into the north-west necessitated a retreat in the early part of 1945 to Sandan in the Kansu Corridor, between the mountains of Mongolia and Tibet. To organise the trek of all the school-pupils, staff, and equipment, including some heavy machines, with the most meagre resources of transport was no small task in itself. And perhaps in the end it was not necessary, the war ending, as it has done, sooner than could have been expected. In such a remote district, far from skilled medical aid, Hogg had no chance of surviving when he caught the germ of the fatal tetanus disease.*

In September the *News Chronicle* of London published an appeal inspired by the Anglican Bishop of Hong Kong, Ronald Hall, and the Reverend George Woods MP:

WANTED SIX MEN READY TO RISK THEIR LIVES

Six courageous men are wanted to go at once to China to work for the China industrial co-operatives. They are to take the place of one who did the work of six – George Hogg, brilliant 30-year-old Oxford graduate who died recently of tetanus in Shandan, in North west China 1500 miles from Chongqing and beyond the reach of medical aid.

If they are willing to take the same risk of disease, endure discomfort, eat only Chinese food and learn to talk the language like a Chinese they should offer their services immediately to the secretary, the Anglo Chinese Development Society, 34 Victoria Street London SW1. Anyone not prepared to take a similar risk need not apply.

Nearly six thousand young men replied to the appeal.

In March the following year, Agnes Smedley wrote from Saratoga Springs in upstate New York, in response to a request from Kathleen for permission to publish Hogg's letters mentioning her in a book about his life. Smedley's letter reads as if she expected it to be intercepted and read by the FBI, which it almost certainly was. FBI agents were trawling through her past, interviewing friends and organisations she had worked for, and following her every step on her lecture tours. They were trying to build a case that she had been not just an open and active communist supporter, but a full-blown Soviet agent. Smedley had always denied membership of the Communist Party, although she freely admitted that she was an ardent supporter of the Chinese communists. She welcomed Kathleen's plan, and said: 'He was a really fine lad, talented, of broad culture, civilised in all his actions and utterly fearless and self-sacrificing in his work in China.'

The most lasting tribute to George Hogg came from the school he had created. He instituted the wall newspaper, and this tribute, jointly written by a number of boys, appeared in the first edition after his death:

George Hogg was a successful man. He learnt how to find what he wanted to do and when he found it he had the strength to make his work a success. He learnt how to live for the school he built up and in it he found great happiness. He is still part of us all and what we have learnt from him will carry us all to success.

EPILOGUE

Two weeks after George Hogg's death, on 6 August 1945, the US Air Force dropped the first atom bomb on Hiroshima. Three days later the second destroyed Nagasaki. On 15 August Japan publicly accepted Allied surrender terms, and on 2 September the instrument of surrender was signed aboard the American flagship USS *Missouri* in Tokyo Bay as American troops began to arrive for the occupation of Japan.

The war with Japan which had dominated Hogg's eight years in China was over. The final stage of the rumbling civil war between nationalists and communists, which had been the inner dynamic of political life in China since Chiang Kai-shek unleashed his death squads against communists in Shanghai in 1927, was about to begin.

Following Hogg's death, Rewi Alley took over as headmaster of the Shandan Bailie School. The sister school at Lanzhou was closed for lack of funds, and sixty students and staff moved to Shandan, doubling the size of the school overnight. The intensifying civil war between communists and nationalists posed a threat to a school which was deemed by the KMT government to be sympathetic to Mao's guerrillas and their cause.

But Chiang Kai-shek had little time to deal with a distant co-operative school on the edge of the Gobi desert. He was bent on final victory over the communists, and outwardly his forces were in a strong strategic position to achieve it. Japan had surrendered without forcing a costly end to the eight years of war, and the Western nations which had so long held sway over China through their concessions had withdrawn all territorial claims, leaving the country as a sovereign state with Chiang as its rightful ruler. The nationalist armed forces now comprised four million men, backed by the most powerful air force in Asia. The warlords had been vanquished. The only challenge to Chiang's supreme power over 450 million people lay with the communists, who were still contained in the north-west around Yenan.

For several months communists and nationalists manoeuvred against each other as President Truman tried to shore up the war-time united front and prevent civil war. An American-brokered ceasefire in January 1946 quickly collapsed, and full-scale fighting resumed. Initially government troops won a series of victories, capturing Yenan in March 1947. Mao and his forces were forced to flee, but they merely melted into the hills, and did not go far. The nationalist victories were deceptive, as the government forces were left in the same vulnerable position that the Japanese had formerly occupied. KMT troops may have held the major cities, rural strongpoints and lines of communication, but the communists retreated to the countryside where they had popular support, and returned to their well-tried guerrilla tactics.

By late 1947 the tide had turned. It was clear to the Western powers, if not to Chiang, that the civil war would end in communist victory. KMT armies were penned into demoralised and poorly supplied garrisons strung out across northern China, and Mao, who had renamed his forces the People's Liberation Army (PLA), could concentrate his guerrillas to pick them off. With popular support throughout the rural areas the guerrillas could move, strike and resupply at will. The KMT forces were destroyed first in Manchuria and then on the north China plain. On 21 January 1949 Chiang Kai-shek officially resigned as

President of the Republic of China. As his military position on the mainland became hopeless, he withdrew to the island of Taiwan, and resumed the title of President. He died there of a heart attack in 1975, aged eighty-seven.

PLA forces reached the Yangtse River in April 1949, and were in Guangzhou on the south coast that autumn. Even before his victorious armies had completed their conquests, Mao proclaimed the establishment of the People's Republic of China, with himself as supreme leader, on 1 October 1949. He did so in Beijing, a capital city restored to its traditional name after being called Beiping for years under the KMT. Despite the communists' years of cultivating chosen correspondents, there was not a single Western journalist present when Mao stood on top of the Tiananmen gate in front of the Forbidden City and made his statement.

In the remote north-west, George Hogg's former pupils faced a perilous time as the communists swept up the Gansu panhandle in the summer of 1949. The nationalists prepared for a stand in Shandan, and began moving troops and artillery into the area around the town. In the chaos of the final months of civil war the demoralised and retreating Kuomintang forces conducted witch-hunts for communist sympathisers, which led to bloody reprisals. The presence of an American teacher, the newly arrived Don Kemp, probably saved the Shandan school from destruction and its staff and pupils from execution. As units of the old Eighth Route Army approached in September 1949, the KMT troops fled to the hills. The town was occupied by the communists without a fight.

The establishment of the People's Republic heralded further changes. In 1952 the Shandan Bailie school was moved to Lanzhou, where it became a training college for apprentice oil-industry workers. Most of Hogg's old boys transferred with the school, and were later to make careers in the oil industry. His four adoptive sons all rejoined their father in Manchuria after the war. In 1953 an earthquake almost completely destroyed Shandan. There was nothing left of George Hogg's school, or of the temples which had formed its base. His grave and mausoleum, although damaged, survived. Today Shandan is a small and unsightly market town, dominated by a sprawling cement works. It is a dusty, polluted place, which has been almost entirely rebuilt since the destruction caused by the earthquake. It has 100,000 inhabitants, the younger generation of whom seem united in their ambition to leave and find work in the regional capital Lanzhou.

In the early 1950s the Chinese government closed down the co-operative movement. Chinese officials openly attacked the 'philanthropic imperialism' of overseas aid organisations, and targeted Indusco as an example. Foreign missionaries were forced to leave the country. Most of those who worked for the co-operative movement and the Bailie schools, both foreign-funded, came under suspicion, and in many cases were harshly treated, during the purges of the Great Proletarian Cultural Revolution.

The Cultural Revolution which began in 1966 and would not run its full course until Mao's death in 1976 affected most of Hogg's old boys. Those in the oil industry were shielded from the worst of the violence, humiliations and dismissals meted out to those labelled as bourgeois, a category which included anyone with educational or professional qualifications, which all Hogg's old boys held. But one way or another, they all suffered in the chaos. Fan Wenhai trained at a geology college in western China, and went on to become a geologist. He was forced to write reports stating that Rewi Alley and George Hogg had collaborated with counter-revolutionaries, a standard and blanket accusation at the time. Many of the old boys were also forced to denounce their headmaster and the school, and both Hogg and Alley were attacked in Red Guard pamphlets and newspapers. Like most schools in China, the Bailie school in Lanzhou was closed during the Cultural Revolution. Hogg's grave was desecrated, as were most statues and artefacts relating to foreign activity in China.

Rewi Alley remained in China, writing books and promoting the government, through the dizzying twists and turns of policy in the Mao era. As an educator and social reformer he became the object of uncritical hero-worship in his native New Zealand, and to some extent remains so to this day. Even he, who had pledged his life to the communist cause in China, was almost forced to leave during the Cultural Revolution. In her masterly account of Alley's life, Dr Anne-Marie Brady says that he made a Faustian choice when he stayed on in China after the communist take-over.

In return for remaining in the country that had become his home, Alley would allow himself to be used for propaganda purposes, even to the point where his personal beliefs dipped completely from view. Though he could not have known it then, the 'covenant' that eventuated between him (and other foreigners who became friends of China in the Mao era) and the CCP was that he would not see, hear or speak evil about China, reporting only the good, and allowing himself to become the political tool of the regime. After 1949 Alley suppressed both his sexual identity and his distinctive individualism. In return the CCP gave him a life vastly superior to that of almost all Chinese people.

Dr Brady was sympathetic to Alley's natural desire for safety and security after years of life in a war zone. But his decision to stay on in China meant that he deliberately ignored government policies that were just as oppressive as those of the old regime. Dr Brady asked: 'What happened to the courage and dedication to a cause that was characteristic of his life before 1949?'

That question posed itself graphically after an estimated thirty-eight million people died in the famine that followed Mao's 'Great Leap Forward' in the years 1958–61. The brutal nation-wide programme to increase industrial output had catastrophic consequences for food production, as Mao well knew. Alley knew it too, since he travelled widely throughout China at a time when millions were dying in the countryside. In his autobiography he says he covered twenty-five thousand miles through fifteen provinces in 1958–59. But he never described what he saw even privately, nor did he seek help for the starving peasantry. Instead he used his travels to write a series of books, one of which was called *Amongst Hills and Streams of Hunan*.

Alley narrowly escaped arrest and expulsion during Mao's final years; his rehabilitation came when Deng Xiaoping attended a dinner for his eightieth birthday in the Great Hall of the People in Beijing in 1977. The Gung Ho co-operative movement was re-categorised as patriotic, and those who had worked for it or for the Bailie schools were rehabilitated. From that moment Alley worked to restore George Hogg's name and reputation in China, and he was the moving force behind the September 1984 reopening of the Bailie school in Shandan.

Today the school lives on in modern buildings in the centre of town which look out over sculptures of Hogg and Alley. The bright and lively pupils know well the story of how George Hogg crossed the mountains with his pupils to rebuild the school in their home town. His restored grave, and that of Alley, lie in a memorial garden at the edge of the town. A small museum nearby contains photographs of Hogg and a painting of him as a young man wearing shorts, a short-sleeved shirt and walking boots. A life-size alabaster bust of Hogg stands in the room, and another is to be found in a room alongside the Silk Route library established in his honour. Among the books in the library are translations of works by Muriel Lester, who continued to work for humanitarian and pacifist causes until her retirement in 1958. She also became one of the more prominent soapbox orators in Hyde Park in London on Sunday mornings, a tradition that continues to this day. She died in 1968.

Rewi Alley, who spoke to me at length about George Hogg in Beijing in 1984, died there in 1987.

Mao's guerrilla commanders Zhu De and Nieh Rong Zhen rose to the most senior positions in the Chinese military. In 1955 both were given the rank of marshal. Zhu De was appointed overall commander of Chinese armed forces during the Korean War, while Nieh Rong Zhen was made responsible for the development of China's nuclear weapons programme. Despite these responsibilities and their senior status, both men were purged, humiliated and dismissed in 1966, the first year of the Cultural Revolution. It was only thanks to Chou En-lai's support that Zhu De was not killed or imprisoned. He died aged eighty-eight in July 1976, just weeks before Mao's own death on 9 September. Nieh Rong Zhen, who had been born a few days before the turn of the twentieth century, died shortly before his ninety-third birthday.

Kathleen Hogg never finished her book about her son's life based on his letters home, but her collection of his letters and writings remains a valuable family archive. Her husband Robert died in 1947. She died twenty years later.

Hogg's brothers and sisters lived long enough to see his rehabilitation by the Chinese and his grave restored. Stephen, the brother to whom he was closest, became a teacher at Frensham Heights preparatory school in Surrey. He was headmaster of the school when he died of a heart attack at the age of sixty-one in 1970.

Hogg's much-loved sister Rosemary survived the longest,

dying in July 2007, at the age of ninety-five. When I visited her in 1986 she spoke of her brother with a passion and clarity of recall undimmed by the fifty years that had passed since she last saw him at Southampton docks.

Xiao Ren continued to write to her English lover until she married a worker in one of the Eighth Route Army's weapons factories in late 1944. Hogg never knew she had married. She was one of the few front-line women guerrillas in the communist forces, operating shoulder-fired grenade-launchers. Ren was involved in numerous clashes with both the Japanese and, after 1945, with the government forces. 'We fought everywhere in Hebei, Hunan and Shandong provinces. There was always a lot of fighting and killing,' she said.

She and her husband, a weapons technician, had four children, and moved to Shanghai in the 1950s. Her husband rose to become a senior marine engineer in Beijing, but during the Cultural Revolution he was sacked in disgrace, imprisoned and tortured as a 'rightist and capitalist roader'. He was sent to a 'reform through labour' camp, and kept there until 1977, when he was released under the 'Right a Wrong' campaign. His health suffered during the years of privation, and Ren and her children were forced from their home in Shanghai and sent to a remote rural area to work in the fields and fend for themselves.

Discussing these traumatic events in the calm of a Beijing restaurant in 2007, she showed no sign of anger. 'Many people suffered much worse than we did,' she said. Her husband died in October 2002, but her children flourish in their various professional careers. Ren is enjoying a happy and lively retirement at the time of writing. She lives alone, but is well looked after by her children. Her enthusiasm for life, like her memory, is unclouded by age.

When the story I wrote about George Hogg's odyssey appeared in the *Sunday Telegraph* in London in March 1985, its publication aroused memories in China and elsewhere. Professor Brian Harland, who became a Fellow of Gonville and Caius College, Cambridge, said in an interview with me before his death in 2003: 'When I met George in Shandan in July 1945 just before he died, I remember thinking that here was the ideal young Englishman. This was 1945, don't forget, when we had just won the war and we were proud of ourselves. George was a handsome, tall young man. He was very open with me as a stranger, and with everyone. I think his public school background made a big difference to what he did, in a funny sort of way. He took on these boys, some as young as seven or eight and some young men aged about seventeen, and he sorted them out. He taught them to think and work as a community. "Gung Ho" was the motto, but it was really getting these highly different and individual boys to understand team spirit. The simple fact was they adored him for it. Of course you could not be in China at that time of corruption, poverty and the constant threat of death without being affected by the politics; it was an intensely political period. But I talked long hours with George about politics and, you know, he was not really concerned with ideology. He had a broad philosophy about how people should work together for the common good, but when you got down to it he was much more John Stuart Mill than Karl Marx. He was a marvellous example of someone who fulfilled the promise of his privileged education and background. He used every bit of his ability to build that school up, to save it and to rebuild it in the face of all kinds of opposition. He was, when I met him, a completely rounded personality.'

Agnes Smedley died in Oxford in 1950, at the age of fifty-eight. At the time she was at the centre of an international controversy over allegations that she had been a spy for the Soviet Union.* In death she was to prove just as controversial as she had been in her turbulent life, and a recent and scholarly biography by Ruth Price (*The Lives of Agnes Smedley*, 2004) establishes beyond reasonable doubt that she was in fact a Soviet spy. She must rank as the only Soviet agent to have actively and publicly proclaimed her support for the communist cause.

Ms Price approached Smedley's biography as a 'self-identified leftist', in her own words, who wished to exonerate her subject of the long-standing Cold War accusations against her. However, her extensive research and examination of papers newly released in Moscow revealed that Smedley had led a life of deception from an early age.

I no longer think of Smedley as the tragic victim of a McCarthyite smear. In truth I consider her as cunning and crafty an operator as her detractors on the right ever alleged . . . That Smedley did damage, there is no question. Her path was littered with people she hurt personally, people whose goodwill she exploited and whose reputations

---

* In September 1947 General Douglas MacArthur, Supreme Commander Allied Powers in Japan, sent a classified report to the Pentagon on a Soviet spy ring that had been run by Richard Sorge in China and Japan in the 1930s and early forties. Using captured Japanese records, MacArthur's intelligence chief, Charles A. Willoughby, claimed – among other things – that Smedley had operated for the Russian secret service as a recruiting officer and as a courier for Sorge's spying in China in the 1930s, and had run an espionage ring in north China from Beijing in the winter of 1932–33. The report led to an FBI investigation, but it was not officially published until February 1948, when it was laid before Congress as an official document authored by the 'National Military Establishment'. Smedley's friends, led by Edgar Snow, sprang to her defence, and shortly after, an army spokesman said the military had made a 'faux pas'. Smedley left the United States for England in 1949, and never returned.

suffered on her behalf because they believed her lies. Moreover, while it does not appear that Agnes's espionage activities visited direct harm on anyone, the beneficiaries of her services, the Soviets, the Chinese communists and, indirectly the German Imperial government – were entities with many crimes on their hands. Still, having come full circle with Smedley, I believe that the principles with which she lived and died ultimately transcend the realm of ideology to embrace humanity's more universal struggle.

The American novelist Katherine Anne Porter was a lifelong friend of Smedley, and, much as she loved her, described her in 1949 as 'a lamentable dupe of the kind our generation and place produced in extraordinary numbers. Agnes had a painful childhood and generally bad experience of life from the beginning – but given her beginnings where else could she have moved so freely and have done better? It is true she has been censured here a little, but she must know that in every country she adores so, she would have been sent to a labour camp or put to death if a man corresponding in power to General MacArthur had accused her of treason.'

George Hogg's UPI mentor Jack Belden also became an FBI suspect in the McCarthyite era of the late 1940s and early fifties, during the witch-hunt to find those who had 'lost China' for the West. Belden left the United Sates to spend an angry exile in Paris, where he died of lung cancer in 1989. Haldore Hanson, another FBI suspect due to his coverage of China for AP, died in Mexico in 1992, aged eighty.

Peter Fleming, the most famous of the English correspondents to have worked in the Hankow press corps, joined the Grenadier Guards during the Second World War, serving with distinction in Norway, Greece and Burma, and then took a senior intelligence post in South-East Asia Command. He retired after the war to a family estate in Oxfordshire, and died while with a shooting party in Argyll, Scotland, in August 1971.

Kathleen Hall died in April 1970 in New Zealand, aged seventy-four. She is still remembered in the town of Songjiazhuang, where she ran her missionary clinic and nursed Hogg through his typhus. The main school in the town bears her name, and in the grounds there is a statue of her with her nurse's bag in one hand and her dog beside her. Her great friend Norman Bethune's name has been given to the local hospital.

Wadham College, Oxford, established a scholarship in George Hogg's name in 1986. A student room in the college has been named after him.

George Hogg's first grave in Shandan had a headstone with the letters 'GAH' and the dates '1915–1945' carved on it. When the grave was restored in 1984 the co-operative movement's 'Gung Ho' insignia was carved at the top of the headstone. Lines from one of Hogg's favourite poems were inscribed below. They are by the First World War poet Julian Grenfell, and are taken from the first verse of his much-anthologised poem 'Into Battle'. Grenfell was killed near Ypres in May 1915, three months to the day after George Hogg was born.

> And life is colour and warmth and light
> And a striving ever more for these
> And he is dead who will not fight
> And who dies fighting has increase.

ACKNOWLEDGEMENTS

I should like to thank the following for their help, guidance and advice.

Mark Thomas, George Hogg's nephew, who with his wife Helena guided me to the family correspondence and was generous both as a host and with his time when I visited him at his home in Finland. Many other members of the Hogg family were very helpful, and patiently put up with my questions. I am especially indebted to Julian Hogg, Vanessa Dingley, Gillian Newell and Hilary Jarvis.

In Beijing, Xiao Lizhi, Nieh Guangchun and Nieh Guanghan spent hours providing detail and background about their life with Hogg. Teresa Huang Wei provided invaluable assistance as interpreter, translator and researcher on my travels in China. In Xianing, Hogg's 'old boys' took the time to have lunch and tell me about their old headmaster. My thanks to Qi Ranmei, Liu Shizhong, Yu Jinzhong, Yang Chunlin, Chen Faxing and Liang Boran. In Shandan, Richard Meinhold provided invaluable background information about the city and its Bailie school.

Dan Smith proved a swift and energetic researcher, and my thanks too to James Saunders, who did much of the early digging in the US archives. Bill Adams tracked down surviving members of Hogg's family in England. Andrew Hunter, the son of Winifred 'Muff' Nelson, was more than helpful in delving into family papers relating to his mother. Miss Pam Weatherley, a former nurse at St George's School and now the archivist, went through hundreds of old rugby team photographs and school reports. Dr Martin Scurr of Notting Hill in London provided the medical background to George Hogg's many illnesses, especially his fatal attack of tetanus. Abigail Mitchell catalogued the bibliography with great care. Rae McGregor, biographer of Kathleen Hall, and Dr Anne-Marie Brady, the biographer of Rewi Alley, looked kindly upon my research and guided me to their own excellent work.

At Wadham College my special thanks to the ever helpful, ever cheerful Jessica Mannix, Development Director, who guided me to sources relevant to Hogg's undergraduate career. My thanks also to Dr Tao Tao Liu, Tutor in Oriental Studies, who very kindly read this book in manuscript, and to Mr Clifford Davies, the college archivist.

John Gittings, my former colleague on the *Guardian* and author of *The Changing Face of China* (Oxford University Press, 2006), also read parts of this book and made many helpful suggestions. Les Hinton, my boss at the time of writing this book, who was then Executive Chairman at News International in London and is now Chief Executive Officer of Dow Jones in New York, was very supportive of the time I spent on the research and writing of this book. Caroline Johnston, my PA, patiently helped with research and endless cups of tea. Linda Seifert, both my friend and my script agent, saw me through the years of writing a film script based on the George Hogg story, without which this book would not have happened. Linda introduced me to Sophie Hicks at Ed Victor's agency, whose enthusiasm for the story lifted me in dark moments. Richard Johnson at HarperCollins provided very considerable help, and Robert Lacey edited the manuscript with care and skill, making an invaluable contribution to the final text.

Finally, my thanks are due to my wife Amanda and to Nicholas and Elizabeth for putting up with me during the writing of this book.

While I thank all the above, the responsibility for this book is entirely mine.

A NOTE ON THE TEXT

In general I have used the Pinyin system of transliteration for Chinese names, which replaced the Wade-Giles system in 1958. I have, however, retained the old and more familiar version of certain names such as Shanghai, Hankow, Yangtse and Canton to avoid confusion. I have also used the old name of Shuangshipu, the town in which George Hogg became headmaster of the Bailie school. Hogg mentions the town frequently in his letters and in his book, so it seemed sensible to retain the name by which he referred to it, rather than to use the modern version, Fengxian. I have used the modern name for the Chinese capital Beijing throughout, although it was variously known as Peking and Peiping in the period covered by the book.

SOURCES

Archives

A key source for this book has been the letters that George Hogg wrote home during his travels in the US, Japan and China from 1937 to 1945. These are held by his nephew Mark Thomas in Finland. The family archive also contains most of Hogg's journalism, including his unpublished articles.

The Ida Pruitt papers in the Arthur and Elisabeth Schlesinger Library at Harvard University.

Muriel Lester's papers at the Swarthmore College Peace Collection in Pennsylvania.

Archives of the *Manchester Guardian* and *The Times*.

Interviews

Rewi Alley
Rosemary Baker
Chen Faxing
Alan Green
Brian Harland
Liang Boran
Liu Shizhong
Lord Lindsay of Birker

Nieh Guangchun
Nieh Guanghan
Qi Ranmei
Mark Thomas
Xiao Lizhi
Yang Chunlin
Yu Jinzhong

Books

Airey, Willis, *A Learner in China*, Caxton Press, 1970

Alley, Rewi, *Yo Banfa!*, New World Press, 1955

Alley, Rewi, *Our Seven – Their Five*, New World Press, 1963

Alley, Rewi, *Fruition*, Caxton Press, 1967

Alley, Rewi, *At 90: Memoirs of my China Years*, New World Press, 1986

Alley, Rewi, *An Autobiography*, New World Press, 1987

Alley, Rewi, *Rewi Alley and Shandan Bailey School*, New World Press, 1997

Auden, W.H., and Isherwood, Christopher, *Journey to a War*, Faber and Faber, 1986

Beasley, William, *The Modern History of Japan*, Weidenfeld and Nicolson, 1973

Belden, Jack, *Retreat with Stilwell*, Alfred A. Knopf, 1943

Belden, Jack, *China Shakes the World*, Monthly Review Press, 1970

Bertram, James, *Unconquered*, Da Capo Press, 1975

Brady, Anne-Marie, *Friend of China: The Myth of Rewi Alley*, Routledge Curzon, 2003

Butterfield, Fox, *China: Alive in the Bitter Sea*, Hodder and Stoughton, 1982

Chang, Jung, *Wild Swans*, HarperCollins, 1991

Chang, Jung, and Halliday, Jon, *Mao: The Unknown Story*, Jonathan Cape, 2005

Clubb, O. Edmund, *Twentieth-Century China*, Columbia University Press, 1964

Eastman, Lloyd, et al., *The Nationalist Era in China 1927–1949*, Cambridge University Press, 1991

Farmer, Rhodes, *Shanghai Harvest*, Museum Press Ltd, 1945

Fenby, Jonathan, *Generalissimo: Chiang Kai-shek and the China he Lost*, The Free Press, 2005

Ferguson, Niall, *The War of the World: History's Age of Hatred*, Penguin Press, 2006

Gillies, Donald, *Radical Diplomat: The Life of Archibald Clark-Kerr, Lord Inverchapel, 1882–1951*, I.B.Tauris, 1999

Gittings, John, *The Changing Face of China*, Oxford University Press, 2006

Hahn, Emily, *China to Me*, Blakiston, 1944

Hanson, Haldor, *Humane Endeavor: The Story of the China War*, Farrar and Rinehart, 1939

Herzstein, Robert E., *Henry R. Luce*, Charles Scribner's Sons, 1994

Hogg, George, *I See a New China*, Little, Brown, 1944

Homer, Joy, *Dawn Watch in China*, Houghton Mifflin, 1941

Hsü, Immanuel C.Y, *The Rise Of Modern China*, Oxford University Press, 1990

King, Marjorie, *China's American Daughter*, Chinese University Press, 2006

Lapwood, Ralph and Nancy, *Through the Chinese Revolution*, People's Books Co-operative Society Ltd, 1954

Lester, Muriel, *It So Happened*, Harper and Brothers, 1947

Lindsay, Michael, *The Unknown War*, Bergström and Boyle, 1975

McGregor, Rae, *Shrewd Sanctity*, Polygraphia Ltd, 2006

Martin, Ralph G., *Henry and Clare*, G.P. Putnam's Sons, 1991

Moise, Edwin E., *Modern China*, Longman, 1994

Moreira, Peter, *Hemingway on the China Front: His WWII Spy Mission with Martha Gellhorn*, Potomac, 2006

Peck, Graham, *Through China's Wall*, William Collins, 1945

Peck, Graham, *Two Kinds of Time*, First Sentry Printing Company, 1967

Price, Ruth, *The Lives of Agnes Smedley*, Oxford University Press, 2004

Schell, Orville, and Esherick, Joseph, *Modern China*, Vintage Sundial Books, 1972

Sergeant, Harriet, *Shanghai*, John Murray, 1999

Smedley, Agnes, *China Correspondent*, Pandora Press, 1984

Snow, Edgar, *Red China Today*, Random House, 1970

Snow, Edgar, *Red Star Over China*, Grove Press, 1981

Tolley, Kemp, *Yangtze Patrol*, Naval Institute Press, 2000

Utley, Freda, *Last Chance in China*, Bobbs-Merrill, 1947

Utley, Freda, *The China Story*, Henry Regnery Company, 1951

White, Theodore H., and Jacoby, Annalee, *Thunder out of China*, William Sloane Associates Inc., 1946

INDEX

Alley, Rewi 63: autobiography 230, 255–6, 268; background 166–7; and co-operative movement 65, 107, 124, 125, 128, 130–1, 166, 169; death 269; decision to remain in communist China 267–8; and development of technical training schools 169–70; and flight of Bailie School 226, 229, 230, 233; and Hogg's arrest and release 225; and Hogg's death 255–6, 257, 258; homosexuality 167, 169, 218–19; relationship with Hogg 166; and Shandan Bailie School 245, 263; in Shanghai 167–8; works to restore Hogg's reputation 268

Amoy 107

Associated Press (AP) 116, 159, 160, 177

Auden, W.H. 46, 59, 60, 168: *Journey to a War* 46, 178

Bailie, Joseph 169

Bailie School (Shuangshipu) 169–70, 192–4, 259: aims of 197, 202; boys at 194–5; feud between north-westerners and north-easterners 201; flea problem 211; improvements by Hogg 192–4; initial antipathy towards Hogg by boys 198; instilling of discipline 199–200, 208; journey to Shandan 17, 236–42; and malaria 208, 217; money and food problems 213–14; preparations for journey 225–6, 231–5; pressure from KMT to recruit boys 224–5, 229, 230–1; rebuilt at Shandan *see* Shandan Bailie School; relationship between Hogg and boys 20, 207, 245; routine and curriculum 197, 198–9, 203–6; selection of pupils 200–1; and singing 205–6; staff 202–3, 208–9

Baker, Cyril 109

Baoji 136, 138, 176–7, 213

Beijing 114–16, 265: economic liberalisation 16; occupation by Japanese 40, 114, 115; opium dens 115; street life 115; student demonstrations (1919) 83

Belden, Jack 59, 66, 74, 96, 97, 130, 273

Bertram, James 95, 96

Bethune, Dr Norman 145–8, 274

Beyond China's City Walls (Hogg) 234

Bolshevik Revolution (1917) 82, 84

Bong (S.J. Jeung) 184–7

Bowra, Maurice 26, 29, 30–1, 33

Boxer Protocol (1901) 49

Boxer Rebellion (1899–1901) 107, 108

Brady, Dr Anne-Marie 167, 267

Braid, Andy 202–3, 231

Buchenwald concentration camp 35

Buddhism 42

Camplin, Alec 169

Canton 103, 107, 110

Capa, Robert 58

Carlson, Captain Evans 94, 121, 131–2

Cathay Hotel (Shanghai) 53

CCP *see* communists/Chinese Communist Party

Chamberlain, Neville 110

Chang, Jung 89

Changsha 99, 223

Chen Tu-hsiu, Professor 82, 84

Chengdu 212, 213

Chenping 163

Chialing River 196

Chiang Chi-hsia 139–41

Chiang Kai-shek 42, 60, 84, 95: background and rise to power 69, 70; and co-operatives 65; and communists 76, 85, 167, 222, 223, 263–4; corruption of administration 87, 180, 186, 222; death 265; fall of government 162; relationship with Stilwell 222, 223–4; resignation 264–5; as supreme commander of Chinese front 222; and *Time* magazine 126, 127; and war against Japanese 49, 50, 53, 68–9, 105, 110, 119, 136–7; and Western press 78, 96

Chieng Wen-shui 148, 149

China: anarchy and power struggle between warlords 69, 83; black market 180, 185; conflict between communists and nationalists 84–5, 167–8, 222–3, 263, 264–5; and gold 147–8; history 69–70; invasion and conquest by Japan 40–2; missionary activity in 107–8; postal service 66; repression of Christian Church in 108; *see also* Sino-Japanese war

Chinese Communist Party *see* communists/Chinese Communist Party

Chinese industrial co-operatives *see* co-operatives

Chingan 238

Chongqing 105, 110, 156–66: bombed by Japanese 156, 157, 160–2, 164; conditions in 158, 159–60; early-warning system 164; foreign community in 164–5

Chou En-lai 55, 59, 78, 86, 98, 120, 134, 226, 269

Churchill, Winston 32

Clark-Kerr, Sir Archibald 64–5, 165

Clark-Kerr, Lady Tita 64

co-operatives (China) 7, 64–5, 99, 124–31, 191, 225: closure of 266; criticised by nationalists as a communist front 129, 130; criticism of 210; funding 124, 125, 127, 129, 130; number 128; problems 128; running costs 127–8; starting up of 19, 124, 125; supported by Soong Meiling 65, 124, 130, 166

co-operatives (Japan) 39, 42

Comintern 84

communists/Chinese Communist Party 90:

appeal of 88; conflict between nationalists and 84–5, 167–8, 222–3, 263, 264–5; co-operation with nationalists 76, 85, 119; formation of Party 83–4; Japanese prisoners policy 93–4; and Long March 57, 79, 85, 86, 120; and 'peasant radicalism' 86–7; repression of Christian Church 108; view of by foreign correspondents 78, 88, 89, 95–6; visited by Americans at Yenan 94–5; at Yenan 85–6, 90; *see also* Mao Tse-tung

Cowley, Malcolm 163

Crozier, William 47, 48

Cultural Revolution 16, 20, 85, 120–1, 266, 269

Czechoslovakia 110

Da Ren 142

deforestation 187, 195

Delta co-operative farm (Rochdale, Mississippi) 38

Deng Xiaoping 16, 20, 121, 268

Durdin, Tillman 51, 53, 59

Edward VIII, King 34

Eighth Route Army 57, 82, 87, 91, 114, 120, 135–6, 145, 222

Fa Ta Si temple (Shandan) 242

Fan Kouqiang 256

Fan Wenhai 237, 240, 245, 255, 256, 266

Farmer, Rhodes 158

fascism 33

Fellowship of Reconciliation 23, 33, 37, 47

Fleming, Ian 59

Fleming, Peter 59–60, 273–4

Fortune magazine 126

Franco, General Francisco 35, 57, 72, 145

Frankfurter Zeitung 62

Gansu 68, 226–7, 249

Gayne, Mark 181–2

Gellhorn, Martha 162

Ghosh cotton-milling machine 213, 231–2, 233–4, 235, 244

Goldwyn, Samuel 125

Gollancz, Victor 62, 250

Graham, Betty 66

Grant, Cecil 26–7

Index

Great Leap Forward 268
Great Wall of China 241
Grenfell, Julian 274
'Gung Ho' slogan 131, 132

Haddon, Brit 126
Hahn, Emily 96, 131, 166; *China to Me* 96
Hall, Kathleen 117–18, 119, 120, 144–7, 274
Hall, Ronald 259
Halliday, Jon 89
Hanchung 148–9, 153
Hankow 53, 54–7, 58–9, 74–5: bombed by
    Japanese 70, 71, 76, 97, 98; decision not to
    fight for by Chiang Kai-shek 105; diseases in
    75, 76; evacuation 97, 98, 100, 101–3, 104;
    falls to Japanese 99, 105–6; foreign
    journalists in 57, 59, 99–100; history 55–6;
    refugees 100; under siege 75–7
Hanson, Haldore 59, 116, 121, 180, 183, 273:
    Humane Endeavor 116
Hanyang 54, 98
Harland, Professor Brian 252–3, 254, 257,
    258–9, 271
Harpenden, Hertfordshire 23–4
Hemingway, Ernest 162–3
Hengyang 223
Himmler, Heinrich 35
Hirohito, Emperor 68, 73, 105
Hiroshima 263
Hitler, Adolf 34–5, 110, 161
Hodgkin, Henry 23
Hoffman, Paul G. 126
Hogg, Barbara (*later* Thomas) (sister) 108–9
Hogg, Daniel (brother) 34, 35, 171
Hogg, Gary (brother) 34, 108, 171
Hogg, George Aylwin
    LIFE BEFORE CHINA
    birth 21; childhood and pacifist upbringing
    18, 21–2, 24–6; education 26–7; at Oxford
    18, 26, 30–4; travels across America 35–9;
    travels in Japan 39–40, 43
    LIFE IN CHINA
    adoptive sons 172–5, 227–8, 266; arrest and
    release 225; articles for *New Statesmen* 111,
    151–2; bus journeys 150–4; as CIC
    inspector in Baoji 175–6, 178, 182; contracts
    anthrax 174, 177–8; contracts paratyphoid

107, 174; contracts tetanus 254–6, 257;
contracts typhus 117–20, 174; and co-
operative movement 17, 19, 129, 136;
correspondent for Associated Press 116,
158, 159, 160, 177; correspondent for
Manchester Guardian 47–8, 67, 71–2, 81, 93,
100, 101–3, 104–6, 109, 111, 112, 123, 159,
221; correspondent for United Press
International 66–7, 72, 74–5, 97, 106; cross-
country trek to Xian 183–4; escapes
Japanese by rickshaw 154–6; expulsion from
Shanghai by Japanese 111, 116; flight to
Shandan with Bailie School 17, 225–7,
228–9, 236–42; friends made on travels
182–3; in Hankow 54–7; as headmaster of
Bailie School 17, 19, 26, 170, 192–5,
197–215, 220 *see also* Bailie School; job with
Van Reekum Bros 54–5, 65; letters home 18,
71–2, 91, 92–3, 94, 103, 109–10, 156–7,
170–1, 172–3, 174–5, 177, 189–90, 210,
215–17, 227–8, 237, 243, 253–4; lives in
mountain cave 210–12, 227; love affair with
Chiang Chi-hsia 139–41; love affair with
Xiao Ren 142–4, 172–3; malaria attacks 217;
meets General Zhu De and spends time
with guerrilla soldiers 132–6; meets Nieh
Rong Zhen and tours communist region
120–3; as 'Ocean Secretary' 19, 138–9,
147–9, 150, 166, 195; and overseas relief
programme after flooding of Yangtse 187–9;
rebuilding of Bailie School at Shandan
243–6; relationship with Alley 166; reviews
of first book 250–1, 253; second book 234;
in Shanghai 44–6, 105; visits Beijing 114–17;
visits Chongqing 156–9; visits communist
headquarters at Yenan 79, 80–2, 90; visits
Shinto shrines at Ise 112–14; writing of
book and attempts to get published 18,
178–82
    PERSONAL LIFE
    character and attributes 18, 27, 29, 210, 215,
    271; death and funeral 256–7, 258;
    honouring of memory of in Shandan 16–17;
    and jazz 75; parental background 22–3;
    political attitudes 91, 109–10; rehabilitation
    by Chinese and restoration of grave 16, 20,
    264, 268, 269; relationship with Agnes

285

Hogg, George Aylwin PERSONAL LIFE – *cont.*
  Smedley 60, 63; relationship with sister
  Rosemary 31; tributes to 29, 259–61;
  vilification of memory of during Cultural
  Revolution and desecration of grave 20, 26,
  266–7
Hogg, Kathleen (*née* Lester) (mother) 22, 24, 25,
  35, 109, 171, 175, 227, 247, 257, 269
Hogg, Robert (father) 21, 24, 171, 175, 257–8,
  269
Hogg, Rosemary (sister) 25, 26, 31, 108, 109,
  170, 269–70
Hogg, Stephen (brother) 25–6, 34, 108, 171, 269
Homer, Joy 114–15
Hong Kong 107
Hou, General 133
Howard, Roy W. 67
Hunan 68
Hunter, Roger 24, 27, 29, 108
hyperinflation 162

I See a New China (Hogg) 18, 178–82, 250–1,
  253
Indusco 125, 129, 131, 210, 266
industrial co-operatives *see* co-operatives
Ise: Shinto shrines at 112–14
Isherwood, Christopher 46–7, 59–60, 168, 178;
  Journey to a War 46, 178

Jacoby, Annalee 159–60
Japan 39–40, 136: belief in racial superiority 40,
  43, 111–12; censorship 40; co-operative
  movement 39, 42; imperial ambitions 41;
  invasion of China 40–2; origins of religious
  faith 112–14; relations with the West 41–2;
  and Shinto 39, 42–3; surrender to Allies
  263; *see also* Sino-Japanese war
Jarvis, Hilary 25
Jeung, S.H. *see* Bong
Johnson, Celia 59

Kagawa, Dr Toyohiko 39–40, 43, 114
K'ang (teacher) 209
Kemp, Don 265
Kobe 39
Kokonor 246
Korea 114

Kung, H.H. 55
Kuo (engineer) 232, 235
Kuomintang (KMT, Nationalist Party) 69, 70,
  83, 84, 87, 110, 120, 222, 224–5, 264
Kwangsi 68

Lacey, Dr 39
Lanzhou 182, 190, 233, 240
Lao Da (Son No.1) *see* Nieh Guangchun
Lao Er (Son No.2) *see* Nieh Guanghan
Lao San (Son No.3) *see* Nieh Guangtao
Lao Si (Son No.4) *see* Nieh Guangpei
Lapwood, Ralph 168, 183–4
'Last Ditchers Club' 77
League of Nations 32
Lederer, Lieutenant William J. 163
Lester, Doris 22
Lester, Muriel (Hogg's aunt) 22, 23, 34, 35, 37,
  39, 47, 55, 179, 269
Life magazine 58, 126, 127, 178
Lindsay, Michael 183–4
Little, Brown & Co 180, 181
Liu Teh-ch'ing 189
London Blitz 156
Long March 57, 79, 85, 86, 120
Loughton, Essex 22–3
Luce, Clare Booth 127, 212
Luce, Henry 58, 78, 125, 125–7, 129, 180, 212
Luoyang 139, 144, 224, 225
Lutheran mission (Hankow) 55

MacArthur, General Douglas 272
McGregor, Rae 145–6
Ma Bufang 227, 242, 249
Manchester Guardian 47–8, 62, 67, 71–2, 81, 93,
  100–3, 105–6, 109, 111, 112, 123, 159, 221,
  259
Manchu dynasty (Qing dynasty) 69, 82, 83
Manchukuo 40
Manchuria 114, 201: conquest of by Japan
  (1931) 40, 42, 49, 201
Mann, Michael 30
Mao Tse-tung 57, 78, 79, 83, 84, 93, 121, 134,
  137, 264: achievements 95; appeal of 88,
  96–7; background 70, 82; death 16, 269;
  establishment of People's Republic of China
  265; extending of territory 97; and Great

Leap Forward 268; as leader of Communist Party 86–7; and Long March 85, 86; and media 87, 88–9, 95, 134

Marxism 82

Mayer, Louis B. 127

Meiji, Emperor 105

Mien-hsien 147

Millican, Frank and Aimee 45, 107, 108

Minami, General 41

Ming dynasty 241

missionaries 107–8

Mitchell, Margaret: *Gone with the Wind* 36, 38

Moreira, Peter: *Ernest Hemingway on the China Front* 163

Munich Agreement (1938) 110

Mussolini, Benito 34–5

Mydans, Carl 178

Mydans, Shelley 178

Nagasaki 263

Nanjing 84: Rape of (1937) 18, 45, 48, 50–1, 53, 116

Nationalist Party *see* Kuomintang

nationalists 80: conflict between communists and 84–5, 167–8, 222–3, 263, 264–5; co-operation with communists 76, 85 119; corruption 87, 180, 186, 222; criticism of co-operatives 129, 130; view of by foreign correspondents 78, 87–8, 96; *see also* Chiang Kai-shek; Kuomintang

Nazi Germany 34

Needham, Dr Joseph 226

Nelson, Robert 'Bosh' 24, 29, 171

Nelson, Winifred 'Muff' (*later* Hunter) 24, 28–9, 36, 108, 190

New Statesman 111, 151–2

News Chronicle 259–60

Nieh Guangchun (Son No. 1) 19–20, 173–4, 205

Nieh Guanghan (Son No. 2) 15, 20, 173–4, 204

Nieh Guangpei (Son No. 4) 173–4, 242, 257

Nieh Guangtao (Son No. 3) 173–4, 257

Nieh Rong Zhen, General 87, 120–1, 135, 269

'ocean carts' 138–9

'ocean devil' 138

Opium Wars 107

Oxford University 21, 30–4, 274: 'King and Country' debate 32

Parker, Gerald 34

Pearl Harbor 136: Japanese attack on (1941) 53, 76, 221

Peck, Graham 195–6: *Through China's Wall* 195; *Two Kinds of Time* 196

Penglai 125

People's Daily 20

People's Liberation Army (PLA) 264, 265

Porter, Katherine Anne 273

Price, Ruth 61–2, 272

Proctor, David 'Dippy' 24, 27, 29

Pruitt, Ida 123, 124–5, 126, 130, 179, 212, 225

Queen Mary 36–7

'Rape of Nanjing' (1937) 18, 45, 48, 50–1, 53, 116

Red Army 134

Red Flag magazine 121

Rockefeller III, John D. 126–7

Roosevelt, Eleanor 125, 126

Roosevelt, President Franklin Delano 94, 224

Roots, Frances 75

Roots, Bishop Logan 55, 65, 100

Ruijin 84–5

St George's School (Harpenden) 21, 24, 26–7

scorched-earth policy 98–9, 105

Scott, C.P. 47

Second World War 129, 136, 141, 225

Selznick, David O. 127

Shandan 16, 229–30, 252, 265: earthquake (1953) 266; local mafia 249; today 266

Shandan Bailie School 263, 265: building of 243–50; move to Lanzhou 265–6; reopening (1984) 268; today 268

Shanghai 44–7, 107, 167–8: Chinese retreat from 50, 53; decadence of 47; during Sino-Japanese war 49–50; impact of war on 35, 45–6, 48, 50; refugees in 46, 48

Shanxi 68

Shinto religion 39, 42–3

Shuangshipu 19, 169, 192, 195, 196–7: Bailie school at *see* Bailie School (Shuangshipu)

Siegmund-Schultze, Friedrich 23
Simpson, Wallis 34
Sino-Japanese war 16, 35, 85: Allied support
  221–2; attack on Japanese mainland by
  Chinese 73; atrocities of Japanese 18, 45, 48,
  50–1, 53, 67, 68, 116; battle of
  T'aierhchuang 58, 67; bombing of
  Chongqing 156, 157, 160–2, 164;
  dynamiting of Yellow River dykes 68, 188;
  end of 263; fall of Hankow 110; impact of
  Pearl Harbor on 221; Japanese bombing
  campaign 72–3, 163–4; Japanese policy of
  total warfare and 'Three All' campaign 116,
  214; moving inland from coastal regions
  strategy 68–9; plague and famine 187;
  progress of 58, 67–8, 73, 110, 136, 223, 224,
  225; Rape of Nanjing 18, 45, 48, 50–1, 53,
  116; and scorched-earth policy 98–9, 105;
  start of 49; united front between
  communists and nationalists 76, 85
Sino-Soviet split 84
Smedley, Agnes 59, 60–2, 64, 79, 100–1, 105:
  background 61–2; *Battle Hymn to China*
  99–100; communist supporter 57, 60–1, 91,
  260; *Daughter of Earth* 57; relationship with
  Hogg 60, 63; Soviet spy allegations 61, 260,
  271–3
Snow, Edgar 57, 59, 88, 96, 124, 130, 131, 168,
  272: *Red Star Over China* 88–9
Snow, Peg 57, 59, 88, 130, 168, 179–80, 212:
  Inside Red China 88, 180
Songjiazhuang 118–20
Soong Ching Ling 124
Soong Meiling (Mme Chiang Kai-shek) 70, 76,
  78, 126, 162, 170: support for co-operatives
  65, 124, 130, 166
Sorge, Richard 53, 272
Soviet Union 35, 84, 161, 221
Spanish Civil War 32, 35, 57, 72, 145
Spectator 250, 251
Stalin, Josef 35, 221
Steele, Art 51, 59, 183
Stennes, Captain Walter 59
Stilwell, General Joseph 74, 222, 223–4
Sun Yat-sen 69, 70, 83, 84, 124
Sunday Telegraph 271
Szechuan 68

T'aierhchuang, battle of 58, 67
Taiping Revolution (1850–65) 107
Terminus Hotel (Hankow) 62–3, 77
Thomas, Donald 108–9
Tianshui 237–8
Tientsin, Treaty of (1858) 56
Time magazine 126, 127
Times Literary Supplement 251, 252
Tolstoy, Leo: *The Kingdom of God is Within You*
  23
Truman, President Harry S. 264

United China Relief (UCR) 126–7
United Press International (UPI) 66–7, 72,
  74–5, 97, 106
Utley, Freda 59

Van Reekum Bros 54–5, 65
Versailles Treaty 82–3

Wadham College (Oxford) 30–4, 274
Wang Feng-jei 176
Whampoa Military Academy 70, 84
White, Theodore 127, 159
Willoughby, Charles A. 272
Woods, Reverend George 246–7, 259
Wuchang 54
Wuhan 54

Xian 80–1, 182, 225
Xiao Ren 99, 142–4, 156, 172–3, 174, 218–19,
  270
Xu Xinliu 124
Xuzhou 58, 67, 73

Yangtse Patrol 62
Yangtse River 54, 56, 158, 187
Yellow River 79, 132–3, 240: dynamiting of
  dykes 68, 188; flooding of 187–9
Yenan 79, 80, 81, 82, 85–6, 87, 90, 91–4, 264
Yenching University 183
Yunnan 68

Zhang Xinyi 240–1
Zhi Fu Zhang 229
Zhu De, General 57, 85, 87, 132, 133, 134, 135,
  269